A Guide to

THE BIG BAND ERA

A Guide to

THE BIG BAND ERA

A Comprehensive Review
of All the Recorded Hits
and All the Hitmakers

David Belaire

 Winged Note Press

A Guide to the Big Band Era

Published in the United States of America by

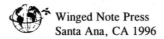 Winged Note Press
Santa Ana, CA 1996

Printed in the United States of America

First Edition

Library of Congress Catalog Card Number:
96-90496

ISBN 0-9653681-0-6

A GUIDE TO THE BIG BAND ERA

Contents

Introduction

(The "Why and How" of this "What, When and Who")

This is a book of lists and facts about popular music in America during twelve years just before the middle of the twentieth century. For the most part, those were years of austerity and sacrifice brought on by the Great Depression and World War II. Other features which made the period unique were that the country had only one president from 1933 to 1945 and that it was the "golden age" for both radio and motion pictures. Coinciding with all this, the country's dance bands enjoyed an era of great popularity, largely caused by a new, upbeat musical style called "swing," introduced by Benny Goodman in 1935.

The new success of the big bands was demonstrated by their increased numbers and ever-increasing attendance at ballrooms, hotel dining rooms, college proms and theaters. Their records were played throughout each day by radio disc jockeys and on juke boxes, which seemed to be everywhere. On radio, in addition to the disc jockey shows, the bands were heard on many evening programs offering live music by itself or as part of variety shows. Late night "remotes" following the eleven o'clock news, presented music by various bands, each in fifteen-minute segments broadcast live from their current venues. An endless procession of musical productions was offered on stage and screen, many of the songs becoming hits and the singers establishing themselves as stars of the entertainment world.

i

As a result, popular music in the 1930s and 1940s probably figured more prominently in the lives of people of all ages than at any other time in America's history. Logically, the music and the many long-established performers were remembered for a very long time.

The writer grew up in that era, one of millions who enjoyed every minute of the popular music of the day he might be able to hear, whenever and from whatever source it might be heard. His enjoyment of band music evolved over the years from being limited to radio and phonograph, to later attending many performances at theaters - especially in New York City - to dancing to music of the big bands in ballrooms, from New York's Pennsylvania Hotel to the Hollywood Palladium. In between, several years of military service provided opportunity to compare notes about popular music with hundreds of other young men. Even while overseas, we were still kept abreast of the latest recorded hits by the much-appreciated Armed Forces Radio.

The point is that from the beginning to the end of that twelve-year musical feast that we thought would never end, recorded music was our principal source. When it came time to write a history of the big band years, the single most important documentation would have been identification of the hundred-or-so recordings per year which became popular and established themselves as part of the musical folklore of this country. Fans who had followed the music closely now wanted to refresh their memories and possibly use the information to search out copies of their most treasured old recordings. The historical record should have been available as well to any researchers and historians, writers and moviemakers, who wanted to know with reasonable certainty: (1) all the recordings which had achieved real popularity; (2) when they were popular and (3) who were all the performers chiefly responsible for making each number popular.

Any of a large number of close observers of this fabulous era of American music could have reconstructed for us the "What, When and Who." Strangely, however, it never appeared, leaving a wide gap in the story of the big band era. Without identification of what it was that we so enjoyed listening to throughout that twelve year period, the years would end up like so much erased tape, or blank pages in a history book.

Granted, there have been books written by a few of the musicians and music critics. For the most part, however, they have been "inside" stories, more meaningful, perhaps, to other members of their profession than to fans. However interesting they may have been, once read, their purpose was served and they were largely forgotten. On the other hand, the kind of book we hoped for would have been a compendium of the big band era - a book loaded with information that we could keep handy and refer to hundreds of times a year. This writer would have worn out at least one copy of such a book, with constant use.

A GUIDE TO THE BIG BAND ERA — Introduction

We waited in a state of frustration for over forty years for someone - anyone - to do it, before finally, out of desperation, undertaking the immense task of compiling this guide, forced to supplement our memory with less-than-adequate sources of information. The likely prospect that if we didn't do it, no one else would, was simply a thought we could not bear and a challenge we could not ignore. The music had been too important a part of our life.

The result is the only book ever compiled which: deals only with the music of the big band era; identifies all the recorded music which achieved real popularity in that period and lists opposite each song title the names of the artist or artists chiefly responsible for making it popular (including the names of bandsingers) and places all of it in chronological order - in effect, creating a twelve-year musical diary.

David Belaire

I

The Big Bands in Profile

Of the hundreds of big bands which made themselves available to play in every city and town of America during that era, the names of the leading ones may be found on the yearly lists of most popular recordings. In all, there were perhaps several dozen "name" bands which recorded most of the songs and instrumentals which became hits. Many of the early favorites among these gave way in the late 1930's to a new group of leaders who made a far greater impact and who held sway to the end.

As the lists of most popular recordings progress through each year, it will be noted that names such as Paul Whiteman, Isham Jones, Rudy Vallee, Ozzie Nelson, Leo Reisman, Victor Young, Johnny Green, Richard Himber and Ray Noble are replaced by those of Benny Goodman, Tommy and Jimmy Dorsey, Glenn Miller, Harry James, Artie Shaw, Woody Herman, Charlie Barnet, Kay Kyser, Sammy Kaye, Freddy Martin, Les Brown, Gene Krupa, Larry Clinton, Russ Morgan, Vaughn Monroe, Dick Jurgens, Alvino Rey and Stan Kenton. There was another small group which was not displaced, each retaining its popularity throughout the era, including the bands of Guy Lombardo, Duke Ellington, Count Basie, Bob Crosby, Glen Gray, Jan Garber, Eddy Duchin, Jimmie Lunceford and Erskine Hawkins. Another early favorite, Hal Kemp, might have been among these had he not

met an untimely death on a California highway during the
Christmas season of 1940.

On the following pages are profiled the several dozen bands
which recorded most of the popular songs. Noted are such
pertinent facts about them as the leader's instrument, if any; the
band's theme song, or songs; its best-remembered vocalists and
a brief commentary regarding the band's style of play and level
of achievement. Notes regarding the longevity of each are in
many instances best estimates, based on the sketchy information available and are included only to help answer the
inevitable question, "I wonder whatever happened to that
band?"

Following the bands are listed the arrangers, those musicians with special music-writing skills who were largely
responsible for the way that each band sounded and also,
therefore, for much of their success. Bandleaders and
arrangers are listed in alphabetical order:

LOUIS ARMSTRONG- (trumpet, vocalist) Theme song:
WHEN IT'S SLEEPY TIME DOWN SOUTH. A charismatic
jazz great and world-renowned entertainer who was the star
attraction in front of bands which themselves were never highly
regarded. He was active in the fullest sense from the early
1920's almost until his passing in 1971.

GUS ARNHEIM- (piano, but did not play in later years)
Theme song: SWEET AND LOVELY. Vocalists: Bing
Crosby, Jimmy Farrell. This bandleader had been well-known
on the west coast since the 1920s, then enjoyed additional

success in Chicago, late in a career which ended in the mid-1940s. Originally a sweet band, it was one of the few of that type which changed to swing, but only in its later years. Arnheim was the first to employ Bing Crosby as a solo vocalist, following the latter's initial success with "The Rhythm Boys" trio in the Paul Whiteman Orchestra.

CHARLIE BARNET- (tenor, alto, soprano saxophone; occasional vocalist) Theme song: REDSKIN RHUMBA. Vocalists: Joe Hostetter, Ford Leary, Bob Carroll, Mary Ann McCall, Lena Horne, Frances Wayne, Kay Starr, Fran Warren. One of the top swing bands. Barnet was a great admirer of Duke Ellington and at times the influence was evident. However, it took the arrangements of Billy May and Skip Martin to finally give the band its own special, identifiable sound. Barnet was active from the early 1930s into the 1960s, but only intermittently after 1946.

BLUE BARRON- (no instrument) Theme song: SOMETIMES I'M HAPPY. Band slogan: "Music of yesterday and today, played the Blue Barron way." Vocalists: Russ Carlyle, Clyde Burke, Jimmy Brown. A sweet band, patterned closely after that of the very successful Sammy Kaye Orchestra, it was active from the early 1930s into the 1960s.

COUNT BASIE- (piano) Instrumental signature: ONE O'CLOCK JUMP. Vocalists: Jimmy Rushing, Helen Humes, Thelma Carpenter. Coached in his youth by "Fats" Waller, William Basie got his start with the Kansas City band of then veteran Benny Moten, where he also acquired the nickname "Count." After forming his own band in 1935, Basie gradually developed a style of rhythm-driven ensemble swing, with simple arrangements allowing for discreet use of solos. This sound became generally considered to be the definitive expression of swing music, especially during the last 20 to 30 years of the band, when it enjoyed considerable success as one of the few remaining swing bands. The band seemed to keep improving and gaining in stature until Basie's passing in 1984.

BUNNY BERIGAN- (trumpet) Theme song: I CAN'T GET STARTED WITH YOU. Vocalists: Ford Leary, Dick Wharton, Ruth Gaylor, Kathleen Lane, Gail Reese, Ruth Bradley, Jayne Dover. This much-loved jazz figure, between stints as a sideman with leading bands, tried leading his own band periodically from 1936 to 1942 with indifferent results. He was denied any further opportunities by severe illness and death, which came at age 33.

BEN BERNIE- (violin, occasional vocalist) Opening and closing theme songs: IT'S A LONESOME OLD TOWN and AU REVOIR, PLEASANT DREAMS. Vocalists: Jackie Heller, Billy Wilson, Ray Hendricks, Don Saxon, Helene Daniels, The Bailey Sisters. He liked to introduce himself as "The Old Maestro." His was a sweet band which was a fixture on radio in the 1930s and was active from the 1920s until his death in 1943.

WILL BRADLEY- (trombone...and it is noteworthy that a fellow trombonist, Glenn Miller, who recruited him for - and played alongside him in - the Ray Noble Orchestra, considered him the best at his instrument.) Theme songs: STRANGE CARGO and (later) THINK OF ME. Vocalists: Ray

McKinley, Carlotta Dale, Terry Allen, Louise Tobin. Unpublicized co-leader of the band was drummer/vocalist Ray McKinley, who was responsible, along with pianist Freddy Slack for the boogie-woogie hits which brought fame to the band in the early 1940s. When Bradley decided to play strictly sweet music, it resulted in the departure of both McKinley and Slack, who formed their own bands. Other musicians were lost to military service about the same time and Bradley disbanded for good. It was ironic that for millions of fans, the name of Will Bradley would always be associated with little else but the boogie-woogie numbers, which was not the music he had wanted to play.

NAT BRANDWYNNE- (piano) Theme song: IF STARS COULD TALK. Vocalists: Buddy Clark, Barry McKinley. A sweet band with a full sound and a solid beat, it had long engagements for many years at New York's prestigious Waldorf Astoria Hotel and was often heard on radio. It was active from the 1930s to the 1970s, the later years in Las Vegas.

LES BROWN- (saxophone and clarinet; also a composer and arranger) Original theme song: DANCE OF THE BLUE DEVILS, was inspired by Les's having graduated from Duke University, whose sports teams use the name "Blue Devils." It was replaced in turn by EVENING STAR, SOPHISTICATED SWING and finally, LEAP FROG, with the melody of SENTIMENTAL JOURNEY later used as the closing number. Band slogan: "Les Brown and His Band of Renown." Vocalists: Betty Bonney, Herb Muse, Ralph Young, Miriam Shaw, Doris Day, Butch Stone, Lucy Ann Polk, Joanne Greer.

Playing swing as well as ballads and with a very personable leader out front, this was a highly successful band, taking its turn in the same ballrooms and on the same radio shows as the other top name bands. It was fully active from the late 1930s to the early 1980s, with much radio work in the postwar years. It often provided music for the shows of comedian Bob Hope, both at home and when the entertainer made his many trips to entertain service personnel at their bases overseas.

HENRY BUSSE- (trumpet) Opening and closing theme songs: HOT LIPS, WHEN DAY IS DONE. Vocalists: Bob Hannon, Don Huston, Dick Wharton.   A sweet band, featuring the leader's muted trumpet, it also played music with a fast, bouncy beat, billed as "Shuffle Rhythm." It had long engagements at some of the most prestigious locations in Chicago and New York, being active from 1929 until the leader's passing in 1955.

CAB CALLOWAY- (vocalist) Theme song: MINNIE THE MOOCHER. This was a band whose primary function was to accompany its leader as he performed his largely exclusive songs in a very distinct and unique crowd-pleasing style, in night clubs, stage shows and films. Nevertheless, if only because of the niche he carved for himself over many years as an extraordinary entertainer, the Cab Calloway band merits a place among the most prominent of the era. Further, there were periods during the forties when it was acknowledged to be a genuinely good swing band. Cab and the band were highly active during the '30s and '40s, then only occasionally so in the '50s and '60s.

FRANKIE CARLE- (piano)   Theme song: SUNRISE
SERENADE.   Vocalists: Gregg Lawrence, Betty Bonney,
Phyllis Lynne, Marjorie Hughes.   After some failed attempts to
lead bands in the '30s and after four years with the Horace
Heidt band, Carle finally was able to form a successful sweet
band in 1944. Radio shows were helpful in its gaining national
recognition and the band was active through the 1950s, then
only occasionally in the 1960s.

BOB CHESTER- (tenor sax)   Opening and closing themes:
SUNBURST and SLUMBER.   Vocalists: Al Stuart, Bill
Darnell, Dolores O'Neill, Bob Haymes, Betty Bradley, Gene
Howard.   The dynamic Mr. Chester dabbled in swing, but his
band is best remembered for sounding like that of Glenn
Miller on several ballads recorded during the early 1940s. It
remained active from 1939 into the early 1950s.

LARRY CLINTON- (Played trumpet, trombone and clarinet,
but rarely with his band; was also an outstanding composer and
arranger.) Theme songs: A STUDY IN BROWN and later,
THE DIPSY DOODLE. Vocalists: Bea Wain, Peggy Mann,
Ford Leary, Terry Allen, Dick Todd.   For having been a
bandleader a relatively short time when he went into military
service as a pilot instructor in 1941, this multi-talented musician made a great impact. In addition to his theme songs, he
wrote other swing numbers which may have revealed his
musical preference.   These included the popular SATAN
TAKES A HOLIDAY and MIDNIGHT IN A MADHOUSE.
He also excelled in adapting the classics to create popular
ballads.   He either wrote or collaborated on several which
became hits, including MY REVERIE, OUR LOVE,

MARTHA and I DREAMT I DWELT IN MARBLE HALLS. Ballads like these, which formed part of a long series of hits by singer Bea Wain in 1938 and 1939, were responsible for this band becoming categorized as a sweet band when it could just as easily have qualified as a fine swing band. Tangible evidence of this was provided by the many instrumentals it recorded. The band existed from 1937 to 1941. A postwar attempt by Larry Clinton to recapture past glory was short-lived.

BOB CROSBY- (vocalist)   Theme song: SUMMERTIME. Other vocalists: Frank Tenille, Kay Weber, Marion Mann, Helen Ward, Dorothy Claire, Liz Tilton, Lucy Ann Polk, Doris Day and the "Bob-O-Links." The Crosby band, although quite versatile, featured and was best known for its dixieland jazz, especially through its band-within-a-band, the "Bobcats." That bouncy, upbeat type of music, while not swing, may have been responsible for the Bob Crosby band making a good showing in the swing (that is, non-sweet) category of magazine polls. The band was active from 1935 to the end of the era. Later, Bob would front dixieland combo's into the 1970s.

XAVIER CUGAT- (violin)   Theme song: MY SHAWL. Vocalists: Don Reid, Pedro Berrios, Carmen Castillo, Abbe Lane, Lina Romay, Dinah Shore, Miguelito Valdes, Del Campo, Buddy Clark. This band was known exclusively for its fine Spanish and Latin-American music. It played the better hotels and clubs from 1935 into the 1970s.

JIMMY DORSEY- (alto sax, clarinet) Instrumental signature

tune: CONTRASTS. Vocalists: Kay Weber, Bob Eberly, Helen O'Connell, Kitty Kallen, Bob Carroll, Anita Boyer. Beginning in 1928 as the Dorsey Brothers Orchestra, the band was left to Jimmy when older brother and leader Tommy simply walked off the bandstand in a fit of anger at his brother and went off to form a new band of his own. Music fans benefitted when both brothers' bands were among the best-loved of the era. Both could swing as well as spotlight their good singers. However, it was during the several years that Bob Eberly and Helen O'Connell sang with Jimmy's band that it enjoyed its greatest popularity. The peak was reached in 1941 when that attractive and talented pair took full advantage of a succession of excellent songs, converting all of them into instant hits (see 1941) which in later years they would often reprise to the delight of audiences and which became part of the regular fare of the "golden oldies" disc jockey shows. In the midst of the war years, Helen O'Connell married, giving up the life of a band singer and Bob Eberly went into military service. Somehow, the band was not the same without the two of them. It underwent even more drastic change, for the better, this time, when the brothers, more mellowed, now, reformed the Dorsey Brothers Orchestra in 1953 and made some beautiful music together until first, Tommy's velvet-toned trombone and then Jimmy's melodious saxophone were lost to music fans, except on record. Separately and together, they had contributed enormously to the musical legacy of the big band years.

TOMMY DORSEY- (trombone) Theme song: I'M GETTING SENTIMENTAL OVER YOU. Vocalists: Cliff Weston, Edythe Wright, Jack Leonard, Allan DeWitt, Frank Sinatra,

Connie Haines, Jo Stafford, the Pied Pipers, Dick Haymes, Stuart Foster, the Sentimentalists. This was a band of consistently high quality, whether playing swing, or, as was more frequent, spotlighting its singers. Tommy's business acumen, as well as his feeling for good music, always meant that he had some of the best musicians, vocalists and arrangers in his employ. Not to be overlooked was his own superb trombone playing, which provided a distinguishing sound for the band, in the same way as did the reed section of Glenn Miller, the trumpet of Harry James and the clarinets of Benny Goodman and Artie Shaw for their bands - all familiar, unmistakeable sounds for the millions of big band fans. In the late 1930s, Tommy was one of the first to adopt the practice of forming a small musical group from members of the regular band, for stylized specialty numbers. He called his group the "Clambake Seven." Later, he also led the way in utilizing a vocal group - first it was the Pied Pipers, later the Sentimentalists - either by themselves, or as vocal backing for the lead singer, which seemed to enhance the presentation of any song. Because of the tie to his theme song and since it also depicted both kinds of music at which he excelled, he liked to be introduced as "The Sentimental Gentleman of Swing."

EDDY DUCHIN- (piano) Theme song: MY TWILIGHT DREAM. Vocalists: Lew Sherwood, the De Marco Sisters, Pete Woolery, Jerry Cooper, Stanley Worth, Johnny Drake, June Robbins, Patricia Norman, Tommy Mercer. This was a sweet band which the leader's handsome appearance, flamboyant piano style and showmanship placed at the forefront of big city hotel bands, from 1931 to 1951.

DUKE ELLINGTON- (piano)   Theme songs: EAST ST. LOUIS TOODLE-OO, SOLITUDE, TAKE THE "A" TRAIN. Vocalists: Ivie Anderson, Herb Jeffries, Ray Nance, Joya Sherrill. This highly-esteemed jazz figure composed many fine instrumentals and songs over a long bandleading career which began in 1918. Working in tandem with Duke, from 1939 until the mid-1960s, was the talented composer and arranger Billy Strayhorn. The stylish writing of both men, interpreted over all those years by Ellington's "all-star" quality musicians, resulted in numerous classic pieces, giving the band a unique quality, greatly admired by other musicians, critics and audiences around the world.

ROBERT "SKINNAY" ENNIS- (drums, trumpet, but best known as a vocalist) Theme song: GOT A DATE WITH AN ANGEL. His was a sweet band, featuring his "breathless" style of vocalizing. He led bands from 1938 to the late 1950s, becoming known nationally through his years on the Bob Hope Show.

SHEP FIELDS- (saxophone, clarinet)   Theme song: RIPPLING RHYTHM. Vocalists: Bob Goday, Charles Chester, Dick Robertson, Jerry Stuart, Hal Derwyn. A most innovative leader of a sweet band, who at one time formed an all-reed orchestra. His band was one of those heard most frequently on late night "remote" broadcasts in the mid-1930s. He enjoyed a successful career into the 1950s.

JAN GARBER- (violin) Theme song: MY DEAR. Slogan: "The Idol of the Air Lanes." Vocalists: Lee Bennett, Fritz Heilbron, Lew Palmer, Russell Brown, Liz Tilton. Another durable sweet band, it built its popularity in the early years by busily recording many of the popular songs. It was active for forty years, beginning in the late 1920s.

BENNY GOODMAN- (clarinet) Opening and closing theme songs: LET'S DANCE and GOODBYE. Slogan: "The King of Swing." Vocalists: Helen Ward, Ray Hendricks, Margaret McCrae, Martha Tilton, Louise Tobin, Helen Forrest, Peggy Lee, Dick Haymes, Art Lund. Benny Goodman earned his rightful place in American popular music's "hall of fame," for having forged a breakthrough in swing and thus inspiring the brightest era of the dance bands; for his virtuosity and musicianship; for his always highly-rated bands and for his ability to find and develop outstanding musicians. A large part of his huge legacy of recorded music includes something unmatched by any other bandleader - a collection of sides made by his trios, quartets, quintets and sextets. This provides evidence of his great devotion to swing and jazz, but despite his emphasis on the fast-paced music, he employed a succession of excellent vocalists, demonstrating that ballads were by no means neglected. After 1946 and into the 1970s, Goodman periodically led specially-organized bands on tours to Europe, the Soviet Union and the Far East. He also performed many times as a classical musician.

GLEN GRAY- (saxophone, clarinet) Theme song: SMOKE RINGS. Slogan: "Glen Gray and the Casa Loma Orchestra." Vocalists: Kenny Sargent, "Pee Wee" Hunt, Clyde Burke, Eugenie Baird, the Le Brun Sisters. This was one of a select few excellent bands in the early '30s, cleverly alternating up-tempo music with slow ballads, as the successful swing bands would do later.   Then, it changed to an entirely sweet style, losing a degree of national popularity in the process. Nevertheless, it always managed to maintain an image of style and class, even in its declining years, which ended about 1950.

JOHNNY GREEN- (piano, composer) Theme song: BODY AND SOUL. Vocalists: Jimmy Farrell, Marjorie Logan. His band was a sweet-styled, hotel-type unit, which meant it maintained an expected formality, as contrasted with some which might have been louder and more jazz-influenced. It was only around at the start of the era and might not have attracted much attention, but for the fact that it was one of the few which were recording the popular songs of the day. This included accompanying Fred Astaire on hit selections from his films.   The name "Johnny Green and His Orchestra" was therefore heard often on radio in disproportion to his ranking among the Whitemans, Grays, Kemps and Lombardos of that period. Add to this circumstance the importance of Green's compositions: BODY AND SOUL, COQUETTE, I COVER THE   WATERFRONT,   I'M   YOURS   and   OUT   OF NOWHERE, plus his later work covering many years as a musical director and conductor in the film industry and Johnny Green's contribution to American popular music before, during and after the big band years may be seen as significant.

LIONEL HAMPTON- (vibraphone, piano, drums) Instrumental signature tune: FLYING HOME.   Vocalists: Dinah Washington, Joe Williams. He was the fourth man added to the original Benny Goodman trio of Benny, Teddy Wilson and Gene Krupa to make a quartet. Jazz great and one of several ex-Goodman sidemen to form his own band, he made a sucessful parlay of swing, jazz and showmanship to remain continually active from 1940 until well into the 1980s.

ERSKINE HAWKINS- (trumpet) Theme songs: SWING OUT and later, TUXEDO JUNCTION. Vocalists: Billy Daniels, James Mitchell, Dolores Brown, Ida James. A good swing band which left the classics, TUXEDO JUNCTION, TIPPIN' IN and AFTER HOURS in its legacy. It was active from the mid-1930s into the 1950s.

HORACE HEIDT- (piano) Theme song: I'LL LOVE YOU IN MY DREAMS. Slogan: "Horace Heidt and His Musical Knights." Vocalists: Ronnie Kemper, Larry Cotton, Gordon MacRae, Lysbeth Hughes, The Four King Sisters. This sweet band evolved into a show band, working almost exclusively on radio and television quiz and variety shows. It was active from the late 1930s into the 1950s.

WOODY HERMAN- (clarinet, alto sax, vocalist) Instrumental signature tune: BLUE FLAME. Early slogan: "The Band That Plays the Blues." Other vocalists: Mary Ann McCall. Muriel Lane, Billie Rogers, Carolyn Grey, Frances Wayne. This was a band which, beginning in 1936, played ballads along with swing, had a certain Ellington influence and soon was rated among the ten best swing bands of the era. Later changing his style to include more of what was then described as "progressive" or "modern" jazz, Woody adopted the name, "Herman's Herd" for his band. Every so often there would be a hiatus, followed by a new edition, "Herd Number Two, Three, Four," etc., comprised of the brightest young musicians Woody could find and which unfailingly managed to create a fresh new sound. Woody remained fully active into the 1980s.

RICHARD HIMBER- (violin) Theme song: IT ISN'T FAIR.
Vocalists: Joey Nash, Stuart Allen. This leader of excellent
sweet dance bands played New York City hotels and on radio
shows from the early thirties to the early forties. It gained
additional recognition by being one of only a few bands to
record some of the better songs of the mid-1930s, such as
STARS FELL ON ALABAMA, AUTUMN IN NEW YORK,
ZING! WENT THE STRINGS OF MY HEART, YOU AND
THE NIGHT AND THE MUSIC and JUST ONE OF THOSE
THINGS.

EARL "FATHA" HINES- (piano)   Theme songs:
CAVERNISM, DEEP FOREST. Vocalists: Walter Fuller,
Herb Jeffries, Billy Eckstine, Sarah Vaughn. This jazz star
reached a modest peak with his band in the early 1940s,
disbanded in 1947, then had a successful career as a solo artist
into the 1970s.

EDDY HOWARD- (vocalist) Opening and closing theme
songs: CARELESS and SO LONG FOR NOW. His band
functioned primarily as accompaniment to his singing, but that
was good enough to produce a number of hit records and to
keep the band active from 1940 into the 1960s.

HARRY JAMES- (trumpet) Theme song: CIRIBIRIBIN.
Vocalists: Frank Sinatra, Connie Haines, Dick Haymes, Helen
Forrest, Kitty Kallen, Johnny McAfee, Jimmy Saunders,
Buddy De Vito. His proficiency and versatility on his instru-
ment were unsurpassed. He led bands which produced much

quality music, both swing and romantic ballads, but it was always his horn which led the way. Whether spewing out notes with a speed and power unmatched by anyone, or caressing them with that great feeling that only he could produce, the James tone was distinctive and instantly recognizable. He left Benny Goodman to start his own band in 1939 and by 1942 the band was breaking attendance records everywhere and coming up with one hit record after another. When Glenn Miller relinquished the No. 1 overall ranking to enter military service, Harry's band was strong enough to seize it and hold on tenaciously to the end of the era. With only brief interruptions, he remained active into the 1980s.

ISHAM JONES- (piano, tenor sax, composer of several hit songs) Theme song: YOU'RE JUST A DREAM COME TRUE. Vocalists: Woody Herman, Eddie Stone, Joe Martin, Kathleen Lane. This was a band which started in 1920 and barely lasted into the big band era. Nevertheless, the stature it attained while playing major venues, especially in the Chicago area and the high regard in which it was held by musicians as well as fans, demand that it be included in any list of prominent bands of the 1930s.

DICK JURGENS- (trumpet) Theme song: DAY DREAMS COME TRUE AT NIGHT. Slogan: "There's that BAND again!" Vocalists: Eddy Howard, Ronnie Kemper, Harry Cool, Buddy Moreno. Although the band was based in Chicago, its recordings featuring Eddy Howard on songs like RAGTIME COWBOY JOE, MY LAST GOODBYE and CARELESS, helped it to gain national recognition as an excellent sweet band. Singers Kemper, Cool and Moreno maintained the standard after Howard left to start his own orchestra in 1940. The band was active from 1938 through the 1960s.

SAMMY KAYE- (sax, clarinet)   Theme song: KAYE'S MELODY. Slogan: "Swing and Sway With Sammy Kaye." Vocalists: Charlie Wilson, Tommy Ryan, Jimmy Brown, Clyde Burke, Allan Foster, Don Cornell, Nancy Norman, Billy Williams, Arthur Wright, Betty Barclay, "The Kaydettes." With much greater emphasis on the "sway" than the "swing," this was one of the more prominent and successful sweet bands, ranking with Guy Lombardo and Kay Kyser. It was active from the 1930s into the 1970s, but on a reduced basis after the 1950s.

HAL KEMP- (sax, clarinet) Theme song: (HOW I'LL MISS YOU) WHEN THE SUMMER IS GONE. Vocalists: Skinnay Ennis, Bob Allen, Maxine Gray, Nan Wynn, Janet Blair. Throughout the 1930's, this was one of the leading sweet bands. With a lightly swinging style, it was more than once voted the favorite of college students. However, its existence was tragically cut short by the death of the leader in an auto accident in December, 1940. Beautiful singer Janet Blair went on to become a movie star.

STAN KENTON- (piano)   Theme song: ARTISTRY IN RHYTHM.   Vocalists: Red Dorris, Anita O'Day, June Christy, Andy Russell, Ann Richardson, Gene Howard, Chris Connor.   From its beginning in 1941 until Stan Kenton's passing in 1979 this band strongly emphasized what was called "progressive jazz," or a conversion of some of the elements of true jazz - the solos and riffs - into written arrangements with modern flourishes for the ensemble playing of a big band. An example might have been a strident saxophone improvisation against a background of trumpets, screeching a repeated riff in unison. While this music jolted the senses of many big band fans, it also gained many adherents and Stan Kenton had a large following. He wisely counterbalanced the occasional wild takeoffs with some of the standard swing band fare - music with a rhythmic beat and excellent vocalists, usually provided with swinging ballads. One could not attend a performance of this band, hear the music and observe the tall, athletic-appearing, obviously intense Stan Kenton in action, without gaining an impression that this was a newer, more modern type of band.

WAYNE KING- (alto sax, clarinet, vocalist) Theme song: THE WALTZ YOU SAVED FOR ME. Other vocalists: Gordon Graham, Buddy Clark. The leader was known as "The Waltz King" and his band was the sweetest of the sweet, specializing in gently-flowing instrumentals. It was enjoyed by the older generation and enough other sedate fans and listeners to keep it as a fixture at the Aragon Ballroom in Chicago and on radio for many years. Its peak years were from the early thirties until the early forties.

GENE KRUPA- (drums) Theme songs: APURKSODY, STARBURST and finally, THAT DRUMMER'S BAND. Vocalists: Irene Daye, Anita O'Day, Howard Dulany, Johnny Desmond, Buddy Stewart, Carolyn Grey. The great drummer and leading swing figure had an excellent band for both swing and ballads. Active except for brief periods between 1938 and the 1960s, it enjoyed its peak of popularity in 1941-42, when Anita O'Day and trumpeter Roy Eldridge were with the band.

KAY KYSER- (no instrument) Theme song: THINKING OF YOU. Vocalists: Harry Babbitt, Ginny Simms, Sully Mason, Merwyn "Ish Kabibble" Bogue, Trudy Erwin, Lucy Ann Polk, Georgia Carroll, Mike Douglas. A sweet and novelty-playing show band, which was very entertaining and very big on radio (Kay Kyser's "College of Musical Knowledge"). Once the "Old Professor" got past his comedy routine, the music was invariably excellent. The band was active from 1934 into the 1950s.

GUY LOMBARDO- (violin) Theme songs: COQUETTE, AULD LANG SYNE. Slogan: "The Sweetest Music This Side of Heaven." Vocalists: Carmen and Lebert Lombardo, (brothers of Guy) The Lombardo Trio, (usually consisting of the two brothers and another member of the band) Kenny Gardner, Billy Leach, Tony Craig, Stuart Foster, Jimmy Brown. Scorned by swing fans as probably "the corniest of the corny," it was nevertheless one of the most successful of all bands and an institution from the late 1920s to the 1960s. It became a decades-long tradition to feature Guy Lombardo's playing of AULD LANG SYNE in a coast-to-coast broadcast each December 31st at midnight. A New Year's Eve wouldn't have seemed complete or "official" without it.

JOHNNY LONG- (violin) Theme song: THE WHITE STAR OF SIGMA NU. (However, the band's greatest hit, IN A SHANTY IN OLD SHANTY TOWN, may have been more closely identified with it.) Vocalists: Bob Houston, "The Four

Teens," Patti Dugan, Helen Young, Paul Harmon, Dave Lambert, Dick Robertson. This was a good sweet band which became known nationally, especially during the war years, through having some exclusive recordings of hit songs played on radio and juke boxes. It was active from 1937 into the 1950s.

VINCENT LOPEZ- (piano) Theme song: NOLA. Vocalists: Johnny Morris, Betty Hutton, Sonny Schuyler. This was another of the sweet bands whose style was largely dictated by the leader's piano. Also typically of such bands, it was employed frequently in hotels. Vincent Lopez and his orchestra played for many years at New York's Hotel Taft and was active from the early 1920s into the 1960s.

JIMMIE LUNCEFORD- (saxophone) Theme songs: JAZZNOCRACY, RHYTHM IS OUR BUSINESS. Vocalists: Willie Smith, Henry Wells, Sy Oliver, Dan Grissom, Trummy Young, "The Delta Rhythm Boys," Joe Thomas. This was a true swing band which won the admiration of its peers. It featured an ensemble style and used a great show of enthusiasm by its members for effect. It was active from 1929 until Lunceford's death in 1947.

ENRIC MADRIGUERA- Theme song: ADIOS. Vocalists: Bob Bunch, Tony Sacco, Patricia Gilmore, Bob Lido. Born in Spain, Madriguera was a child prodigy on the violin. His musical prowess led to concert tours, then a position as conductor of the Cuban Philharmonic Orchestra. Moving to New York City, he formed a Latin-American dance band there in 1929 and remained active into the 1950s.

FREDDY MARTIN- (tenor sax) Theme song: TONIGHT WE LOVE -adapted from First Movement, Piano Concerto No. 1 in B-flat Minor (Tchaikovsky). Vocalists: Elmer Feldkamp, Terry Shand, Eddie Stone, Glen Hughes, Bob Haymes, Artie Wayne, Clyde Rogers, Merv Griffin, Stuart Wade, "The Martin Men." This was a leading sweet band which managed a more modern sound than most, due in large part to a fine sax section, led by Martin's own much-admired playing. Although based for many years at the Cocoanut Grove in the Ambassador Hotel in Los Angeles, it also traveled widely and was nationally known through radio shows and hit records. It was active from 1932 into the 1960s.

CLYDE McCOY- (trumpet) Theme song: SUGAR BLUES. Vocalists: Bud Prentiss, Wayne Gregg, Dick Lee, The Four Bennett Sisters. A sweet band, most famous for the "wah-wah" trumpet style of Clyde McCoy, it was active from the 1920s into the 1960s.

HAL McINTYRE- (sax, clarinet) Theme song: MOON MIST. Vocalists: Carl Denny, Jack Lathrop, Al Nobel, Gloria Van, Helen Ward, Ruth Gaylor. Hal graduated from the Glenn Miller band to lead a good one of his own, featuring ballads and occasional swing, from 1941 until 1959.

GLENN MILLER- (trombone) Opening and closing theme songs: MOONLIGHT SERENADE, SLUMBER SONG. Vocalists: Ray Eberle, Tex Beneke, Marion Hutton, Dorothy Claire, Paula Kelly, Skip Nelson, Kay Starr, "The Modernaires." Glenn Miller formed a band in 1937 and tried for two years to obtain a certain sound from his reed section. When he finally found it in a combination of saxophones and one clarinet, the distinctive sound also thrilled and delighted millions of big band fans. They made the band easily No. 1 in popularity for three and a half years, (early 1939 to September, 1942) or until Glenn volunteered for military service. Besides its nightly prime time radio programs, it was heard often via remote broadcasts from wherever it might be playing. It was in constant demand at the leading ballrooms, college campuses, hotels and movie theaters. It made two very popular movies: *Sun Valley Serenade* and *Orchestra Wives*. There were periods when one third of the records on juke boxes were by the Miller band. More than any other band, this one produced great recordings in a variety of moods. Its swing instrumentals, including: IN THE MOOD, (arguably the most famous and best-loved swing number of all time) TUXEDO JUNCTION, PENNSYLVANIA 6-5000, ANVIL CHORUS, LITTLE BROWN JUG, SONG OF THE VOLGA BOATMEN, AMERICAN PATROL and STRING OF PEARLS, became hits soon after the country's disc jockeys had played them a few times. Another kind of instrumental was a Miller trademark, much-loved by his fans. This was the sometimes slow, sometimes sprightly, but always melodious type, in which the famous reed section was usually quite evident, including numbers like: SUNRISE SERENADE, LONDONDERRY AIR, FALLING LEAVES, ADIOS, PAVANNE, MISSOURI WALTZ, BEAUTIFUL OHIO, ALICE BLUE GOWN and the theme song, MOONLIGHT SERENADE. In a third, equally popular category, were the novelty songs, including: CHATTANOOGA CHOO-CHOO, ELMER'S TUNE, DON'T SIT UNDER THE APPLE TREE, KALAMAZOO and JUKE BOX SATURDAY NIGHT. But,

impressive as it was, all of the foregoing was more than offset
by the great number of beautiful, romantic ballads sung by Ray
Eberle, (the younger brother of Bob Eberly retained the family
spelling) either alone or backed by "The Modernaires." Small
wonder, then, that this band was dominant for so long.

VAUGHN MONROE- (trumpet, vocalist) Theme song:
RACING WITH THE MOON. Other vocalists: Marilyn Duke,
The Four Lee Sisters, The Norton Sisters, "The Moon Maids,"
"The Moon Men," "Ziggy" Talent. This was a highly successful sweet band which featured the vocalizing of the handsome
Monroe and his group of singers, made a number of movies,
had many hit records and was featured in prime time radio
shows. Among sweet bands, Guy Lombardo had the greatest
longevity, but perhaps only Kay Kyser appealed to a wider
audience than Vaughn Monroe. The band was active from
1940 through the late 1950s.

RUSS MORGAN- (piano, trombone, sax, guitar, organ, vibra-
harp, vocalist, composer, arranger) Theme song: DOES
YOUR HEART BEAT FOR ME? Slogan: "Music In the
Morgan Manner." Other vocalists: Jack Fulton, Judy
Richards, Jimmy Lewis, Mert Curtis, Lewis Julian, Bernice
Parks, "The Morganaires," Gloria Whitney, Al Jennings.
Morgan guided his sweet band through more than 30 successful
years, from the 1930s to the 1960s. At any given time
throughout, there was probably a currently popular Russ
Morgan recording being featured on radio and juke box.

OZZIE NELSON- (saxophone, vocalist) Theme song:
LOYAL SONS OF RUTGERS. Other vocalists: Harriet

Hilliard, Rose Ann Stevens. Ozzie Nelson began his professional bandleading career in 1930, just after Rudy Vallee and they were similar in many respects. Nelson did not cause as great a sensation in the entertainment world as Vallee, but in the early big band years, when few were as yet recording all the popular songs, Ozzie's records proved very timely and welcome selections. He married his singer, Harriet Hilliard, in 1935 and in 1944 they gave up the band life to play themselves on radio - a concept which they later adapted easily to television for many more years.

RAY NOBLE- (piano, composer, arranger) Opening and closing theme songs: THE VERY THOUGHT OF YOU, GOODNIGHT SWEETHEART. Vocalists: Al Bowlly, "The Freshmen," Howard Phillips, Tony Martin, Larry Stewart, "Snooky" Lanson, Buddy Clark. This English songwriter/bandleader came to America just prior to the start of the era to lead a ready-made sweet band, organized for him by Glenn Miller and comprising several of the better sidemen of that period, including pianist Claude Thornhill, trombonist Will Bradley and Miller himself. It held forth for a few years in one of the most prestigious venues then available - the Rainbow Room, at the top of the 65-story RCA Building in New York's recently-completed Rockefeller Center. During that time, the band was one of the small number providing recordings of currently popular songs. Noble disbanded about 1937 to do studio work in California, later led bands on radio variety shows into the 1950s.

RED NORVO- (xylophone, vibraphone) Theme song: MR. AND MRS. SWING. Vocalists: Mildred Bailey, Terry Allen.

Norvo led smaller bands and combo's and occasionally played with some of the leading swing bands, such as those of Benny Goodman and Woody Herman. He led a full band of his own from 1936 to 1939 and was a talented and respected jazz figure, who, with his wife, singer Mildred Bailey, played an important part in the 1930s world of popular music.

TONY PASTOR- (tenor sax, vocalist)   Theme song: BLOSSOMS.   Other vocalists: Dorsey Anderson, Johnny McAfee, Eugenie Baird, Betty and Rosemary Clooney, Peggy Mann. Tony's band featured ballads with some excursions into jazz, while he continued a tradition of novelty singing he had begun with Artie Shaw. The band was active from 1939 to 1957.

LOUIS PRIMA- (trumpet, vocalist)   Theme song: WAY DOWN YONDER IN NEW ORLEANS. Other vocalists: Lily Ann Carol, Keely Smith. This band specialized in novelty songs, either by Louis alone, or, as in later years, with his then wife, Keely Smith. The band was active from 1939 into the 1960s.

LEO REISMAN- (violin)   Theme song: WHAT IS THIS THING CALLED LOVE? Vocalists: (as from 1935) Sally Singer, Phil Dewey, Frank Luther, Felix Knight, Lee Wiley, Joan Whitney, Sara Horn, Anita Boyer. The band also accompanied Fred Astaire in recording hit songs from the latter's films. This was a sweet band which was active from 1921 into the early 1940s. It had a history of producing recordings of good songs from films and Broadway musicals, which others inexplicably overlooked.

ALVINO REY- (electric guitar) Opening and closing theme songs: BLUE REY, NIGHTY NIGHT. Vocalists: The Four King Sisters, (Alyce, Donna, Louise and Yvonne) Bill Schallen. This was a good, sweet dance band, made uniquely attractive by two features: first, the unusual effects which Alvino was able to produce from his instrument; second, the King Sisters, whose singing enhanced the band's performance, whether they sang together or in solo spots, as Alyce and Yvonne often did. The band was active from 1938 through the 1970s.

JAN SAVITT- (violin) Theme songs: QUAKER CITY JAZZ, IT'S A WONDERFUL WORLD. Slogan: "The Shuffle Rhythm of Jan Savitt and His Top Hatters." Vocalists: George "Bon-Bon" Tunnell, Phil Brito, Clyde Burke, Allan De Witt, Carlotta Dale, Gloria De Haven. This band played swing as well as sweet, but its bouncy "Shuffle Rhythm" set it apart. It was active from 1937 until Savitt's untimely death in 1948.

ARTIE SHAW- (clarinet) Theme song: NIGHTMARE. Vocalists: Tony Pastor, Peg La Centra, Billie Holday, Helen Forrest, Pauline Byrne, Anita Boyer, Lena Horne, Paula Kelly, Georgia Gibbs, Dolores O'Neill, Mel Torme, Kitty Kallen. It was inevitable that Artie Shaw, with another good, clarinet-led swing band, would be compared with his great contemporary, Benny Goodman. In fact, by 1938, when Shaw recorded his hit version of BEGIN THE BEGUINE, fans of both bands were about evenly divided. Then, in November, 1939, with his band at the peak of its popularity, Shaw abruptly departed the big band scene for an extended vacation, during which his musicians and singer Helen Forrest found employment elsewhere. Upon his return, he formed a new band, this time including a large number of violinists. Before he left again in early 1942 to lead a band in the Navy, Shaw made a number of fine recordings, including a big hit with FRENESI, (which he always claimed to detest) but somehow was never mentioned again as being among the leaders, who by then included Glenn Miller, Harry James, Tommy and Jimmy Dorsey, as well as his old rival, Goodman. However, despite the interruptions in the band's existence and changes in its style, its impact as a swing band in the late 1930s was such that many would always regard that band as their favorite of the big band years.

FREDDY SLACK- (piano)   Theme song: STRANGE CARGO. (previously the Will Bradley theme, conceded to Freddy when he left that band) Vocalists: Ella Mae Morse, Margaret Whiting, Liza Morrow, "The Mellowaires." Freddy Slack's special contribution was that he was an exponent of the boogie woogie style and as such, made some of the most memorable recordings of the big band era. With the Will Bradley-Ray McKinley band, there were: BEAT ME DADDY, EIGHT TO THE BAR; SCRUB ME MAMA, WITH A BOOGIE BEAT; DOWN THE ROAD A PIECE and CELERY STALKS AT MIDNIGHT. With his own band and singer Ella Mae Morse, he made: COW COW BOOGIE; MR. FIVE BY FIVE and THE HOUSE OF BLUE LIGHTS. Miss Morse's unusual and pleasing style proved to be the perfect conduit for such songs, gaining much popularity for both the band and herself. The band was active for about ten years, dating from early 1941.

CHARLIE SPIVAK- (trumpet) Theme song: STARDREAMS. Vocalists: Garry Stevens, Tommy Mercer, Irene Daye, Jimmy Saunders, June Hutton, "The Stardusters." This was a better-than-average sweet band, reaching a high level of prominence during the war years. Good singers, song selection and the distinctive mellow tone of Charlie's trumpet helped to give it much of its appeal. It was active from 1940 into the 1950s.

JACK TEAGARDEN- (trombone, vocalist) Theme songs: I GOT A RIGHT TO SING THE BLUES, BASIN STREET BLUES. Other vocalists: Dolores O'Neill, Kitty Kallen, David Allen. This leading exponent of the blues enjoyed great stature as a jazz trombonist. He worked with Paul Whiteman from 1933 to 1938 and led bands of his own from 1939 into the 1960s, his name and talent always an attraction.

CLAUDE THORNHILL- (piano, composer, arranger) Theme song: SNOWFALL. Vocalists: Jimmy Farrell, Maxine Sullivan, Dick Harding, Lillian Lane, Fran Warren, Chris Connor, "The Snowflakes." From 1937 into the mid-1950s, with interruptions for military service and free lance work, Claude Thornhill produced some of the most original and pleasing music, interspersed with modern jazz, created by any band. While his genius was unquestioned and his music certainly admired, in retrospect it seems not to have received as much acclaim nor the band as much success as it deserved, possibly a result of his absence from the big band scene for long periods.

ORRIN TUCKER- (saxophone, vocalist) Theme song: DRIFT-ING AND DREAMING. Other vocalists: Bonnie Baker,

Scottee Marsh, Helen Lee. This was just a good sweet band of modest success when in 1939 Tucker chose to revive a song from 1917: OH! JOHNNY, OH! JOHNNY, OH! The "little girl" voice of singer Bonnie Baker made it one of those instant sensations, nearly approaching the furor over THE MUSIC GOES 'ROUND AND AROUND (Riley and Farley, 1935) and BEI MIR BIST DU SCHOEN (The Andrews Sisters, 1937). It gave the band, which was active from the mid-1930s to the mid-1950s, increased popularity for several years.

TOMMY TUCKER- (piano, but did not play with the band; vocalist) Theme song: I LOVE YOU (OH, HOW I LOVE YOU). Slogan: "It's Tommy Tucker Time!" Other vocalists: Don Brown, Amy Arnell. This was yet another good, if not outstanding sweet band. It achieved its greatest popularity during the war years, when the attractive Amy Arnell had some hit songs and was a favorite of servicemen. The band was active from the late 1930s into the 1950s.

RUDY VALLEE- (saxophone, vocalist) Theme song: MY TIME IS YOUR TIME. In the late 1920s, this enterprising bandleader had success in New York City clubs and on radio when fresh out of college. In fact, his success derived from his collegiate style, including singing through a megaphone and a repertoire of college-inspired songs, such as BETTY COED, THE STEIN SONG and THE WHIFFENPOOF SONG. This led in turn to his appearing in movie musicals and subsequently enjoying a multi-faceted business career which continued into the 1970s.

FRED WARING- (vocalist) Theme song: SLEEP. Other vocalists: Tom Waring, (brother) Clare Hanlon, Johnny "Scat" Davis, Rosemary and Priscilla Lane. Featuring singers, including a glee club, this band was simply part of *The Fred Waring Show,* one of the music staples on radio during many of the big band years. As such, it was in a category apart from the typical big band. It seldom recorded after 1932 and did not compete with the Dorseys, Lombardos, et al, for bookings at the dance venues.

CHICK WEBB- (drums) Theme song: LET'S GET TOGETHER. Vocalist: Ella Fitzgerald. This was a swing and jazz band, strong on rhythm. On at least one occasion, it was said to have been declared the winner in a head-to-head competition with some bigger-name swing bands. However, perhaps its greatest fame came from having been the vehicle for launching the singing career of Ella Fitzgerald. Her 1938 hit with the band, A-TISKET, A-TASKET, was a sensation, catapulting her to instant fame and subsequently to a very long and successful career as one of America's premier singers of popular song. Chick Webb died in 1939 at age 30 and Ella led the band for a few years afterward.

TED WEEMS- (violin and trombone, but did not play with the band) Theme song: OUT OF THE NIGHT. Vocalists included Perry Como and Marvell (Marilyn) Maxwell. This was a smaller, though popular sweet band, which featured its singers along with whistler Elmo Tanner and was most effective in the smaller rooms. It was active from the late 1920s into the 1960s.

PAUL WHITEMAN-(violin) Theme song: RHAPSODY IN BLUE. Vocalists: "The Rhythm Boys" trio, which included Bing Crosby in his first singing job; Johnny Mercer, Morton Downey, Mildred Bailey, Red McKenzie. Despite his long-time label as the "Jazz King" and the fact that he employed many fine jazz soloists, a performance of the Paul Whiteman Orchestra was not a likely place at which to hear jazz. With an average 25 members, it was instead an oversized dance band, easily the most famous prior to 1935 and the swing revolution. Having been active since 1919, Whiteman entered the Big Band Era as an "elder statesman," devoting more time to radio and movies and less to dances and making records. He remained active into the 1950s.

VICTOR YOUNG- (violin, composer) Theme song: A GHOST OF A CHANCE. Vocalists: Paul Small, Hal Burke, Milton Watson, Frank Luther, Dick Robertson, "The Tune Twisters." Two other beautiful compositions by Victor Young, in addition to his theme song, were STELLA BY STARLIGHT and MY FOOLISH HEART. He was radio conductor for Al Jolson and his orchestra provided accompaniment on many recording dates for Bing Crosby, Connie Boswell and The Boswell Sisters. He was also another of the small group who did most of the early recording.

The Arrangers and Bandleaders For Whom They Worked

For various reasons, musicians moved about from band to band and because of their varying styles and abilities, this often affected the way the bands sounded. However, even more influential in the way they sounded were the arrangers. These were musicians with a special talent for writing music for the various instruments and who were employed to adapt songs or instrumentals to the style desired by the bandleader. In certain instances they may also have been commissioned to create an original piece of music, or may simply have done this voluntarily. Creativeness was their stock in trade and outstanding hits were achievements for which they would be credited for the rest of their lives and beyond.

Several of these gentlemen gained considerable recognition, such as Fletcher Henderson, for his arrangements for Benny Goodman; Sy Oliver, for his work with Tommy Dorsey; Jerry Gray, for important creations for both Artie Shaw and Glenn Miller; Billy May for Charlie Barnet and others and Ed Sauter and Bill Finegan, also for their work with several of the leading bands. But, by and large, the arrangers did not receive nearly as much credit as they deserved for such demanding, specialized, generally excellent and often brilliant work. For every BEGIN THE BEGUINE, OPUS No. 1 and 'S WONDERFUL for which a Jerry Gray, Sy Oliver or a Ray Conniff would be credited repeatedly by disc jockeys, so that not only their individual names, but the arranging craft itself gained recognition, there were a hundred other beautiful arrangements whose creators were left unidentified. Take a number as huge in importance as TAKE THE "A" TRAIN. Most fans knew that it belonged to Duke Ellington, but it is really questionable whether many knew it had been arranged by one Billy Strayhorn.

Now, so many years later, when it's even becoming difficult to find records or sheet music of many old songs and instrumentals, credit for the best-known arrangements of these numbers is even harder to trace. In an effort to keep the identities of the busiest and best-known arrangers as well-preserved as possible, we have compiled the following representative list. Shown are the bandleaders for whom each of them worked. It will be noted that some eventually became bandleaders, while others were bandleaders from beginning to end:

CHARLIE ALBERTINE- Bobby Byrne, Sammy Kaye, Les Elgart

AL AVOLA- Tony Pastor, Frankie Carle

CHARLIE BARNET- for his own orchestra

BILL BORDEN- Claude Thornhill

LES BROWN- Jimmy Dorsey, Larry Clinton and for his own band.

BOB BURNET- Charlie Barnet

SONNY BURKE- Jimmy Dorsey, Charlie Spivak

RALPH BURNS- Woody Herman, Benny Goodman

TUTTI CAMARATA- Paul Whiteman, Charlie Barnet, Jimmy Dorsey, Glen Gray

BENNY CARTER- Charlie Barnet

BILL CHALLIS- Paul Whiteman, Fletcher Henderson, Dorsey Brothers, Glen Gray

LARRY CLINTON- Isham Jones, Glen Gray, Tommy
    Dorsey, Jimmy Dorsey, Bunny Berigan and for his own
    orchestra.
FRANK COMSTOCK- Les Brown
RAY CONNIFF- Bunny Berigan, Artie Shaw, Alvino Rey,
    Vaughn Monroe
FRANK DeVOL- Horace Heidt, Alvino Rey
TOMMY DORSEY- for his own orchestra
GEORGE DUNING- Kay Kyser
DUKE ELLINGTON- Did most of the arranging for his band,
    although the contributions of Billy Strayhorn were
    considerable.
BUD ESTES- Charlie Barnet
GIL EVANS- Claude Thornhill
JERRY FIELDING- Alvino Rey, Tommy Dorsey, Charlie
    Barnet, Kay Kyser
BILL FINEGAN- Glenn Miller, Tommy Dorsey, Horace
    Heidt
RALPH FLANAGAN- Charlie Barnet, Hal McIntyre, Tony
    Pastor, Gene Krupa, Blue Barron, Sammy Kaye
ANDY GIBSON- Charlie Barnet, Harry James
GENE GIFFORD- Glen Gray
JERRY GRAY- Artie Shaw, Glenn Miller
JIMMY GRIER- Gus Arnheim
BOB HAGGART- Bob Crosby
GEORGE HANDY- Alvino Rey
BUSTER HARDING- Teddy Wilson, Artie Shaw, Cab
    Calloway, Benny Goodman, Count Basie, Glenn Miller,
    Tommy Dorsey
LENNIE HAYTON- Artie Shaw

NEAL HEFTI- Charlie Barnet, Bobby Byrne, Earl Hines,
    Woody Herman, Charlie Spivak, Alvino Rey
FLETCHER HENDERSON- Charlie Barnet, Benny Goodman
    and for his own band
BILL HOLMAN- Charlie Barnet, Stan Kenton
BEN HOMER- Les Brown
HARRY JAMES- For his own orchestra
GORDON JENKINS- Isham Jones
BUDD JOHNSON- Tony Pastor
DICK JONES- Tommy Dorsey, Glen Gray
DEAN KINCAIDE- Bob Crosby, Charlie Barnet, Tommy
    Dorsey, Benny Goodman, Ray McKinley, Muggsy Spanier
JOHNNY MANDEL- Alvino Rey, Artie Shaw
SKIP MARTIN- Charlie Barnet, Les Brown, Glenn Miller
MATTY MATLOCK- Bob Crosby, Harry James
DAVE MATTHEWS- Woody Herman, Hal McIntyre
BILLY MAY- Charlie Barnet, Glenn Miller
GLENN MILLER- Ben Pollack, Dorsey Brothers, Red
    Nichols, Ray Noble and for his own orchestra
BILLY MOORE- Charlie Barnet
RUSS MORGAN- Fletcher Henderson, Louis Armstrong,
    Chick Webb, Dorsey Brothers, Freddy Martin and for
    his own orchestra
GERRY MULLIGAN- Gene Krupa, Stan Kenton
JAMES MUNDY- Benny Goodman, Earl Hines, Count Basie,
    Gene Krupa, Bob Crosby, Paul Whiteman
SY OLIVER- Jimmie Lunceford, Tommy Dorsey
GLENN OSSER- Charlie Barnet, Bunny Berigan, Bob
    Crosby, Benny Goodman, Paul Whiteman, Shep Fields
MEL POWELL- Benny Goodman, Glenn Miller Army Air
    Corps Band

LOU QUADLING- Kay Kyser, Gus Arnheim
DON REDMAN- Fletcher Henderson, Jimmy Dorsey, Count
    Basie, Harry James
NELSON RIDDLE- Tommy Dorsey, Bob Crosby, Charlie
    Spivak, Alvino Rey
HARRY RODGERS- Artie Shaw, Glen Gray
PETE RUGOLO- Charlie Barnet, Stan Kenton
BILL RUSSO- Stan Kenton
EDGAR SAMPSON- Chick Webb, Benny Goodman, Artie
    Shaw, Teddy Wilson, Red Norvo
EDDIE SAUTER- Charlie Barnet, Benny Goodman, Artie
    Shaw, Woody Herman, Red Norvo, Tommy Dorsey,
    Ray McKinley
BOBBY SHERWOOD- Charlie Barnet and for his own
    orchestra
AXEL STORDAHL- Tommy Dorsey
BILLY STRAYHORN- Duke Ellington
CLAUDE THORNHILL- Skinnay Ennis and for his own
    orchestra
JOHN SCOTT TROTTER- Hal Kemp
LARRY WAGNER- Glen Gray
HENRY WELLS- Andy Kirk, Jimmie Lunceford, Teddy
    Powell
PAUL WESTON- Bob Crosby, Tommy Dorsey

Some famous arrangements and their creators:

AMAPOLA - Tutti Camaratta, for Jimmy Dorsey
GREEN EYES - Tutti Camaratta, for Jimmy Dorsey
YOURS - Tutti Camaratta, for Jimmy Dorsey
TANGERINE - Tutti Camaratta, for Jimmy Dorsey
MY REVERIE -Larry Clinton, for his own orchestra
DEEP PURPLE - Larry Clinton, for his own orchestra
'S WONDERFUL -Ray Conniff, For Artie Shaw
SONG OF INDIA -Tommy Dorsey, for his own orchestra
LITTLE BROWN JUG -Bill Finegan, for Glenn Miller
BEGIN THE BEGUINE -Jerry Gray, for Artie Shaw
PENNSYLVANIA 6-5000 - Jerry Gray, for Glenn Miller
TUXEDO JUNCTION - Jerry Gray, for Glenn Miller
A STRING OF PEARLS - Jerry Gray, for Glenn Miller
ST. LOUIS BLUES MARCH -Jerry Gray, Ray McKinley and
    Glenn Miller, for the Army Air Corps Band
STAR DUST -Lennie Hayton, for Artie Shaw
CHRISTOPHER COLUMBUS -Fletcher Henderson, for
    Benny Goodman
KING PORTER STOMP -Fletcher Henderson, for
    Benny Goodman
FLIGHT OF THE BUMBLE BEE -Harry James, for his own
    orchestra
CARNIVAL OF VENICE -Harry James, for his own
    orchestra
BOOGIE-WOOGIE -Dean Kincaide, for Tommy Dorsey
I'VE GOT MY LOVE TO KEEP ME WARM -Skip Martin,
    for Les Brown
CHEROKEE -Billy May, for Charlie Barnet
SKYLINER -Billy Moore, for Charlie Barnet

OPUS No. 1 -Sy Oliver, for Tommy Dorsey
THE JERSEY BOUNCE -Mel Powell, for Benny Goodman
MISSION TO MOSCOW - Mel Powell, for Benny Goodman
DON'T BE THAT WAY -Edgar Sampson, for Benny
    Goodman
STOMPIN' AT THE SAVOY -Edgar Sampson, for Benny
    Goodman
I LET A SONG GO OUT OF MY HEART -Billy Strayhorn,
    for Duke Ellington
TAKE THE "A" TRAIN -Billy Strayhorn, for Duke Ellington

II

The Years

Here begin the yearly lists of hit recordings. To help the reader understand exactly how they have been structured, we offer the following explanations:

In the yearly lists, after each song title, the bandleader's name is listed first, followed by the vocalist's name in parentheses, e. g., "Bob Crosby (Frank Tenille)" or "(Vocal) and His Orchestra," if the bandleader himself was the vocalist, e.g., "Bob Crosby (Vocal) and His Orchestra" or "Instrumental" if there was no vocal, e.g., "Bob Crosby (Instrumental)."

If the recording artists were independent singers or groups, the names are (usually) listed by themselves without mention of accompanists, such as "Bing Crosby," "Frances Langford," "Connie Boswell," "The Boswell Sisters," etc. The reason for this is that the records of these and other independent artists were sold, or listed on juke boxes, or requested of disc jockeys without regard to the accompanists, which in any case were often changed, from one recording session to another. Certain exceptions have been made when it appeared that the combination of independent singer and accompanying orchestra was one worth noting.

Perhaps most importantly, it should be explained that

39

the trimesters in which it is indicated that songs were popular, were those in which they first attracted attention by being played repeatedly on radio, which in itself qualified a song as a popular hit. Using trimesters is merely a means of separating the songs into groups as an aid to chronological placement. It was never possible to be more precise, such as indicating a day or a week when a song became popular. Recording dates are well-documented, but the dates when recordings were issued and when they began to receive radio and juke box play, and further, whether they caught on immediately, are facts not readily ascertainable, at least not with certainty. Neither "chart dates" or dates when songs first appeared on *Your Hit Parade* can be relied upon 100% as dates when songs actually became known to the average listener. In any case, songs seemed to succeed each other much like seasons of the year. When some would start to fade, new ones would be introduced - which makes our use of trimesters appropriate if not sharply precise. While the periods of popularity of some songs may not have extended beyond, or even as long as three months, that of others, such as PAPER DOLL and I'LL BE SEEING YOU, was prolonged for up to six months. Just as a song's popularity may have carried over from one trimester to the next, it may also have been divided between the end of one year and the early weeks or months of the next. In those instances, as with trimesters, an effort was made to place those songs in the periods when it appeared that interest in them was greatest - which was more likely to have been at the beginning, rather than in the later months of their popularity.

To find a hit from any of these years: the Index of Songs and Instrumentals at the back of this book permits the reader to quickly determine the quarter of the year when the song was popular. Turning to that year's lists, the quarter and then the song title may be easily located. Alongside will be noted the artist or artists either mainly responsible for or contributing to the song's popularity.

1 9 3 5

The Most Popular Recordings

January - March

SOLITUDE -Duke Ellington (Instrumental)

P. S. I LOVE YOU -Rudy Vallee (Vocal) and His Orchestra

THE OBJECT OF MY AFFECTION -Jimmy Grier (Pinky
Tomlin); The Boswell Sisters; Glen Gray (Pee Wee Hunt);
Jan Garber (Lee Bennett)

YOU'RE THE TOP -Paul Whiteman (Peggy Healy and John
Hauser)

STAY AS SWEET AS YOU ARE -Jimmy Grier (Pinky
Tomlin); Guy Lombardo (Carmen Lombardo)

JUNE IN JANUARY -Bing Crosby

I GET A KICK OUT OF YOU -Paul Whiteman (Ramona
Davies); Leo Reisman (Sally Singer)

WITH EVERY BREATH I TAKE -Bing Crosby

ANYTHING GOES -Paul Whiteman (Ramona Davies)

LOVE IS JUST AROUND THE CORNER -Bing Crosby

AUTUMN IN NEW YORK -Richard Himber (Joey Nash)

ZING! WENT THE STRINGS OF MY HEART -Richard
Himber (Joey Nash); Victor Young (Hal Burke)

ISLE OF CAPRI -Ray Noble (Al Bowlly); Freddy Martin
(Elmer Feldkamp)

BLUE MOON -Glen Gray (Kenny Sargent); Benny Goodman
(Helen Ward)

YOU AND THE NIGHT AND THE MUSIC -Richard
Himber (Libby Holman)
ON THE GOOD SHIP LOLLIPOP -Rudy Vallee (Vocal) and
His Orchestra
WHEN I GROW TOO OLD TO DREAM -Glen Gray (Kenny
Sargent)
CLOUDS -Ray Noble (Al Bowlly)
I WON'T DANCE -Eddy Duchin (Lew Sherwood); Johnny
Green (Marjorie Logan and Jimmy Farrell); Guy
Lombardo (The Lombardo Trio)
LOVELY TO LOOK AT -Eddy Duchin (Lew Sherwood);
Guy Lombardo (The Lombardo Trio); Leo Reisman
(Phil Dewey)
WHAT'S THE REASON (I'M NOT PLEASIN' YOU?) -Guy
Lombardo (Carmen Lombardo)
SOON -Bing Crosby
IT'S EASY TO REMEMBER -Bing Crosby
LOOKIE, LOOKIE, LOOKIE, HERE COMES COOKIE -
Glen Gray (Pee Wee Hunt)
LULLABY OF BROADWAY (Academy Award-winner from
the film, *Gold Diggers of 1935*) -Dick Powell, Hal Kemp
(Bob Allen); Dorsey Brothers Orchestra (Bob Crosby);
The Boswell Sisters
FLOWERS FOR MADAME -Ray Noble (Al Bowlly); Bob
Crosby (Frank Tenille)

April - June

THE LITTLE THINGS YOU USED TO DO -Johnny Green
(Marjorie Logan)

ABOUT A QUARTER TO NINE -Ozzie Nelson (Vocal) and
His Orchestra; Johnny Green (Jimmy Farrell); Victor
Young (Hal Burke)
SHE'S A LATIN FROM MANHATTAN -Victor Young (Hal
Burke); Johnny Green (Jimmy Farrell); Ozzie Nelson
(Vocal) and His Orchestra
LIFE IS A SONG (LET'S SING IT TOGETHER) -Ruth
Etting; Freddy Martin (Elmer Feldkamp); Connie Boswell;
Victor Young (Milton Watson)
LOVE AND A DIME -Jan Garber (Fritz Heilbron)
YOU'RE A HEAVENLY THING -Benny Goodman (Helen
Ward)
TELL ME THAT YOU LOVE ME -Frank Parker; Freddy
Martin (Elmer Feldkamp); Russ Morgan (Jack Fulton)
THE LADY IN RED -Xavier Cugat (Don Reid); Louis Prima
(Vocal) and His Orchestra
IN A LITTLE GYPSY TEA ROOM -Bob Crosby (Frank
Tenille); Jan Garber (Lee Bennett); Louis Prima (Vocal)
and His Orchestra
IN THE MIDDLE OF A KISS -Hal Kemp (Skinnay Ennis);
Connie Boswell
SEEIN' IS BELIEVIN' -Guy Lombardo (Carmen Lombardo);
Connie Boswell; Rudy Vallee (Vocal) and His Orchestra
I'LL NEVER SAY "NEVER AGAIN" AGAIN -Benny
Goodman (Helen Ward); Ozzie Nelson (Vocal) and His
Orchestra
CHASING SHADOWS -Dorsey Brothers (Bob Eberly);
Connie Boswell; Louis Prima (Vocal) and His Orchestra
RHYTHM OF THE RAIN -Dorsey Brothers (Kay Weber)
THRILLED -Hal Kemp (Skinnay Ennis)

July - September

EAST OF THE SUN (AND WEST OF THE MOON) -Bob
   Crosby (Frank Tenille)
LET'S SWING IT -Ray Noble (Al Bowlly)
PARIS IN THE SPRING -Ray Noble (Al Bowlly); Freddy
   Martin (Elmer Feldkamp)
AND THEN SOME -Ozzie Nelson (Vocal) and His Orchestra;
   Bob Crosby (Vocal) and His Orchestra
I'M GONNA SIT RIGHT DOWN AND WRITE MYSELF A
   LETTER -Fats Waller
EVERY LITTLE MOVEMENT -Dorsey Brothers (Kay
   Weber)
I COULDN'T BELIEVE MY EYES -Freddy Martin (Elmer
   Feldkamp)
LOVE ME FOREVER -Russ Morgan (Vocal) and His
   Orchestra
YOU'RE ALL I NEED -Eddy Duchin (Lew Sherwood);
   Jimmy Dorsey (Bob Eberly)
LULU'S BACK IN TOWN -Fats Waller; Dick Powell
CHEEK TO CHEEK -Fred Astaire, with the Leo Reisman
   Orchestra; Eddy Duchin (Lew Sherwood); Guy Lombardo
   (Carmen Lombardo)
TOP HAT, WHITE TIE AND TAILS -Fred Astaire, with the
   Johnny Green Orchestra; Ray Noble (Al Bowlly); The
   Boswell Sisters
PAGE MISS GLORY -Hal Kemp (Skinnay Ennis)
(OOH!) WHAT A LITTLE MOONLIGHT CAN DO -Teddy
   Wilson (Billie Holiday)

I'M IN THE MOOD FOR LOVE -Little Jack Little (Vocal)
   and His Orchestra; Frances Langford; Paul Whiteman
   (Ramona Davies)
DOUBLE TROUBLE -Ray Noble (Vocal with The Four
   Freshmen) and His Orchestra
THE ROSE IN HER HAIR -Russ Morgan (Vocal) and His
   Orchestra
ISN'T THIS A LOVELY DAY? -Fred Astaire, with the
   Johnny Green Orchestra; Guy Lombardo (Carmen
   Lombardo)
THE PICCOLINO -Fred Astaire, with the Leo Reisman
   Orchestra; Ray Noble (Al Bowlly)
TRUCKIN' -Fats Waller
I WISHED ON THE MOON -Bing Crosby; Ray Noble (Al
   Bowlly)
FROM THE TOP OF YOUR HEAD TO THE TIP OF YOUR
   TOES -Bing Crosby; Hal Kemp (Skinnay Ennis)
WITHOUT A WORD OF WARNING -Bing Crosby
I FEEL A SONG COMIN' ON -Frances Langford
ACCENT ON YOUTH -Duke Ellington (Instrumental); Jan
   Garber (Lee Bennett)
RHYTHM AND ROMANCE -Fats Waller

October - December

BROADWAY RHYTHM -Guy Lombardo (Instrumental);
   Richard Himber (Stuart Allen)
YOU ARE MY LUCKY STAR -Tommy Dorsey (Eleanor
   Powell, guest vocalist); Eddy Duchin (Lew Sherwood);
   Connie Boswell

THE GENTLEMAN OBVIOUSLY DOESN'T BELIEVE
(IN LOVE) -Jimmy Dorsey (Kay Weber)

I'VE GOT A FEELIN' YOU'RE FOOLIN' -Jimmy Dorsey
(Bob Eberly); Eddy Duchin (Lew Sherwood); Tommy
Dorsey (Eleanor Powell, guest vocalist)

ROLL ALONG, PRAIRIE MOON -Smith Ballew (Vocal) and
His Orchestra; Bob Crosby (Vocal) and His Orchestra

ON TREASURE ISLAND -Tommy Dorsey (Edythe Wright);
Bing Crosby; Bob Crosby (Frank Tenille)

RED SAILS IN THE SUNSET -Guy Lombardo (Carmen
Lombardo); Bing Crosby; Ray Noble (Al Bowlly)

I FOUND A DREAM -Enric Madriguera (Tony Sacco); Bob
Crosby (Frank Tenille)

HERE'S TO ROMANCE -Enric Madriguera (Tony Sacco);
Bob Crosby (Frank Tenille); Buddy Clark

BEGIN THE BEGUINE -Xavier Cugat (Don Reid)

TWENTY FOUR HOURS A DAY -Teddy Wilson (Billie
Holiday)

DON'T GIVE UP THE SHIP -Dick Powell; Tommy Dorsey
(Cliff Weston)

THANKS A MILLION -Dick Powell; Bob Crosby (Vocal)
and His Orchestra

TAKE ME BACK TO MY BOOTS AND SADDLE -Bing
Crosby; Tommy Dorsey (Cliff Weston)

I'M SITTIN' HIGH ON A HILLTOP -Bob Crosby (Vocal)
and His Orchestra; Guy Lombardo (Carmen
Lombardo)

A LITTLE BIT INDEPENDENT -Freddy Martin (Elmer
Feldkamp); Fats Waller; Bob Crosby (Vocal) and His
Orchestra

JUST ONE OF THOSE THINGS -Richard Himber (Stuart
     Allen)
WHERE AM I? -Ray Noble (Al Bowlly); Little Jack Little
     (Vocal) and His Orchestra
NO OTHER ONE -Benny Goodman (Helen Ward); Bob
     Crosby (Vocal) and His Orchestra
EENIE, MEENIE, MINEY, MO -Benny Goodman (Helen
     Ward); Bob Crosby (Vocal) and His Orchestra
THE MUSIC GOES 'ROUND AND AROUND -Riley and
     Farley "Onyx Club Boys" Orchestra (Sung by Joe Riley
     and Eddie Farley)
WITH ALL MY HEART -Hal Kemp (Skinnay Ennis); Glen
     Gray (Kenny Sargent); Ray Noble (Al Bowlly)

     Among each year's crop of song hits there of course were
always some whose popularity was greater and longer-lasting
than that of the others. Those were the songs which obtained
more sales of sheet music and recordings and were heard on
radio disc jockey shows and juke boxes for months, while the
average song was heard briefly and was gone. Some would
have such lasting appeal that they were performed by a
succession of artists over several decades. Sometimes, however, fame for a song was fleeting, so that while it may have
been one of the biggest hits of its year, it did not graduate into
the ranks of the standards or classics, which endured for years.
While identifying all the hits of every year, it is also revealing
to note those which were outstanding at the time, as well as
those which outlasted the rest.

     With perfect timing, the weekly radio show, *Your Hit*

Parade began its long run this year, providing future historians a record at least of how its surveys measured the comparative popularity of the year's favorites. For example, the *Hit Parade's* top ten for 1935, based on point allocations for most appearances and most weeks in first place were: RED SAILS IN THE SUNSET; IN A LITTLE GYPSY TEA ROOM; CHEEK TO CHEEK; EAST OF THE SUN (AND WEST OF THE MOON); YOU ARE MY LUCKY STAR; CHASING SHADOWS; LIFE IS A SONG; WHAT'S THE REASON? (I'M NOT PLEASIN' YOU?); IN THE MIDDLE OF A KISS and ON TREASURE ISLAND.

Causing one of the greatest sensations ever was Riley and Farley's THE MUSIC GOES 'ROUND AND AROUND, heard just before year-end and a few weeks into 1936.

Among this year's songs which proved to have the most lasting power were: SOLITUDE; I GET A KICK OUT OF YOU; EAST OF THE SUN (AND WEST OF THE MOON); BEGIN THE BEGUINE; CHEEK TO CHEEK; I'M IN THE MOOD FOR LOVE and JUST ONE OF THOSE THINGS.

Instrumental "Collector's Items"

GROWLIN'	-Charlie Barnet
NAGASAKI	-Charlie Barnet
SUGARFOOT STOMP	-Dorsey Brothers
WEARY BLUES	-Dorsey Brothers
STOP LOOK AND LISTEN	-Jimmy Dorsey
DUSK IN UPPER SANDUSKY	-Jimmy Dorsey

ADMIRATION	-Duke Ellington
FAREWELL BLUES	-Duke Ellington
LET'S HAVE A JUBILEE	-Duke Ellington
MOONLIGHT FIESTA	-Duke Ellington
SHOWBOAT SHUFFLE	-Duke Ellington
MERRY-GO-ROUND	-Duke Ellington
REMINISCING IN TEMPO	-Duke Ellington
JAPANESE SANDMAN	-Benny Goodman (Full Band)
BLUE SKIES	-Benny Goodman (Full Band)
DEAR OLD SOUTHLAND	-Benny Goodman (Full Band)
SOMETIMES I'M HAPPY	-Benny Goodman (Full Band)
THREE LITTLE WORDS	-Benny Goodman (Full Band)
KING PORTER STOMP	-Benny Goodman (Full Band)
JAZZ ME BLUES	-Benny Goodman (Full Band)
BODY AND SOUL	-Benny Goodman (Trio)
AFTER YOU'VE GONE	-Benny Goodman (Trio)
WHO?	-Benny Goodman (Trio)
SOME DAY SWEETHEART	-Benny Goodman (Trio)
ALONE	-Jimmie Lunceford
RUNNIN' WILD	-Jimmie Lunceford
FOUR OR FIVE TIMES	-Jimmie Lunceford
BLACK AND TAN FANTASY	-Jimmie Lunceford
RHYTHM IS OUR BUSINESS	-Jimmie Lunceford
PHANTOM FANTASY	-Russ Morgan
TIDAL WAVE	-Russ Morgan
SLIPHORN SAM	-Russ Morgan
MIDNIGHT OIL	-Russ Morgan
WAY DOWN YONDER IN NEW ORLEANS	-Ray Noble
CHINATOWN MY CHINATOWN	-Ray Noble

BUGLE CALL RAG   -Ray Noble
DINAH   -Ray Noble

Developments This Year in Popular Music

- New bands getting started this year included those of William "Count" Basie, Bob Crosby, Tommy Dorsey and Ray Noble. There were unusual circumstances relating to the Crosby, Dorsey and Noble endeavors. Only this year, Bob Crosby had joined the Dorsey Brothers' band as vocalist, undoubtedly with high hopes residing in all parties that he might follow in the footsteps of his famous brother Bing. Then, he received an offer for him to lend the prestige of the Crosby name as leader of a band of excellent musicians who had been left temporarily leaderless. Thus began the Bob Crosby Orchestra, which gained prominence in the first half of the big band era.

- Replacing Bob Crosby as vocalist with the Dorsey Brothers Orchestra was Bob Eberly, who would become quite possibly the male band singer most admired by his peers.

- The Dorsey Brothers band became the Jimmy Dorsey band, when Tommy capped one of the brothers' frequent arguments by storming off the stage at a performance and never returning. By September, Tommy was recording with his own new band.   •

- Ray Noble was   a 30-year-old English bandleader, songwriter and musical director of a leading record company when he decided to try his luck in America. To help organize a band, he obtained the services of Glenn Miller, who was still a few years away from forming his own orchestra. Glenn was also scheduled to be a trombonist and arranger with the band and employed several other all-star caliber musicians, including Will Bradley as another trombonist, Charlie Spivak on trumpet and Claude Thornhill on piano. Noble brought his own drummer and his great vocalist, Al Bowlly, from England. The band gained the added advantage of a booking at the prestigious Rainbow Room, high atop the new RCA Building in New York's recently completed Rockefeller Center. It remained a fixture there for a few years, while at the same time busily recording many of the top tunes of the day, which helped greatly in making the band well known. The success of the Ray Noble Orchestra proved a timely contribution to the launching of the big band era, as were such Noble compositions as GOODNIGHT SWEETHEART, THE TOUCH OF YOUR LIPS, THE VERY THOUGHT OF YOU, GOT A DATE WITH AN ANGEL, LOVE IS THE SWEETEST THING, I HADN'T ANYONE TILL YOU and CHEROKEE.

- The Glen Gray Orchestra, also known as the Casa Loma Orchestra, or Glen Gray and His Casa Loma Orchestra, was joined this year by Larry Clinton, who could play trumpet, trombone and clarinet, but perhaps was most valued as an arranger. The band this year had the distinction of being the first to appear on stage at the New York Paramount Theater, that motion picture palace on Times Square, which later became a coveted booking for every band, group and singer of the big band era, for the valuable publicity it would bring.

- Singer Frances Langford got her first big break this year, with an important role in the movie, *Every Night At Eight*, with Alice Faye and George Raft. In it, she sang I'M IN THE MOOD FOR LOVE, which became a hit and helped to establish her as one of the leading singers of this era.

- Making several notable recordings this year, as they had done throughout the early 1930s, were the three Boswell Sisters, Connie, Helvetia and Martha, from New Orleans. In addition, Connie, who was a victim of poliomyelitis, was successful as a soloist and also made recordings with Bing Crosby. As a trio, the girls helped to inspire many other girl singing groups. The Andrews Sisters readily credited the Boswells for setting an example of proficiency for them to strive to equal.

- In August, at the end of a discouraging series of engagements between New York and Los Angeles, the Benny Goodman band scored a rousing success at the Los Angeles Palomar Ballroom. This was always considered to be the breakthrough for swing music. Swing in turn led to increased interest in the big bands and a rapid expansion of every facet of their business.

- Just before Christmas, the entire nation was captivated by a "nonsense" song, THE MUSIC GOES 'ROUND AND AROUND. Mike Riley and Eddie Farley, leaders of an 8-piece band, "The Onyx Club Boys," were responsible for composing and singing this frivolous ditty, which, during its first days of release, was played over and over by radio disc jockeys nationwide, as public demand was insatiable. Evening variety shows were soon vying with each other to present Riley and Farley to perform it in person. If ever there was a song sensation, it was this one and fascination with it continued for a few weeks into the new year. Then, it quickly faded, along with Riley and Farley and their Onyx Club Boys, almost never to be heard again.

1 9 3 6

The Most Popular Recordings

January - March

ALONE -Tommy Dorsey (Cliff Weston); Hal Kemp (Bob Allen)

MOON OVER MIAMI -Eddy Duchin (Lew Sherwood); Jan Garber (Lee Bennett); Dick Robertson; Buddy Clark; Connie Boswell

LIGHTS OUT -Eddy Duchin (Lew Sherwood); Victor Young (Dick Robertson)

I FEEL LIKE A FEATHER IN THE BREEZE -Hal Kemp (Skinnay Ennis); Jan Garber (Lee Bennett); Richard Himber (Stuart Allen)

THE BROKEN RECORD -Guy Lombardo (The Lombardo Trio)

DINNER FOR ONE PLEASE JAMES -Ray Noble (Al Bowlly); Hal Kemp (Skinnay Ennis and Maxine Gray)

LITTLE GIRL BLUE -Paul Whiteman (Donald Novis and Gloria Grafton)

THE MOST BEAUTIFUL GIRL IN THE WORLD -Paul Whiteman (Instrumental)

MY ROMANCE -Paul Whiteman (Donald Novis and Gloria Grafton)

PLEASE BELIEVE ME -Tommy Dorsey (Buddy Gately)

I'M SHOOTING HIGH -Alice Faye; Tommy Dorsey
(Edythe Wright)
A BEAUTIFUL LADY IN BLUE -Ray Noble (Al Bowlly);
Jan Garber (Lew Palmer)
CLING TO ME -Ozzie Nelson (Vocal) and His Orchestra
I'M BUILDING UP TO AN AWFUL LETDOWN -Fred
Astaire; Eddy Duchin (Lew Sherwood)
YOU HIT THE SPOT -Frances Langford; Richard Himber
(Stuart Allen)
I'M GONNA SIT RIGHT DOWN AND WRITE MYSELF A
LETTER (From 1935) Continued popularity through new
recordings by Hal Kemp (Skinnay Ennis) and The Boswell
Sisters
IT'S BEEN SO LONG -Benny Goodman (Helen Ward);
Freddy Martin (Terry Shand); Bunny Berigan (Chick
Bullock)
WAH HOO -Paul Whiteman (Durelle Alexander)
LET YOURSELF GO -Fred Astaire; Ray Noble (Al Bowlly
and The Freshmen); The Boswell Sisters
I'M PUTTING ALL MY EGGS IN ONE BASKET -Fred
Astaire; Jan Garber (Lee Bennett); The Boswell Sisters
GOODY GOODY -Benny Goodman (Helen Ward); Bob
Crosby (Vocal) and His Orchestra
LOST -Hal Kemp (Bob Allen); Buddy Clark; Jan Garber (Lee
Bennett)
WHAT'S THE NAME OF THAT SONG? -Bob Crosby
(Vocal) and His Orchestra; Paul Whiteman (John
Hauser)
LET'S FACE THE MUSIC AND DANCE -Fred Astaire;
Ray Noble (Al Bowlly)

April - June

THE TOUCH OF YOUR LIPS -Bing Crosby; Ray Noble (Al
    Bowlly); Hal Kemp (Skinny Ennis); Buddy Clark; Jan
    Garber (Lee Bennett)
YOU STARTED ME DREAMING -Tommy Dorsey (Joe
    Dixon); Wingy Manone (vocal) and His Orchestra)
A MELODY FROM THE SKY -Frances Langford; Eddy
    Duchin (Pete Woolery); Freddy Martin (Elmer Feldkamp);
    Jan Garber (Lee Bennett)
LOVE IS LIKE A CIGARETTE -Duke Ellington (Ivie
    Anderson)
TORMENTED -Richard Himber (Stuart Allen)
I GOT PLENTY O' NUTTIN' -Bing Crosby; Guy Lombardo
    (The Lombardo Trio)
IT AIN'T NECESSARILY SO -Bing Crosby; Guy Lombardo
    (The Lombardo Trio)
YOU (GEE BUT YOU'RE WONDERFUL) -Tommy Dorsey
    (Edythe Wright); Jimmy Dorsey (Bob Eberly)
ALL MY LIFE -Benny Goodman Trio (Helen Ward); Teddy
    Wilson (Ella Fitzgerald); Fats Waller
(THERE IS) NO GREATER LOVE -Duke Ellington (Ivie
    Anderson); Isham Jones (Woody Herman); Guy Lombardo
    (The Lombardo Trio)
IS IT TRUE WHAT THEY SAY ABOUT DIXIE? -Al
    Jolson; Jimmy Dorsey (Bob Eberly); Ozzie Nelson (Vocal)
    and His Orchestra
ROBINS AND ROSES -Bing Crosby; Tommy Dorsey
    (Edythe Wright); Jimmy Dorsey (Kay Weber)
IT'S A SIN TO TELL A LIE -Fats Waller; Victor Young
    (Dick Robertson)

TWILIGHT ON THE TRAIL -Bing Crosby

WOULD YOU? -Bing Crosby; Richard Himber (Stuart Allen);

I'SE A-MUGGIN' -Stuff Smith; Hal Kemp (Skinnay Ennis)

SHE SHALL HAVE MUSIC -Buddy Clark; Rudy Vallee (vocal) and His Orchestra

CHRISTOPHER COLUMBUS -The Benny Goodman and Fletcher·Henderson Orchestras (Instrumentals)

THE GLORY OF LOVE -Benny Goodman (Helen Ward); Nat Brandwynne (Buddy Clark); Rudy Vallee (Vocal) and His Orchestra

THERE'S A SMALL HOTEL -Benny Goodman (Helen Ward); Hal Kemp (Maxine Gray); Paul Whiteman (Durelle Alexander)

YOU CAN'T PULL THE WOOL OVER MY EYES -Benny Goodman (Helen Ward); Ted Weems (Perry Como)

TAKE MY HEART -Bing Crosby; Nat Brandwynne (Buddy Clark); Eddy Duchin (Jerry Cooper); Jan Garber (Russell Brown)

ON THE BEACH AT BALI-BALI -Tommy Dorsey (Edythe Wright); Connie Boswell; Shep Fields (Charles Chester)

July - September

THESE FOOLISH THINGS REMIND ME OF YOU -Benny Goodman (Helen Ward); Nat Brandwynne (Buddy Clark); Teddy Wilson (Billie Holiday)

LET'S SING AGAIN -Fats Waller

CROSS PATCH -Bob Crosby (Vocal) and His Orchestra; Fats Waller

STOMPIN' AT THE SAVOY -Benny Goodman
   Instrumental)

WHEN I'M WITH YOU -Hal Kemp (Skinnay Ennis); Charlie
   Barnet (Bob Parks); Ray Noble (Al Bowlly)

NO REGRETS -Tommy Dorsey (Jack Leonard); Glen Gray
   (Kenny Sargent); Artie Shaw (Wes Vaughn); Teddy
   Wilson (Billie Holiday)

RENDEZVOUS WITH A DREAM -Jan Garber (Russell
   Brown)

SAN FRANCISCO -Tommy Dorsey (Edythe Wright)

DID I REMEMBER? -Tommy Dorsey (Edythe Wright); Dick
   Powell; Shep Fields (Charles Chester); Jan Garber (Russell
   Brown)

A STAR FELL OUT OF HEAVEN -Hal Kemp (Bob Allen);
   Charlie Barnet (Joe Hostetter); Ben Bernie (Ray
   Hendricks)

YOU'RE NOT THE KIND -Fats Waller

SHOE SHINE BOY -Bing Crosby

ME AND THE MOON -Bing Crosby; Hal Kemp (Skinnay
   Ennis); Shep Fields (Dick Robertson); Richard Himber
   (Stuart Allen)

KNOCK-KNOCK, WHO'S THERE? -Vincent Lopez (Johnny
   Morris, Maxine Tappan and Stanley Worth); Ted Weems
   Orchestra (Band Vocal)

BYE-BYE, BABY -Charlie Barnet (The Barnet Modernaires);
   Fats Waller; Nat Brandwynne (Buddy Clark)

UNTIL TODAY -Nat Brandwynne (Buddy Clark)

UNTIL THE REAL THING COMES ALONG -Charlie
    Barnet (Vocal) and His Orchestra; Jan Garber (Russell
    Brown); Fats Waller; Andy Kirk (Pha Terrell)
    (Pha was pronounced "Fay." This song became Andy
    Kirk's theme song.)
SING, BABY, SING -Charlie Barnet (Vocal) and His
    Orchestra
I'M AN OLD COWHAND -Bing Crosby
WHEN DID YOU LEAVE HEAVEN? -Tony Martin;
    Frances Langford; Charlie Barnet (Joe Hostetter); Guy
    Lombardo (Carmen Lombardo)
I CAN'T ESCAPE FROM YOU -Bing Crosby
SUMMERTIME -Billie Holiday
EMPTY SADDLES -Bing Crosby
THE WAY YOU LOOK TONIGHT (Academy Award-
    winning song from the film, *Swingtime,* with Fred Astaire
    and Ginger Rogers) -Fred Astaire; Bing and Dixie Lee
    Crosby; Guy Lombardo (Carmen Lombardo)
PICK YOURSELF UP -Fred Astaire

October - December

A FINE ROMANCE -Fred Astaire; Bing and Dixie Lee
    Crosby; Guy Lombardo (Carmen Lombardo); Billie
    Holiday
YOU TURNED THE TABLES ON ME -Benny Goodman
    (Helen Ward); Jan Garber (Russell Brown)
I'LL SING YOU A THOUSAND LOVE SONGS -Russ
    Morgan (Vocal) and His Orchestra; Eddy Duchin (Jimmy
    Newell)

SOUTH SEA ISLAND MAGIC -Bing Crosby; Artie Shaw
(Peg La Centra)
SONG OF THE ISLANDS -Bing Crosby
ON A COCOANUT ISLAND -Shep Fields (Charles Chester);
Victor Young (Dick Robertson)
ORGAN GRINDER'S SWING -The Benny Goodman and
Jimmie Lunceford Orchestras (Instrumentals)
DID YOU MEAN IT? -Charlie Barnet (Vocal) and His
Orchestra
(IF YOU CAN'T SING IT) YOU'LL HAVE TO SWING IT -
Chick Webb (Ella Fitzgerald)
IN THE CHAPEL IN THE MOONLIGHT -Nat Brandwynne
(Buddy Clark); Richard Himber (Stuart Allen); Shep Fields
(Mary Jane Walsh)
TO YOU SWEETHEART ALOHA -Guy Lombardo (Lebert
Lombardo)
IT'S DE-LOVELY -Hal Kemp (Skinnay Ennis); Eddy Duchin
(Jerry Cooper); Shep Fields (Charles Chester); Will
Osborne (Vocal) and His Orchestra
I'VE GOT YOU UNDER MY SKIN -Frances Langford, with
the Jimmy Dorsey Orchestra; Hal Kemp (Skinnay Ennis);
Ray Noble (Al Bowlly)
PENNIES FROM HEAVEN -Bing Crosby
LET'S CALL A HEART A HEART -Bing Crosby; Artie
Shaw (Peg La Centra)
ONE, TWO, BUTTON YOUR SHOE -Bing Crosby; Artie
Shaw (Tony Pastor); Ray Noble (Al Bowlly)
SO DO I -Bing Crosby; Shep Fields (Charles Chester)
EASY TO LOVE -Frances Langford, with the Jimmy Dorsey
Orchestra; Ray Noble (Al Bowlly); Shep Fields (Dick
Robertson)

The year's most popular songs, according to appearances on *Your Hit Parade*: DID I REMEMBER?; THE WAY YOU LOOK TONIGHT; ALONE; LOST; IS IT TRUE WHAT THEY SAY ABOUT DIXIE?; PENNIES FROM HEAVEN; GOODY GOODY; IN THE CHAPEL IN THE MOON-LIGHT; LIGHTS OUT and WHEN I'M WITH YOU.

Those whose popularity seemed to last longest through having been the most recorded over the years were: THESE FOOL-ISH THINGS REMIND ME OF YOU; I'VE GOT YOU UNDER MY SKIN; THE WAY YOU LOOK TONIGHT; PENNIES FROM HEAVEN; EASY TO LOVE and IT'S A SIN TO TELL A LIE.

Instrumental "Collector's Items"

MUSKRAT RAMBLE	-Bob Crosby
DIXIELAND SHUFFLE	-Bob Crosby
PAGAN LOVE SONG	-Bob Crosby
SUGAR FOOT STRUT	-Bob Crosby
BIG CHIEF DESOTO	-Bob Crosby
SAVOY BLUES	-Bob Crosby
PARADE OF THE MILK BOTTLE CAPS	-Jimmy Dorsey
MUTINY IN THE BRASS SECTION	-Jimmy Dorsey
THE SKELETON IN THE CLOSET	-Jimmy Dorsey
DIPPER MOUTH BLUES	-Jimmy Dorsey
THAT'S A-PLENTY	-Tommy Dorsey
ROYAL GARDEN BLUES	-Tommy Dorsey
AFTER YOU'VE GONE	-Tommy Dorsey
IN THE GROOVE	-Tommy Dorsey

UPTOWN DOWNBEAT	-Duke Ellington
IN A JAM	-Duke Ellington
CLARINET LAMENT	-Duke Ellington
ECHOES OF HARLEM	-Duke Ellington
GET HAPPY	-Benny Goodman (Full Band)
I KNOW THAT YOU KNOW	-Benny Goodman (Full Band)
I'VE FOUND A NEW BABY	-Benny Goodman (Full Band)
SWINGTIME IN THE ROCKIES	-Benny Goodman (Full Band)
WHEN BUDDHA SMILES	-Benny Goodman (Full Band)
LOVE ME OR LEAVE ME	-Benny Goodman (Full Band)
BUGLE CALL RAG	-Benny Goodman (Full Band)
ALEXANDER'S RAGTIME BAND	-Benny Goodman (Full Band)
SOMEBODY LOVES ME	-Benny Goodman (Full Band)
JAM SESSION	-Benny Goodman (Full Band)
DINAH	-Benny Goodman (Quartet)
EXACTLY LIKE YOU	-Benny Goodman (Quartet)
MOONGLOW	-Benny Goodman (Quartet)
SWEET SUE (JUST YOU)	-Benny Goodman (Quartet)
MELANCHOLY BABY	-Benny Goodman (Quartet)
WHISPERING	-Benny Goodman (Quartet)
MORE THAN YOU KNOW	-Benny Goodman (Trio)
NOBODY'S SWEETHEART	-Benny Goodman (Trio)
CHINA BOY	-Benny Goodman (Trio)
OH LADY BE GOOD	-Benny Goodman (Trio)
BIG JOHN'S SPECIAL	-Erskine Hawkins
THE GOOSE HANGS HIGH	-Woody Herman
OLD FASHIONED SWING	-Woody Herman
MY BLUE HEAVEN	-Jimmie Lunceford
I GOT RHYTHM	-Red Norvo
OH LADY BE GOOD	-Red Norvo

SUGAR FOOT STOMP   -Artie Shaw
THOU SWELL   -Artie Shaw

Developments This Year in Popular Music

- After having introduced swing music to the nation in
1935, Benny Goodman further established his style as a potent
new force in popular music. Besides recording a number of
popular songs featuring his fine vocalist, Helen Ward, he made
the swing hits STOMPIN' AT THE SAVOY and CHRISTO-
PHER COLUMBUS, as well as many jazz numbers, utilizing
either a trio or a quartet, featuring himself, Teddy Wilson on
piano, Gene Krupa on drums and Lionel Hampton on vibraphone, as the fourth member.   Many of these recordings
became treasured "collector's items."

- Helen Ward, who was one of the girl singers most
admired by her peers and fellow musicians, recorded several of
the year's biggest hits with the Goodman band, including: IT'S
BEEN SO LONG; GOODY GOODY; THE GLORY OF
LOVE; YOU CAN'T PULL THE WOOL OVER MY EYES;
THESE FOOLISH THINGS REMIND ME OF YOU and
YOU TURNED THE TABLES ON ME. THESE FOOLISH
THINGS, one of this year's songs which became a standard,
was from a London musical.

- With all of the above, it was a strong year for Benny
Goodman and probably the one during which his band was the
clear leader.

- New bands formed this year and destined for prominence included those of Benny Berigan, Woody Herman and Artie Shaw.

- Tommy Dorsey began the year with a new male singer named Jack Leonard, who would establish himself as one of the finest and would remain with the band for four years.

- The Shep Fields band was touring with the Veloz and Yolanda dance team this year when its "Rippling Rhythm" style attracted many new fans. Soon, the band was heard often on radio and became one of the busiest in the recording studios.

- In late October, the musical *Red, Hot and Blue* opened on Broadway with Ethel Merman, Jimmy Durante and a new-comer named Bob Hope. Hope made a few guest appearances on radio that fall and winter and was heard singing a Cole Porter song from the show, entitled IT'S DE-LOVELY. There was little indication at the time that this London, England-born, ex-prizefighter from Cleveland was going to become an American icon.

- Bob Hope's future movie travel-companion, Bing Crosby, (*Road to Morocco, Road to Zanzibar*, etc.) was already a giant in music, radio and films. The Crosby voice was so admired that nearly every young American male could be heard at one time or another trying to imitate it. It should be noted that all of Bing Crosby's years as America's number one entertainer, his biggest years coincided with the Big Band Era. Throughout the period, his records competed on even terms, sharing time on radio disc jockey shows and on the country's juke boxes with all the best that the bands were offering. On the label of any record he made with a big band and there were quite a few, it was Bing Crosby who got top billing.

- By coincidence, at the end of the year, singer-actress Dorothy Lamour, a future co-star with Crosby and Hope, made her movie debut in a starring role in *Jungle Princess*. In the film she sang MOONLIGHT AND SHADOWS and received favorable reviews for both her singing and acting. However, her initial fame resulting from this film derived from the native wrap-around dress known as a "sarong," which she wore in the role and which was adopted as a new style by fashion designers.

1 9 3 7

The Most Popular Recordings

January - March

WHEN MY DREAM BOAT COMES HOME -Shep Fields
(Bob Goday); Guy Lombardo (Lebert Lombardo)

THE NIGHT IS YOUNG (AND YOU'RE SO BEAUTIFUL)
-Jan Garber (Russell Brown); Wayne King Orchestra
(Instrumental)

WITH PLENTY OF MONEY AND YOU -Henry Busse (Bob
Hannon); Hal Kemp (Skinnay Ennis); Dick Powell

GOODNIGHT MY LOVE -Alice Faye; Benny Goodman
(Frances Hunt); Shep Fields (Bob Goday); Hal Kemp
(Skinnay Ennis)

THIS YEAR'S KISSES -Alice Faye; Dick Powell; Hal Kemp
(Skinnay Ennis); Benny Goodman (Margaret McCrae)

MOONLIGHT AND SHADOWS -Dorothy Lamour; Bing
Crosby; Shep Fields (Bob Goday); Eddy Duchin (Lew
Sherwood)

MARIE (From 1929) -Tommy Dorsey (Jack Leonard, with
Band Chorus)

SONG OF INDIA (From 1894) -Tommy Dorsey swing
instrumental

TRUST IN ME -Artie Shaw (Peg La Centra); Connie Boswell

DEDICATED TO YOU -Tommy Dorsey (Jack Leonard);
Andy Kirk (Pha Terrell)

I'VE GOT MY LOVE TO KEEP ME WARM -Alice Faye;
    Ray Noble (Howard Phillips); Dick Powell; Mildred
    Bailey
SERENADE IN THE NIGHT -Connie Boswell; Shep Fields
    (Bob Goday)
YOU'RE LAUGHING AT ME -Glen Gray (Kenny Sargent);
    Hal Kemp (Bob Allen); Mildred Bailey; Dick Powell
SLUMMING ON PARK AVENUE -Alice Faye; Red Norvo
    (Mildred Bailey); Ray Noble (The Merry Macs)
BOO HOO -Guy Lombardo (The Lombardo Trio)
LAMPLIGHT -Hal Kemp (Skinnay Ennis)
LITTLE OLD LADY -Ray Noble (Al Bowlly); Shep Fields
    (Bob Goday)
WHAT WILL I TELL MY HEART? -Bing Crosby; Hal
    Kemp (Bob Allen); Guy Lombardo (Carmen Lombardo)
THEY ALL LAUGHED -Fred Astaire; Tommy Dorsey
    (Edythe Wright); Ozzie Nelson (Vocal) and His Orchestra)

April - June

TOO MARVELOUS FOR WORDS -Bing Crosby; Glen Gray
    (Kenny Sargent)
WHERE ARE YOU? -Tommy Dorsey (Jack Leonard); Connie
    Boswell; Mildred Bailey; Shep Fields (Bob Goday)
SHALL WE DANCE? -Fred Astaire
THE DONKEY SERENADE -Allan Jones
SEPTEMBER IN THE RAIN -Guy Lombardo (Carmen
    Lombardo); Artie Shaw (Peg La Centra)
CARELESSLY -Teddy Wilson (Billie Holiday)

THE LOVE BUG WILL BITE YOU -Guy Lombardo
(Carmen Lombardo); Artie Shaw (Tony Pastor); Jimmy
Dorsey (Ray McKinley)
NEVER IN A MILLION YEARS -Alice Faye; Bing Crosby;
Glen Gray (Kenny Sargent); Mildred Bailey
THERE'S A LULL IN MY LIFE -Alice Faye; Glen Gray
(Kenny Sargent); Duke Ellington (Ivie Anderson); Mildred
Bailey; The Andrews Sisters
TWILIGHT IN TURKEY -Raymond Scott Quintet; Tommy
Dorsey Clambake Seven; Artie Shaw Orchestra
(all instrumentals)
BLUE HAWAII -Bing Crosby
LET'S CALL THE WHOLE THING OFF -Fred Astaire;
Eddy Duchin (Jerry Cooper); Shep Fields (Bob Goday)
SWEET LEILANI (Academy Award-winning song from the
film, *Waikiki Wedding*) -Bing Crosby
JOHNNY ONE-NOTE -Hal Kemp (Skinnay Ennis); Artie
Shaw and Victor Young Orchestras (Instrumentals)
THEY CAN'T TAKE THAT AWAY FROM ME -Fred
Astaire; Tommy Dorsey (Jack Leonard); Jimmy Dorsey
(Bob Eberly) Ozzie Nelson (Vocal) and His Orchestra
ROCKIN' CHAIR (From 1930) -A popular revival by Mildred
Bailey
IT LOOKS LIKE RAIN IN CHERRY BLOSSOM LANE -
Sammy Kaye (Tommy Ryan); Guy Lombardo (Lebert
Lombardo); Shep Fields (Bob Goday)
A SAILBOAT IN THE MOONLIGHT -Guy Lombardo
(Carmen Lombardo); Charlie Barnet (Kurt Bloom)
THE MERRY-GO-ROUND BROKE DOWN -Russ Morgan
(Jimmy Lewis); Eddy Duchin (Lew Sherwood); Jimmie
Lunceford (Sy Oliver); Shep Fields (Bob Goday)

July - September

THE YOU AND ME THAT USED TO BE -George Hall
    (Dolly Dawn); Mal Hallet (Teddy Grace)
CARAVAN -Duke Ellington (Instrumental); Bunny Berigan
    (Instrumental)
PECKIN' -Bing Crosby; Benny Goodman (Instrumental)
WHERE OR WHEN -Hal Kemp (Bob Allen); Guy Lombardo
    (Carmen Lombardo); Benny Goodman Trio (Instrumental)
SATAN TAKES A HOLIDAY -Tommy Dorsey
    (Instrumental)
I KNOW NOW -Dick Powell; Guy Lombardo (Carmen
    Lombardo)
GONE WITH THE WIND -Claude Thornhill (Maxine
    Sullivan); Horace Heidt (Larry Cotton)
SO RARE -Gus Arnheim (Jimmy Farrell); Guy Lombardo
    (Carmen Lombardo)
THE FIRST TIME I SAW YOU -Bunny Berigan (Ford
    Leary); Jimmie Lunceford (Dan Grissom)
SMARTY -Bing Crosby; Fats Waller
MY CABIN OF DREAMS -Tommy Dorsey (Edythe Wright);
    Frances Langford; Gus Arnheim (Jimmy Farrell); George
    Hall (Dolly Dawn)
STARDUST ON THE MOON -Tommy Dorsey (Edythe
    Wright); Woody Herman (Vocal) and His Orchestra
ALL YOU WANT TO DO IS DANCE -Bing Crosby; Jimmy
    Dorsey (Bob Eberly); Artie Shaw (Peg La Centra)
AFRAID TO DREAM -Artie Shaw (Peg La Centra); Benny
    Goodman (Betty Van); Connie Boswell
THE BIG APPLE -Tommy Dorsey Clambake Seven (Edythe
    Wright); Ozzie Nelson (Vocal) and His Orchestra

HAVE YOU GOT ANY CASTLES, BABY? -Tommy Dorsey
(Jack Leonard); George Hall (Dolly Dawn); Dick Powell
YOU CAN'T HAVE EVERYTHING -Bob Crosby (Kay
Weber)
THE LOVELINESS OF YOU -Hal Kemp (Bob Allen); Russ
Morgan (Mert Curtis)
IT'S THE NATURAL THING TO DO -Bing Crosby; Artie
Shaw (Peg La Centra); Horace Heidt (The King Sisters);
Mildred Bailey
HARBOR LIGHTS -Frances Langford; Claude Thornhill
(Jimmy Farrell); Shep Fields (Bob Goday)
WHISPERS IN THE DARK -Connie Boswell; Bob Crosby
(Kay Weber); Hal Kemp (Bob Allen)
THAT OLD FEELING -Connie Boswell; Shep Fields (Bob
Goday)
REMEMBER ME? -Bing Crosby; Hal Kemp (Skinnay Ennis)
THE MOON GOT IN MY EYES -Bing Crosby; Jimmy
Dorsey (Bob Eberly); Hal Kemp (Bob Allen); Artie Shaw
(Peg La Centra)

October - December

ROSES IN DECEMBER -Ozzie Nelson (Harriet Hilliard);
Dick Powell; Bunny Berigan (Ruth Gaylor)
JOSEPHINE -Tommy Dorsey Clambake Seven (Jack
Leonard); Russ Morgan (Vocal) and His Orchestra; Wayne
King Orchestra; Ozzie Nelson (Vocal) and His Orchestra
CAN I FORGET YOU? -Bing Crosby; Guy Lombardo
(Carmen Lombardo); Artie Shaw (Peg La Centra);
Ozzie Nelson (Vocal) and His Orchestra

THE ONE ROSE (THAT'S LEFT IN MY HEART) -Bing
Crosby; Larry Clinton (Bea Wain)
SAIL ALONG SILVERY MOON -Bing Crosby
YOU CAN'T STOP ME FROM DREAMING -Ozzie Nelson
(Vocal) and His Orchestra; Dick Powell; Teddy Wilson
Orchestra (Instrumental)
BLOSSOMS ON BROADWAY -Shep Fields (Bob Goday);
Connie Boswell; George Hall (Dolly Dawn); Dick
Robertson (Vocal) and His Orchestra
THE FOLKS WHO LIVE ON THE HILL -Bing Crosby;
Ozzie Nelson (Vocal with Harriet Hilliard) and His
Orchestra; Guy Lombardo (Carmen Lombardo)
I STILL LOVE TO KISS YOU GOODNIGHT -Bing Crosby;
Hal Kemp (Skinnay Ennis); Shep Fields (Bob Goday)
VIENI, VIENI -Rudy Vallee (Vocal) and His Orchestra);
Horace Heidt (Lysbeth Hughes)
BASIN STREET BLUES (From 1929) -Bing Crosby and
Connie Boswell teamed up on this popular revival
IF IT'S THE LAST THING I DO -Tommy Dorsey (Jack
Leonard); Artie Shaw (Bea Wain); Frances Langford
ONCE IN AWHILE -Tommy Dorsey (Jack Leonard and The
Three Esquires); Frances Langford; Ozzie Nelson (Harriet
Hilliard); Horace Heidt (Larry Cotton)
NICE WORK IF YOU CAN GET IT -Fred Astaire; Shep
Fields (Bob Goday); Bob Crosby (Vocal) and His
Orchestra; The Andrews Sisters
THE LADY IS A TRAMP -Tommy Dorsey Clambake Seven
(Edythe Wright); Artie Shaw (Tony Pastor)
EBB TIDE -Claude Thornhill (Barry McKinley); Bunny
Berigan (Gail Reese); Connie Boswell; Ozzie Nelson
(Vocal) and His Orchestra

THERE'S A GOLD MINE IN THE SKY -Bing Crosby;
   Horace Heidt (Larry Cotton); Mildred Bailey
ROSALIE -Artie Shaw (Tony Pastor); Sammy Kaye (Tommy
   Ryan); Horace Heidt (Lysbeth Hughes); Leo Reisman (Lee
   Sullivan)
LOCH LOMOND (From Scotland, 1881) -ClaudeThornhill
   (Maxine Sullivan)
TRUE CONFESSION -Larry Clinton (Bea Wain); Connie
   Boswell; Sammy Kaye (Charlie Wilson)
A FOGGY DAY -Fred Astaire; Bob Crosby (Kay Weber);
   Hal Kemp (Skinnay Ennis)
WHO? (From 1925) -Popular revival by Tommy Dorsey (Jack
   Leonard, with band chorus)
HAVE YOU MET MISS JONES? -Artie Shaw (Tony Pastor);
   Glen Gray (Kenny Sargent); Sammy Kaye (Tommy Ryan);
   Leo Reisman (Lee Sullivan)
BOB WHITE (WHATCHA GONNA SWING TONIGHT?) -
   Benny Goodman (Martha Tilton); Bing Crosby and Connie
   Boswell

Of this year's favorite songs, the following achieved the
greatest popularity, based on their number of appearances in
the weekly radio survey, *Your Hit Parade* : ONCE IN
AWHILE; IT LOOKS LIKE RAIN IN CHERRY BLOSSOM
LANE; BOO HOO; SEPTEMBER IN THE RAIN; THAT
OLD FEELING; WHISPERS IN THE DARK; A SAILBOAT
IN THE MOONLIGHT; GOODNIGHT, MY LOVE;
ROSALIE; HARBOR LIGHTS.

HARBOR LIGHTS enjoyed an extended new period of
popularity in 1950, while recording artists over the years made

standards of ONCE IN AWHILE; THAT OLD FEELING; TOO MARVELOUS FOR WORDS and WHERE OR WHEN. Duke Ellington's CARAVAN became one of the longer-lasting instrumental favorites to emerge from the big band era, while Les Brown and Jimmy Dorsey made instrumental hits in the postwar years of this year's ballads, I'VE GOT MY LOVE TO KEEP ME WARM and SO RARE.

Instrumental "Collector's Items"

SURREALISM	-Charlie Barnet
OVERHEARD IN A COCKTAIL LOUNGE	-Charlie Barnet
ONE O'CLOCK JUMP	-Count Basie
JOHN'S IDEA	-Count Basie
HONEYSUCKLE ROSE	-Count Basie
SWINGIN' AT THE DAISY CHAIN	-Count Basie
ROSELAND SHUFFLE	-Count Basie
TIME OUT	-Count Basie
TOPSY	-Count Basie
OUT THE WINDOW	-Count Basie
DANCE OF THE BLUE DEVILS	-Les Brown
SWAMP FIRE	-Les Brown
RIGMAROLE	-Les Brown
MIDNIGHT IN A MADHOUSE	-Larry Clinton
A STUDY IN BROWN	-Larry Clinton
THE BIG DIPPER	-Larry Clinton
SOUTH RAMPART STREET PARADE	-Bob Crosby
GIN MILL BLUES	-Bob Crosby
LITTLE ROCK GETAWAY	-Bob Crosby
ROLLIN' HOME	-Tommy Dorsey
BEALE STREET BLUES	-Tommy Dorsey

CANADIAN CAPERS	-Tommy Dorsey
STOP LOOK AND LISTEN	-Tommy Dorsey
BLACK BUTTERFLY	-Duke Ellington
THE NEW BIRMINGHAM BREAKDOWN	-Duke Ellington
SCATTIN' AT THE KIT-KAT	-Duke Ellington
THE NEW EAST ST. LOUIS TOODLE-OO	-Duke Ellington
ROCKING IN RHYTHM	-Duke Ellington
AZURE	-Duke Ellington
ALL GOD'S CHILLUN GOT RHYTHM	-Duke Ellington
JUBILESTA	-Duke Ellington
DIMINUENDO IN BLUE	-Duke Ellington
CRESCENDO IN BLUE	-Duke Ellington
HARMONY IN HARLEM	-Duke Ellington
DUSK IN THE DESERT	-Duke Ellington
I WANT TO BE HAPPY	-Benny Goodman (Full Band)
CHLO-E (SONG OF THE SWAMP)	-Benny Goodman (Full Band)
PECKIN'	-Benny Goodman (Full Band)
SING SING SING (1&2, orig. version)	-Benny Goodman (Full Band)
LIFE GOES TO A PARTY	-Benny Goodman (Full Band)
IDA SWEET AS APPLE CIDER	-Benny Goodman (Quartet)
TEA FOR TWO	-Benny Goodman (Quartet)
RUNNIN' WILD	-Benny Goodman (Quartet)
SMILES	-Benny Goodman (Quartet)
LIZA	-Benny Goodman (Quartet)

I'M A DING DONG DADDY	
FROM DUMAS	-Benny Goodman (Quartet)
AVALON	-Benny Goodman (Quartet)
EVERYBODY	
LOVES MY BABY	-Benny Goodman (Trio)
CASA LOMA STOMP	-Glen Gray
DOCTOR JAZZ	-Woody Herman
DUPREE BLUES	-Woody Herman
IT HAPPENED DOWN	
IN DIXIELAND	-Woody Herman
DOUBLE OR NOTHING	-Woody Herman
POWERHOUSE	-Hal Kemp
FOR DANCERS ONLY	-Jimmie Lunceford
I GOT RHYTHM	-Glenn Miller
COMMUNITY SWING	-Glenn Miller
DOIN' THE JIVE	-Glenn Miller
DINNER MUSIC FOR A PACK	
OF HUNGRY CANNIBALS	-Raymond Scott Quintet
MY BLUE HEAVEN	-Artie Shaw
CREAM PUFF	-Artie Shaw
SWING HIGH SWING LOW	-Artie Shaw
COPENHAGEN	-Artie Shaw
SOBBIN' BLUES	-Artie Shaw
AT SUNDOWN	-Artie Shaw
SKELETON IN THE CLOSET	-Artie Shaw
BORN TO SWING	-Artie Shaw
SYMPHONY IN RIFFS	-Artie Shaw
I SURRENDER DEAR	-Artie Shaw
UBANGI	-Artie Shaw
NIGHT AND DAY	-Artie Shaw
BLUE SKIES	-Artie Shaw

SOMEDAY SWEETHEART	-Artie Shaw
THE BLUES (1&2)	-Artie Shaw
SHINDIG	-Artie Shaw
THE BIG DIPPER	-Artie Shaw

Developments This Year in Popular Music

- It was in the first week of this year that a slender young trumpet player joined Benny Goodman's band, coming over from Ben Pollack's organization, the same band which had produced Goodman himself and many other big band stars. Born in Georgia and reared in Texas as the son of circus performers, this young man was Harry James and he soon dazzled the music world with his ability. He remained with Benny for two full years, then left to lead his own band, which, for the last few years of the era was the most popular in the country, due largely to his own talent and appeal.

- For two weeks in March, the Benny Goodman band appeared at New York's Paramount Theater. Throughout its stay, the assistance of city police was required to maintain control over the large number of enthusiastic young swing fans who lined up outside the theater each morning, long before the boxoffice opened.   Once inside, they remained to sit impatiently through the film at least twice, in order to cheer each Goodman performance, many dancing in the aisles. Reports of the tremendous enthusiasm demonstrated during this session soon spread across the country, giving the band - and swing music - another large boost in popularity.

- ONE O'CLOCK JUMP, which he recorded this year, would become associated with Count Basie as his composition and signature tune. Harry James helped to establish it further when he recorded it with a 9-piece all-star group in January, 1938 and that version became a million-seller.

- Similarly, Goodman's swing classic, SING SING SING, which he recorded in July on two sides, had to await the stellar, full-length performance at Carnegie Hall in January of 1938, before attracting the attention which skyrocketed it to fame.

- In the Spring, Bunny Berigan's new band opened in the roof ballroom of New York's Hotel Pennsylvania.

- The bands of Les Brown, Larry Clinton, Sammy Kaye, Johnny Long, Jan Savitt and Claude Thornhill began making their important musical contributions this year. Glenn Miller also made an attempt, but was dissatisfied with the band he had organized and broke it up to begin anew in 1938.

- In a never-ending search for just the right "fit" in the important role of band singer, vocalists played "Musical Chairs" this year. Frances Hunt (GOODNIGHT MY LOVE) began the year with Benny Goodman, having replaced Margaret MacRae (THIS YEAR'S KISSES). She in turn was followed btiefly by Betty Van (AFRAID TO DREAM) who gave way to Martha Tilton. Martha and Benny's band proved to be a perfect "fit" and her first of many hits was BOB WHITE. Kay Weber moved from Jimmy Dorsey to Bob Crosby in mid-year as his first girl singer. Anita Bradley replaced Peg La Centra with Artie Shaw, following brief stints by Louise Farrell and Bea Wain, the latter ultimately settling in as another perfect fit for a series of hit recordings with Larry Clinton. In his first year, Sammy Kaye was employing three boy singers: Jimmy Brown, Tommy Ryan and Charlie Wilson. Jan Savitt hired George "Bon-Bon" Tunnell and Carlotta Dale to sing with his new band, while ClaudeThornhill began by featuring the vocals of Jimmy Farrell, who was later succeeded by Barry McKinley and Maxine Sullivan.

- Alternately recording with husband Red Norvo and with her own orchestra, Mildred Bailey usually received top billing and unfailingly turned out strong performances. She was one of the singing stars of the era, yet remained somewhat under-rated.

- This was Tommy Dorsey's second full year leading a band without the partnership of his brother Jimmy and his band established itself strongly among the leaders. Giving impetus to that rise was a masterful blend of swing and ballads sung by the fine vocalists Jack Leonard and Edythe Wright. At some point in most numbers would be heard the unmistakeably smooth sound of the Dorsey trombone. A listener was invariably left wondering how Tommy managed to store enough breath in his lungs to be able to play such long, uninterrupted passages.

The band had a typical year's work in the recording studios, making 60 to 70 sides, several of which would gain considerable popularity. However, one of the pairings made in January resulted in a double big band "classic," doing more than anything else this year to focus attention on the Tommy

Dorsey Orchestra. On one side was MARIE, in which novel use was made of the band members to chant rhythmically in the background, behind the lyric sung by Jack Leonard. It didn't really matter whether the words interjected by the chorus related to the song's message or not. They were well-chosen, timely and smile-provoking. It was a clever new vocal presentation and the overall effect was pleasingly different and attention-getting. By itself, MARIE might well have sold a million copies. On the flip side, however, was a swing number for all time, which ensured the first million-seller of the big band years. Tommy himself led a group effort in the arrangement of SONG OF INDIA, one of the most impressive instrumentals of the entire era.

- By this time, there were many young swing fans, who, along with the musicians, were developing a special vocabulary of swing slang. Following are some of the most widely-used expressions:

Swing Slang:
cats -musicians in a swing band
corn -uninspired, usually sweet music, good only for sedate
      dancing; adjective: corny
cut a rug -dance to swing music
disc (also "platter") -a phonograph record
eighty-eight -a piano
groovy -good, pleasing; initially applied to swing music, later
      to anything pleasing
hepcat -a very knowledgeable swing fan
hot licks -impressive solos by swing musicians
ickie -person oblivious to swing

in the groove -condition of musicians inspired to top
    performance on a swing number
jam -verb meaning to swing out, or produce swing music
jam session -informal gathering of musicians dedicated to
    playing swing music
jitterbug -dancer of swing dances; verb: to swing dance
jive -slang for swing music (later also to tease or fabricate)
jump -for a band to reach a high level of swing expertise
kicking out -description of a swing musician's solo
    improvisation
knocked-out -to be so engrossed in the music as to block out
    everything else
licorice stick -a clarinet
long-hair -one who prefers classical music, or an intellectual
    with disdain for swing
one-nighter -a one-night engagement for a band
out of this world -incredibly good, usually in reference to a
    band's performance, but also used as a superlative,
    descriptive of anything or anyone
scat singer -a singer who improvises by emitting sounds or
    meaningless syllables, either in place of, or between a song's
    actual words
send -the act of impressing listeners, by a musician or band
skins (or "hides") -drums
slush pump (or "bone") -trombone
solid jive -swing music found to be especially pleasing
square -one not attuned to, or not appreciative of swing music

1 9 3 8

The Most Popular Recordings

January - March

YOU'RE A SWEETHEART -Dolly Dawn; Artie Shaw
(Anita Bradley); Tommy Dorsey Clambake Seven
(Edythe Wright); Ozzie Nelson (Vocal) and His
Orchestra

I DOUBLE DARE YOU -Larry Clinton (Bea Wain); Woody
Herman (Vocal) and His Orchestra; Russ Morgan
(Bernice Parks)

BEI MIR BIST DU SCHOEN -The Andrews Sisters; Benny
Goodman Quartet (Martha Tilton)

THE DIPSY DOODLE -Tommy Dorsey (Edythe Wright);
Sammy Kaye (Jimmy Brown)

IN THE STILL OF THE NIGHT -Tommy Dorsey (Jack
Leonard); Leo Reisman (Lee Sullivan)

I CANT GET STARTED (From 1936) -Bunny Berigan
(Vocal) and His Orchestra

THE MOON OF MANAKOORA -Dorothy Lamour; Bing
Crosby

I FALL IN LOVE WITH YOU EVERY DAY -Jimmy
Dorsey (Bob Eberly); Larry Clinton (Bea Wain); George
Hall (Dolly Dawn)

(OUR) LOVE IS HERE TO STAY -Larry Clinton (Bea
Wain); Jimmy Dorsey (Bob Eberly); Red Norvo
(Mildred Bailey)

WHISTLE WHILE YOU WORK -The Seven Dwarfs (From
the sound track of *Snow White and the Seven Dwarfs*);
Guy Lombardo (The Lombardo Trio); Shep Fields (Bob
Goday)

THANKS FOR THE MEMORY (Academy Award-winning
song from the film, *The Big Broadcast of 1938*) -Bob
Hope and Shirley Ross; Benny Goodman (Martha Tilton);
Shep Fields (Bob Goday); Mildred Bailey (Vocal) and Her
Orchestra

GOODNIGHT ANGEL -Artie Shaw (Anita Bradley); Hal
Kemp (Bob Allen)

I CAN DREAM CAN'T I? -Tommy Dorsey (Jack Leonard)

I SEE YOUR FACE BEFORE ME -Guy Lombardo (Carmen
Lombardo); Glen Gray (Kenny Sargent); Mildred Bailey;
Ozzie Nelson (Vocal) and His Orchestra

MARTHA -Larry Clinton (Bea Wain)

I DREAMT I DWELT IN MARBLE HALLS -Larry Clinton
(Bea Wain)

SENT FOR YOU YESTERDAY AND HERE YOU COME
TODAY -Count Basie (Jimmy Rushing)

PLEASE BE KIND -Benny Goodman (Martha Tilton); Red
Norvo (Mildred Bailey); Frances Langford; Bob Crosby
(Kay Weber)

TI-PI-TIN -Horace Heidt (Larry Cotton and Lysbeth Hughes);
Guy Lombardo (The Lombardo Trio)

HEIGH-HO! -The Dwarfs' Marching Song, sound track from
Snow White and the Seven Dwarfs ; Horace Heidt (The
King's Men & Glee Club)

ALL OF ME (From 1932) -Jimmy Dorsey (Helen O'Connell)

YOU'RE AN EDUCATION -Larry Clinton (Bea Wain)

HOW'DJA LIKE TO LOVE ME? -Larry Clinton (Bea Wain);
George Hall (Dolly Dawn); Horace Heidt (The Four King
Sisters); Jimmy Dorsey (Don Mattison)

April - June

YEARNING (JUST FOR YOU) (From 1928) -Popular
revival by Tommy Dorsey (Jack Leonard, with Band
Chorus)
LOVE WALKED IN -Jimmy Dorsey (Bob Eberly); Sammy
Kaye (Tommy Ryan); Jan Garber (Russell Brown)
YOU COULDN'T BE CUTER -Tommy Dorsey (Edythe
Wright)
JOSEPH JOSEPH - The Andrews Sisters
ON THE SENTIMENTAL SIDE -Bing Crosby; Jimmy
Dorsey (Bob Eberly)
MY HEART IS TAKING LESSONS -Bing Crosby; Glen
Gray (Pee Wee Hunt)
AT A PERFUME COUNTER -Jimmy Dorsey (Bob Eberly);
Larry Clinton (Bea Wain)
DON'T BE THAT WAY -Benny Goodman (Instrumental);
Bing Crosby
CRY, BABY, CRY -Larry Clinton (Bea Wain); Sammy Kaye
(The Three Barons)
CATHEDRAL IN THE PINES -Shep Fields (Jerry Stewart)
I LET A SONG GO OUT OF MY HEART -Duke Ellington
(Instrumental); Benny Goodman (Martha Tilton); Mildred
Bailey (Vocal) and Her Orchestra
FERDINAND THE BULL -Larry Clinton (Bea Wain);
Horace Heidt (The Four King Sisters)

LOVELIGHT IN THE STARLIGHT -Dorothy Lamour; Jan
  Savitt (Carlotta Dale); Horace Heidt (Larry Cotton)
YOU LEAVE ME BREATHLESS -Tommy Dorsey (Jack
  Leonard); Connie Boswell; Mildred Bailey; Ozzie Nelson
  (Vocal) and His Orchestra
SAYS MY HEART -Tommy Dorsey (Edythe Wright); Red
  Norvo (Mildred Bailey); Ozzie Nelson (Harriet Hilliard);
  The Andrews Sisters
MUSIC, MAESTRO, PLEASE -Tommy Dorsey (Edythe
  Wright)
OH! MA-MA (THE BUTCHER BOY) -The Andrews Sisters
IT'S THE DREAMER IN ME -Bing Crosby; Benny Goodman
  (Martha Tilton)

July - September

I MARRIED AN ANGEL -Larry Clinton (Bea Wain); Buddy
  Clark; Sammy Kaye (Jimmy Brown); The Andrews Sisters
SPRING IS HERE -Blue Barron (Russ Carlyle); Buddy Clark
FLAT FOOT FLOOGIE (WITH THE FLOY FLOY) - Slim
  Gaillard and Slam Stewart; Benny Goodman (Band
  Chorus)
JOHN SILVER -Jimmy Dorsey (Instrumental, with some
  vocalizing by the band)
I HADN'T ANYONE TILL YOU -Ray Noble (Tony Martin);
  Tommy Dorsey (Jack Leonard); Jimmy Dorsey (Bob
  Eberly); Benny Goodman (Martha Tilton)
ANY OLD TIME -Artie Shaw (Billie Holiday)
WHEN MOTHER NATURE SINGS HER LULLABY -Bing
  Crosby

I'M GONNA LOCK MY HEART -Larry Clinton (Bea Wain);
    Kay Kyser (Sully Mason); Teddy Wilson (Billie Holiday)
NOW IT CAN BE TOLD -Bing Crosby; Tommy Dorsey
    (Jack Leonard); Mildred Bailey (Vocal) and Her Orchestra
A-TISKET, A-TASKET -Chick Webb (Ella Fitzgerald)
THE GYPSY IN MY SOUL -Bing Crosby
YOU GO TO MY HEAD -Larry Clinton (Bea Wain); Glen
    Gray (Kenny Sargent)
 GARDEN OF THE MOON -Jimmy Dorsey (Bob Eberly);
    Dick Jurgens (Eddy Howard); Red Norvo (Mildred Bailey)
LOVE IS WHERE YOU FIND IT -Jimmy Dorsey (Bob
    Eberly); Kay Kyser (Harry Babbitt); Mildred Bailey; The
    Andrews Sisters; Sammy Kaye (Charlie Wilson)
WHAT GOES ON HERE IN MY HEART? -Benny Goodman
    (Martha Tilton); Gene Krupa (Irene Daye); Dick Jurgens
    (Eddy Howard)
A LITTLE KISS AT TWILIGHT -Benny Goodman (Martha
    Tilton); Dick Jurgens (Eddy Howard)
FROM NOW ON -Frances Langford; Les Brown (Miriam
    Shaw)
I'LL SEE YOU IN MY DREAMS (From 1924) -Popular
    revival by Tommy Dorsey (Jack Leonard, with Band
    Chorus)
I'VE GOT A POCKETFUL OF DREAMS -Bing Crosby
INDIAN LOVE CALL -Artie Shaw (Tony Pastor, with vocal
    effects by the band members)
STOP BEATIN' 'ROUND THE MULBERRY BUSH -
    Tommy Dorsey (Edythe Wright); Kay Kyser (Sully
    Mason); Les Brown (Herb Muse)
SO HELP ME -Kay Kyser (Harry Babbitt); Mildred Bailey
    (Vocal) and Her Orchestra

I'VE GOT A DATE WITH A DREAM -Benny Goodman
(Martha Tilton)
ALEXANDER'S RAGTIME BAND (From 1911) -Popular
revival by Bing Crosby, with Connie Boswell
ON THE BUMPY ROAD TO LOVE -OzzieNelson (Vocal)
and His Orchestra

October - December

SHADRACH -Larry Clinton (Ford Leary, with Band Chorus)
CHANGE PARTNERS -Fred Astaire; Jimmy Dorsey (Bob
Eberly); Larry Clinton (Dick Todd); Ozzie Nelson (Vocal)
and His Orchestra)
I USED TO BE COLOR BLIND -Fred Astaire; Hal Kemp
(Bob Allen); Mildred Bailey (Vocal) and Her Orchestra
THE LAMBETH WALK -Russ Morgan (Jimmy Lewis); Al
Donahue (Paula Kelly)
MEXICALI ROSE -Bing Crosby
I WON'T TELL A SOUL (I LOVE YOU) -Andy Kirk (Pha
Terrell); Artie Shaw (Helen Forrest)
AT LONG LAST LOVE -Larry Clinton (Bea Wain); Frances
Langford; Glen Gray (Kenny Sargent); Kay Kyser (Ginny
Simms)
SMALL FRY -Bing Crosby, with Johnny Mercer
BOOGIE WOOGIE -Tommy Dorsey (Instrumental)
WHILE A CIGARETTE WAS BURNING -Buddy Rogers
(Vocal) and His Orchestra: Sammy Kaye (Charlie Wilson)
SILVER ON THE SAGE -Bing Crosby; Dick Jurgens (Eddy
Howard)
HEART AND SOUL -Larry Clinton (Bea Wain); Connie
Boswell; Al Donahue (Paula Kelly)

MY REVERIE (Based on Claude De Bussy's REVERIE, from 1895) -Larry Clinton (Bea Wain)

MY OWN -Tommy Dorsey (Edythe Wright); Gene Krupa (Irene Daye); George Hall (Dolly Dawn)

WHO BLEW OUT THE FLAME? -Larry Clinton (Bea Wain); Red Norvo (Mildred Bailey); Ozzie Nelson (Vocal) and His Orchestra

ALL ASHORE -Sammy Kaye (Tommy Ryan); Jan Garber (Lee Bennett)

SUMMERTIME (From 1935) -Bing Crosby; Bob Crosby (Instrumental - Theme Song)

SUMMER SOUVENIRS -Larry Clinton (Bea Wain); Connie Boswell

WHEN I GO A-DREAMIN' -Benny Goodman (Martha Tilton); Kay Kyser (Harry Babbitt)

DAY AFTER DAY (From 1932) -Artie Shaw (Helen Forrest)

TWO SLEEPY PEOPLE -Bob Hope and Shirley Ross; Kay Kyser (Harry Babbitt and Ginny Simms); Bob Crosby (Vocal with Marion Mann) and His Orchestra

DEEP IN A DREAM -Artie Shaw (Helen Forrest); Bob Crosby (Marion Mann); Kay Kyser (Ginny Simms)

HAVE YOU FORGOTTEN SO SOON? -Tommy Dorsey (Jack Leonard); Kay Kyser (Ginny Simms); Red Norvo (Mildred Bailey); Les Brown (Miriam Shaw); Sammy Kaye (Charlie Wilson)

SIXTY SECONDS GOT TOGETHER -Hal Kemp (Skinnay Ennis); Kay Kyser (Harry Babbitt)

YOU MUST HAVE BEEN A BEAUTIFUL BABY -Bing Crosby; Tommy Dorsey Clambake Seven (Edythe Wright); Russ Morgan (Vocal) and His Orchestra

OLD FOLKS -Bing Crosby; Larry Clinton (Bea Wain)

HOORAY FOR HOLLYWOOD -Johnny "Scat" Davis
THIS CAN'T BE LOVE -Benny Goodman (Martha Tilton);
    Les Brown (Miriam Shaw) Frances Langford; Horace
    Heidt (Larry Cotton)
JEEPERS CREEPERS -Larry Clinton (Ford Leary); Al
    Donahue (Paula Kelly)
JUST A KID NAMED JOE -Bing Crosby; Jan Savitt (George
    "Bon-Bon" Tunnell); Johnny Long (Jack Edmondson)
THE FUNNY OLD HILLS -Bing Crosby
GIRL FRIEND OF THE WHIRLING DERVISH -Guy
    Lombardo (Lombardo Trio)
HAWAIIAN WAR CHANT -Tommy Dorsey (Instrumental)
ANGELS WITH DIRTY FACES -Tommy Dorsey (Edythe
    Wright)
GET OUT OF TOWN -Frances Langford; Les Brown
    (Miriam Shaw); Sammy Kaye (Charlie Wilson)
MY HEART BELONGS TO DADDY -Larry Clinton (Bea
    Wain); Mary Martin, guest vocalist with the Eddy Duchin
    Orchestra
SEPTEMBER SONG -Walter Huston
SING FOR YOUR SUPPER -Benny Goodman (Martha
    Tilton); Les Brown (Miriam Shaw); Horace Heidt (Charles
    Goodwin)

The most popular songs of the year, based on most appear-
ances and most times in first place on the weekly radio survey,
Your Hit Parade , were: MY REVERIE; TI-PI-TIN; I'VE
GOT A POCKETFUL OF DREAMS; LOVE WALKED IN;
MUSIC, MAESTRO, PLEASE; SAYS MY HEART;
THANKS FOR THE MEMORY; YOU'RE A SWEET-

HEART, PLEASE BE KIND and YOU MUST HAVE BEEN
A BEAUTIFUL BABY.

On the other hand, standing up best in the test of time were:
YOU GO TO MY HEAD; SEPTEMBER SONG; SUMMER-
TIME and CHANGE PARTNERS, with THANKS FOR THE
MEMORY; I HADN'T ANYONE TILL YOU; THIS CAN'T
BE LOVE and MUSIC, MAESTRO, PLEASE also receiving a
fair share of attention.

Instrumental "Collector's Items"

STRUTTIN' WITH SOME BARBECUE	-Louis Armstrong
STOP LOOK AND LISTEN	-Charlie Barnet
IN A JAM	-Charlie Barnet
SWINGING DOWN TO RIO	-Charlie Barnet
JUMP-JUMP'S HERE	-Charlie Barnet
DO YOU WANT TO JUMP CHILDREN?	-Charlie Barnet
JUMPIN' AT THE WOODSIDE	-Count Basie
SWINGIN' THE BLUES	-Count Basie
SHORTY GEORGE	-Count Basie
EVERY TUB	-Count Basie
BLUE AND SENTIMENTAL	-Count Basie
DOGGIN' AROUND	-Count Basie
TEXAS SHUFFLE	-Count Basie
HOW LONG BLUES	-Count Basie
THE DIRTY DOZENS	-Count Basie
HEY LAWDY MAMA	-Count Basie
PANASSIE STOMP	-Count Basie
SOPHISTICATED LADY	-Bunny Berigan
PINE TOP'S BOOGIE WOOGIE	-Les Brown

SOBBIN' BLUES	-Les Brown
WOLVERINE BLUES	-Bob Crosby
DIGA DIGA DOO	-Bob Crosby
HONKY TONK TRAIN BLUES	-Bob Crosby
AT THE JAZZ BAND BALL	-Bob Crosby
DOGTOWN BLUES	-Bob Crosby
LOUISE, LOUISE	-Bob Crosby
PANAMA	-Bob Crosby
ROYAL GARDEN BLUES	-Bob Crosby
SQUEEZE ME	-Bob Crosby
MARCH OF THE BOBCATS	-Bob Crosby
CAN'T WE BE FRIENDS?	-Bob Crosby
YOU'RE DRIVING ME CRAZY	-Bob Crosby
DARKTOWN STRUTTERS' BALL	-Jimmy Dorsey
CHINATOWN MY CHINATOWN	-Tommy Dorsey
THE SHEIK OF ARABY	-Tommy Dorsey
I NEVER KNEW	-Tommy Dorsey
PANAMA	-Tommy Dorsey
WASHBOARD BLUES	-Tommy Dorsey
SYMPHONY IN RIFFS	-Tommy Dorsey
TIN ROOF BLUES	-Tommy Dorsey
DOWN HOME RAG	-Tommy Dorsey
DAVENPORT BLUES	-Tommy Dorsey
LIGHTLY AND POLITELY	-Tommy Dorsey
STEPPIN' INTO SWING SOCIETY	-Duke Ellington
NEW BLACK AND TAN FANTASY	-Duke Ellington
RIDING ON A BLUE NOTE	-Duke Ellington
LOST IN MEDITATION	-Duke Ellington
BRAGGIN' IN BRASS	-Duke Ellington
SWINGTIME IN HONOLULU	-Duke Ellington
DINAH'S IN A JAM	-Duke Ellington

PYRAMID	-Duke Ellington
A BLUES SERENADE	-Duke Ellington
PRELUDE TO A KISS	-Duke Ellington
LAMBETH WALK	-Duke Ellington
HIP CHIC	-Duke Ellington
BUFFET FLAT	-Duke Ellington
MIGHTY LIKE THE BLUES	-Duke Ellington
ONE O'CLOCK JUMP	-Benny Goodman (Full Band)
MAKE BELIEVE	-Benny Goodman (Full Band)
BLUE ROOM	-Benny Goodman (Full Band)
LULLABY IN RHYTHM	-Benny Goodman (Full Band)
BIG JOHN'S SPECIAL	-Benny Goodman (Full Band)
I NEVER KNEW	-Benny Goodman (Full Band)
SWEET SUE (JUST YOU)	-Benny Goodman (Full Band)
MY MELANCHOLY BABY	-Benny Goodman (Full Band)
WRAPPIN' IT UP	-Benny Goodman (Full Band)
MARGIE	-Benny Goodman (Full Band)
RUSSIAN LULLABY	-Benny Goodman (Full Band)
BUMBLE BEE STOMP	-Benny Goodman (Full Band)
CIRIBIRIBIN	-Benny Goodman (Full Band)
TOPSY	-Benny Goodman (Full Band)
SMOKE HOUSE	-Benny Goodman (Full Band)
FAREWELL BLUES	-Benny Goodman (Full Band)
MY HONEY'S LOVIN' ARMS	-Benny Goodman (Full Band)
IT HAD TO BE YOU	-Benny Goodman (Full Band)
BACH GOES TO TOWN	-Benny Goodman (Full Band)
I'LL ALWAYS BE IN LOVE WITH YOU	-Benny Goodman (Full Band)
UNDECIDED	-Benny Goodman (Full Band)
SWEET GEORGIA BROWN	-Benny Goodman (Quartet)
'S WONDERFUL	-Benny Goodman (Quartet)

BLUES IN YOUR FLAT	-Benny Goodman (Quartet)
SWEET LORRAINE	-Benny Goodman (Trio)
CALLIOPE BLUES	-Woody Herman
TWIN CITY BLUES	-Woody Herman
LAUGHING BOY BLUES	-Woody Herman
LULLABY IN RHYTHM	-Woody Herman
INDIAN BOOGIE WOOGIE	-Woody Herman
ONE O'CLOCK JUMP	-Harry James All-Stars
PRELUDE TO A STOMP	-Gene Krupa
JAM ON TOAST	-Gene Krupa
WIRE BRUSH STOMP	-Gene Krupa
RHYTHM JAM	-Gene Krupa
BYE BYE BLUES	-Gene Krupa
WALKIN' AND SWINGIN'	-Gene Krupa
DIPPER MOUTH BLUES	-Glenn Miller
BY THE WATERS OF MINNETONKA	-Glenn Miller
KING PORTER STOMP	-Glenn Miller
SUGARFOOT STOMP	-Jan Savitt
THAT'S A-PLENTY	-Jan Savitt
FUTURISTIC SHUFFLE	-Jan Savitt
QUAKER CITY JAZZ	-Jan Savitt
TOY TRUMPET	-Artie Shaw
POWER HOUSE	-Artie Shaw
AZURE	-Artie Shaw
THE CALL OF THE FREAKS	-Artie Shaw
IN THE SHADE OF THE NEW APPLE TREE	-Artie Shaw
BLUE FANTASY	-Artie Shaw
MEADE LUX SPECIAL	-Artie Shaw

I CAN'T BELIEVE THAT YOU'RE
   IN LOVE WITH ME   -Artie Shaw
NON-STOP FLIGHT   -Artie Shaw
SOFTLY, AS IN A MORNING SUNRISE   -Artie Shaw
THE CHANT   -Artie Shaw
BACK BAY SHUFFLE   -Artie Shaw
NIGHTMARE   -Artie Shaw

Developments This Year in Popular Music

- Swing continued to gain in popularity and was now well
beyond any concept of being a musical fad or novelty.   In
January, Benny Goodman conducted the first performance by
any swing band in that most highbrow of locales, New York's
Carnegie Hall - yet another breakthrough for him.   The fact
that his band was invited to play there was newsworthy
enough, but the quality of the performance drew such raves
from everyone in attendance that it was recognized as a
landmark event in the annals of American popular music.
Other concerts were later held, some including Benny Goodman and some at the same Carnegie Hall, but this one always
held a special place for all who remembered it.   Twelve years
later, a long-playing album of the complete performance was
issued and enjoyed brisk sales, testifying to both its fame and
its quality.

In all, twenty-three numbers were performed on that
occasion by: a) the Goodman Trio, consisting of Benny on
clarinet, Teddy Wilson at the piano and Gene Krupa on drums;
b) the Quartet, which saw the addition of Lionel Hampton on
vibraphone and c) the full orchestra. In an effort to present a

broader range of musical talent, Benny reached outside his band, inviting several musicians of all-star caliber from other bands to contribute on some of the evening's selections. These included Count Basie on piano, with his all-star sidemen, Buck Clayton (trumpet); Lester Young (tenor); Freddie Green (guitar) and Walter Page (bass). On loan from Duke Ellington were: Cootie Williams (trumpet); Johnny Hodges (alto) and Harry Carney (baritone sax). Prominent among the many memorable numbers were: DON'T BE THAT WAY, ONE O'CLOCK JUMP, STOMPIN' AT THE SAVOY and SING SING SING. The latter had been recorded the previous year on two sides, each of more than three minutes' duration. At Carnegie, it was played through in its entirety and Gene Krupa's long, spectacular solo toward the end caused the audience to erupt in spontaneous, unrestrained cheering. It was a thrilling moment, not only for those present, but vicariously for millions more who read about it and heard recordings of the performance. It was possibly the highlight of an evening full of outstanding individual and collective performances, causing SING SING SING to come immediately to mind whenever the first and most famous swing concert would be recalled.

- At this time there were two magazines devoted to news of the big bands: *Downbeat* and *Metronome* . Both inaugurated polls this year to determine which bands were the favorites among fans. The results revealed that among swing bands most highly regarded were: Artie Shaw, Benny Goodman, Tommy Dorsey, Bob Crosby, Count Basie, Duke Ellington, Jimmy Dorsey, Glen Gray, Jimmie Lunceford, Red Norvo and Gene Krupa. The favorite sweet bands were: Glen Gray, Hal

Kemp, Tommy Dorsey, Kay Kyser, Guy Lombardo, Horace Heidt, Wayne King, Larry Clinton, Russ Morgan, Ray Noble, Will Osborne, Glenn Miller and Sammy Kaye.

It is interesting to note how highly the polls rated the Crosby unit as a "swing" band. This may have been "painting with a broad brush," so to speak, in deference to its Dixieland jazz group, the "Bobcats." Many fans may have concluded that if Dixieland wasn't "sweet" music, it must therefore be "swing." Swing was still new and not yet clearly defined in the minds of all listeners.

Also worthy of note is the appearance of the Tommy Dorsey and Glen Gray bands on both the sweet and swing lists in these polls, evidence of their versatility.

However, what these polls, conducted during the year rather than at the end, failed to reflect, was how much air time each of these bands obtained in 1938. The *Downbeat* poll must have been taken later, since it more accurately indicates that by late in the year, popular new records by the bands of Artie Shaw and Larry Clinton had obtained quite extensive play by disc jockeys and that the bands of Glenn Miller and Gene Krupa were becoming well-known. Larry Clinton easily had the greatest number of hit records. This was attributable in large part to his girl singer, Bea Wain, who recorded two dozen songs and saw nearly all of them become hits, including MY REVERIE, the year's top song on the *Your Hit Parade* weekly radio survey.

-In mentioning air time, recognition must also be given to

the Andrews Sisters, Patti, LaVerne and Maxine, from Min-
neapolis, Minnesota. The girls' first big hit, BEI MIR BIST
DU SCHOEN, (It means "you're grand," according to the
lyrics) carried over into this year and they quickly followed it
with JOSEPH, JOSEPH and OH! MA-MA. In addition, their
versions this year of TI-PI-TIN, SAYS MY HEART, I
MARRIED AN ANGEL and LOVE IS WHERE YOU FIND
IT, recorded initially by some of the bands, were also big
sellers for the girls, whose special sound and style were fast
endearing themselves to the public. This formula of exclusive
hits combined with cover recordings of the hits of various
bands would be their key to success throughout the big band
years and beyond. Although they recorded an occasional
ballad, their specialty was the fast-paced novelty song, through
which they would weave jazzy vocal effects and in effect,
swing. Their style was considered at that time to be "hep" and
"modern" and along with the swing bands, they helped to
change the musical tastes of many Americans during the late
1930s.

Half a century or more after the fact, many readers may
find it difficult to imagine that one hundred or more songs
could gain real popularity in one year. That is to say, popular
enough to still be recognized, decades later. Nevertheless, it
was true, year after year. Contributing to a song's popularity
was the fact that it might be recorded by several artists, as seen
on our yearly lists. In addition, disc jockeys, becoming
increasingly numerous, tended to mimic each other's selections, assuring wide saturation for a limited number of each
month's new recordings. Songs from Broadway and Hollywood musicals gained an edge through the national publicity

obtained from that exposure and often that provided the incentive for bands and independent singers to record them. Bing Crosby would record songs from his films and also sing them on his weekly radio show, the Kraft Music Hall, giving them three-pronged exposure.

- In addition to newly-written songs, there was a yearly complement of revivals, with old songs occasionally enjoying a second period of popularity, thanks to excellent new arrangements by such bands as those of Tommy Dorsey and Artie Shaw, who specialized in resurrecting old songs, usually with great success. Two of the biggest hits of the big band era were crafted this year from older numbers - Jerry Gray's arrangement for Artie Shaw of Cole Porter's BEGIN THE BEGUINE (1935) and Dean Kincaide's remodeling of PINE TOP'S BOOGIE WOOGIE (1929) into Tommy Dorsey's BOOGIE WOOGIE.

- When he formed his present band in March of this year, Glenn Miller employed two men who would figure prominently in the band's success. One was tenor sax player and novelty vocalist Gordon "Tex" Beneke, while the other was singer Ray Eberle. Ray was the younger brother of Bob Eberly, Jimmy Dorsey's excellent vocalist, who had begun spelling the family name with a "y" to avoid the tendency of some to mispronounce it. That such a young, inexperienced singer as Eberle would land a job with the band which was destined to become the best had to be the result of a rare occurrence and it was. His path crossed with that of Glenn Miller in a New York club one night when Ray went to visit his brother at the moment when Glenn had dropped by on a night to listen to Jimmy Dorsey's band. Upon entering, Ray passed the table where Glenn was seated with friends. Glenn glanced up at the young man and struck by his strong resemblance to his brother, a large-framed, dark and handsome fellow, gasped in astonishment that if Bob weren't on the stage singing, he'd have been certain that he had just walked by the table. On being told that this was Bob's younger brother and also being in need of a boy singer, Glenn asked if anyone knew whether the young man could sing. No one knew, nor was the nineteen-year-old himself much help, in his modesty, when asked. So, based solely upon his relationship and resemblance to one of the best singers in the business, Ray Eberle was offered a chance to audition with the Glenn Miller band and another important chapter in big band history was begun. He later revealed that he was paid thirty-five dollars per week and fifteen dollars for a recording, two for twenty-five. Years later, Harry James told an interviewer that when he employed Frank Sinatra in 1939, he paid him $75.00 weekly and in less than a year's time, Tommy Dorsey was able to obtain Frank's services with a higher offer, making him one of the highest paid bandsingers. This proved nothing more than that "poor" Ray Eberle spent his career as the principal voice of the leading band of its time, comparatively underpaid. However, if he eventually learned of that circumstance, he might have been somewhat pacified by the knowledge that as Miller's lead vocalist, his status and resulting fame were no doubt the envy of everyone in his profession.

- In addition to Glenn Miller's new band, others getting started this year were those of Gene Krupa, Skinnay Ennis and Alvino Rey.

1 9 3 9

The Most Popular Recordings

January - March

THEY SAY -Artie Shaw (Helen Forrest); Mildred Bailey (Vocal) and Her Orchestra; Connie Boswell; Sammy Kaye (Tommy Ryan)

THANKS FOR EVERYTHING -Artie Shaw (Helen Forrest)

THE UMBRELLA MAN -Kay Kyser (Ginny Simms, Harry Babbitt); Guy Lombardo (The Lombardo Trio); Sammy Kaye (The Three Barons and Band Chorus)

F. D. R. JONES -Hal Kemp (Skinnay Ennis); Chick Webb (Ella Fitzgerald); Cab Calloway (Vocal) and His Orchestra

I HAVE EYES -Bing Crosby; Artie Shaw (Helen Forrest); Benny Goodman (Martha Tilton); Les Brown (Herb Muse)

'T AIN'T WHAT YOU DO (IT'S THE WAY THAT YOU DO IT) -Jimmie Lunceford (Trummy Young, Band Chorus); Harry James (Jack Palmer)

WHAT IS THIS THING CALLED LOVE (From 1930) -Artie Shaw (Instrumental)

COULD BE -Glen Gray (Pee Wee Hunt); Sammy Kaye (The Three Barons)

THINKING OF YOU -Kay Kyser (Harry Babbitt) Theme Song

HURRY HOME -Frances Langford; Sammy Kaye (Charlie
   Wilson); Kay Kyser (Harry Babbitt); Bob Crosby (Vocal)
   and His Orchestra); Jan Savitt (Carlotta Dale)
DEEP PURPLE -Larry Clinton (Bea Wain); Artie Shaw
   (Helen Forrest); Bing Crosby; Jimmy Dorsey (Bob
   Eberly); Kay Kyser (Ginny Simms)
BLAME IT ON MY LAST AFFAIR -Mildred Bailey; Count
   Basie (Helen Humes); Harry James (Bernice Byers)
PENNY SERENADE -Guy Lombardo (The Lombardo Trio);
   Sammy Kaye (Jimmy Brown); Dick Jurgens (Eddy
   Howard); Horace Heidt (Larry Cotton)
BETWEEN A KISS AND A SIGH -Artie Shaw (Helen
   Forrest); Bing Crosby; Tommy Dorsey (Edythe Wright);
   Kay Kyser (Harry Babbitt)
CUCKOO IN THE CLOCK -Kay Kyser (Sully Mason);
   Benny Goodman (Johnny Mercer); Glenn Miller (Marion
   Hutton)
STAR DUST (From 1929) -Bing Crosby
YOU'RE A SWEET LITTLE HEADACHE -Bing Crosby;
   Benny Goodman (Martha Tilton); Artie Shaw (Helen
   Forrest); Les Brown (Miriam Shaw)
DOES YOUR HEART BEAT FOR ME? Russ Morgan
   (Instrumental) Theme Song
I GET ALONG WITHOUT YOU VERY WELL -Larry
   Clinton (Bea Wain); Jimmy Dorsey (Bob Eberly); Red
   Norvo (Mildred Bailey); Charlie Barnet (Judy Ellington)
I CRIED FOR YOU (From 1923) -Glen Gray (Kenny
   Sargent); Bing Crosby
BLUE MOON (FROM 1934) -Tommy Dorsey (Jack Leonard,
   Band Chorus)

(I'M AFRAID) THE MASQUERADE IS OVER -Larry
    Clinton (Bea Wain); Jimmy Dorsey (Bob Eberly); Horace
    Heidt (Larry Cotton)
TWO O'CLOCK JUMP -Harry James (Instrumental)
GOTTA GET SOME SHUTEYE -Kay Kyser (Harry Babbitt);
    Glen Gray (Pee Wee Hunt)
I'M IN LOVE WITH THE HONORABLE MR. SO-AND-SO
    Artie Shaw (Helen Forrest); Frances Langford
FALLING IN LOVE WITH LOVE -Frances Langford
HEAVEN CAN WAIT -Tommy Dorsey (Jack Leonard); Glen
    Gray (Clyde Burke); Kay Kyser (Harry Babbitt)
UNDECIDED -Chick Webb (Ella Fitzgerald); Benny
    Goodman (Instrumental)
LAZY BONES (From 1933) -Glen Gray (Pee Wee Hunt and
    Louis Armstrong, guest vocalist)

April - June

SUNRISE SERENADE -Glenn Miller and Glen Gray
    (Instrumentals)
HOLD TIGHT - HOLD TIGHT -The Andrews Sisters
LITTLE SIR ECHO -Bing Crosby; Dick Jurgens (Eddy
    Howard); Guy Lombardo (Carmen Lombardo); Horace
    Heidt (Emily Stevenson and Larry Cotton)
GOD BLESS AMERICA -Kate Smith
IF I HAD MY WAY (From 1913) -Bing Crosby; Glen Gray
    (Kenny Sargent)
EAST SIDE OF HEAVEN -Bing Crosby; Kay Kyser (Harry
    Babbitt); Sammy Kaye (Jimmy Brown)

LITTLE SKIPPER -Tommy Dorsey (Jack Leonard); Horace
    Heidt (Larry Cotton); Ozzie Nelson (Vocal) and His
    Orchestra
I SURRENDER DEAR (From 1930) -Bing Crosby
OUR LOVE -Larry Clinton (Bea Wain); Tommy Dorsey
    (Jack Leonard); Jimmy Dorsey (Bob Eberly)
DON'T WORRY 'BOUT ME -Hal Kemp (Bob Allen); Les
    Brown (Miriam Shaw)
WHAT GOES UP MUST COME DOWN -Bob Crosby
    (Vocal) and His Orchestra; Les Brown (Miriam Shaw);
    Horace Heidt (Tony Russell)
TEARS FROM MY INKWELL -Glen Gray (Kenny Sargent);
    Kay Kyser (Ginny Simms); Sammy Kaye (Tommy Ryan)
THAT SLY OLD GENTLEMAN -Bing Crosby; Kay Kyser
    (Ginny Simms); Mildred Bailey (Vocal) and Her
    Orchestra; Sammy Kaye (Jimmy Brown)
AND THE ANGELS SING -Benny Goodman (Martha Tilton);
    Glenn Miller (Ray Eberle); Bing Crosby; Mildred Bailey
ALL OF ME (From 1932) -Jimmy Dorsey (Helen O'Connell)
THREE LITTLE FISHIES -Kay Kyser (Harry Babbitt, Ginny
    Simms, Merwyn Bogue); Guy Lombardo (Carmen
    Lombardo, Larry Owen, Fred Henry); Hal Kemp (The
    Smoothies)
DON'T WORRY 'BOUT ME -Bob Crosby (Marion Mann);
    Hal Kemp (Bob Allen); Les Brown (Miriam Shaw);
    Horace Heidt (Larry Cotton)
PENTHOUSE SERENADE -Bob Crosby (Marion Mann)
WISHING -Glenn Miller (Ray Eberle); Hal Kemp (Skinnay
    Ennis); Horace Heidt (Larry Cotton and The Heidt Lights)
(AT THE) WOODCHOPPERS' BALL -Woody Herman
    (Instrumental)

THE LADY'S IN LOVE WITH YOU -Glenn Miller (Tex
    Beneke); Benny Goodman (Martha Tilton); Gene Krupa
    (Irene Daye)
I NEVER KNEW HEAVEN COULD SPEAK -Hal Kemp
    (Bob Allen); Bob Crosby (Marion Mann)
IF I DIDN'T CARE -The Ink Spots
RAGTIME COWBOY JOE -Dick Jurgens (Eddy Howard);
    Pinky Tomlin
ALL I REMEMBER IS YOU -Tommy Dorsey (Jack
    Leonard); Jimmy Dorsey (Helen O'Connell); Artie Shaw
    (Helen Forrest); Kay Kyser (Harry Babbitt)
PAVANNE -Glenn Miller (Instrumental)
STRANGE ENCHANTMENT -Dorothy Lamour
WELL ALL RIGHT -The Andrews Sisters
(ALLA EN) EL RANCHO GRANDE (From 1934) -Bing
    Crosby, with The Foursome
S'POSIN' (From 1929) -Bing Crosby
BEER BARREL POLKA -The Andrews Sisters; The Will
    Glahe Polka Band (Instrumental)
LITTLE BROWN JUG (From 1869) -Glenn Miller
    (Instrumental)
STAIRWAY TO THE STARS -Glenn Miller (Ray Eberle);
    Kay Kyser (Harry Babbitt); Jimmy Dorsey (Bob Eberly);
    Al Donahue (Paula Kelly)

July - September

WHITE SAILS (BENEATH A YELLOW MOON) -Al
    Donahue (Paula Kelly); Sammy Kaye (Clyde Burke);
    Ozzie Nelson (Vocal) and His Orchestra

MOON LOVE -Glenn Miller (Ray Eberle); Al Donahue
(Paula Kelly); Sammy Kaye (Clyde Burke); Mildred
Bailey; Horace Heidt (Larry Cotton)
BLUE EVENING -Glenn Miller (Ray Eberle); Frances
Langford; Hal Kemp (Bob Allen)
IT'S FUNNY TO EVERYONE BUT ME -The Ink Spots;
Jimmy Dorsey (Bob Eberly); Harry James (Frank Sinatra)
JUST FOR A THRILL -The Ink Spots; Bob Chester (Kathleen
Lane)
I POURED MY HEART INTO A SONG -Artie Shaw (Helen
Forrest); Jimmy Dorsey (Bob Eberly); Tommy Dorsey
(Jack Leonard); Horace Heidt (Larry Cotton)
SOUTH AMERICAN WAY -The Andrews Sisters
ESPECIALLY FOR YOU -Orrin Tucker (Bonnie Baker);
Jimmy Dorsey (Helen O'Connell)
THE LAMP IS LOW -Glenn Miller (Ray Eberle); Tommy
Dorsey (Jack Leonard); Jimmy Dorsey (Bob Eberly);
Mildred Bailey (Vocal) and Her Orchestra
TO YOU -Glenn Miller (Ray Eberle); Tommy Dorsey (Jack
Leonard); Al Donahue (Paula Kelly)
YOU TAUGHT ME TO LOVE AGAIN -Tommy Dorsey
(Jack Leonard); Gene Krupa (Irene Daye); Jan Savitt
(Carlotta Dale)
GIRL OF MY DREAMS (From 1928) -Bing Crosby
THE JUMPIN' JIVE -Cab Calloway (Vocal) and His
Orchestra; The Andrews Sisters
COMES LOVE -Artie Shaw (Helen Forrest); Jimmy Dorsey
(Helen O'Connell); Harry James (Connie Haines)
MY LAST GOODBYE -Dick Jurgens (Eddy Howard); Glenn
Miller (Ray Eberle)

OVER THE RAINBOW (Academy Award-winning song from *The Wizard of Oz*) -Judy Garland; Glenn Miller (Ray Eberle); Larry Clinton (Bea Wain); Bob Crosby (Teddy Grace); Horace Heidt (Larry Cotton)

DING-DONG, THE WITCH IS DEAD! -Glenn Miller (Marion Hutton)

THE MAN WITH THE MANDOLIN -Glenn Miller Marion Hutton); Frances Langford; Horace Heidt (Larry Cotton and The Heidt Lights)

OH! YOU CRAZY MOON -Glenn Miller (Ray Eberle); Tommy Dorsey (Jack Leonard); Kay Kyser (Ginny Simms); Bob Crosby (Vocal) and His Orchestra

TRAFFIC JAM -Artie Shaw (Instrumental)

CINDERELLA STAY IN MY ARMS -Glenn Miller (Ray Eberle)

YOU CAN DEPEND ON ME (From 1932) -Dick Jurgens (Eddy Howard); Count Basie (Jimmie Rushing)

DAY IN, DAY OUT -Artie Shaw (Helen Forrest); Tommy Dorsey (Jack Leonard); Bob Crosby (Helen Ward); Kay Kyser (Harry Babbitt)

COQUETTE (From 1928) -The Ink Spots

A MAN AND HIS DREAM -Bing Crosby; Tommy Dorsey (Jack Leonard); Jimmy Dorsey (Bob Eberly); Artie Shaw (Helen Forrest); Kay Kyser (Harry Babbitt)

WHO'S SORRY NOW? (From 1923) -Glenn Miller (Ray Eberle)

JUST ONE MORE CHANCE (From 1931) -Bing Crosby

MOONLIGHT SERENADE -Glenn Miller (Instrumental-Theme Song)

IF I HAD YOU (From 1928) -Jimmy Dorsey (Bob Eberly)

MELANCHOLY MOOD -Artie Shaw (Helen Forrest); Harry
   James (Frank Sinatra); Bob Crosby (Vocal) and His
   Orchestra
AN APPLE FOR THE TEACHER -Bing Crosby and Connie
   Boswell; Horace Heidt (The Heidt Lights)
MY ISLE OF GOLDEN DREAMS (From 1916) -GlennMiller
   (Instrumental)

October - December

IN THE MOOD -Glenn Miller (Instrumental)
IN AN 18th CENTURY DRAWING ROOM -Raymond Scott
   Quintet (Instrumental)
WHAT'S NEW? -Bing Crosby; Benny Goodman (Louise
   Tobin); Hal Kemp (Nan Wynn); Kay Kyser (Ginny
   Simms); Bob Crosby (Instrumental, originally titled I'M
   FREE)
CHEROKEE -Charlie Barnet (Instrumental)
BLUE ORCHIDS -Tommy Dorsey (Jack Leonard); Glenn
   Miller (Ray Eberle); Jimmy Dorsey (Bob Eberly); Horace
   Heidt (Larry Cotton)
BABY ME -Glenn Miller (Kay Starr); Sammy Kaye (The
   Three Barons)
ARE YOU HAVING ANY FUN? -Tommy Dorsey (Edythe
   Wright); Jimmy Dorsey (Helen O'Connell); Horace Heidt
   (The Heidt Lights)
IF I KNEW THEN (WHAT I KNOW NOW) -Dick Jurgens
   (Eddy Howard); Bing Crosby; Woody Herman (Vocal)
   and His Orchestra; Sammy Kaye (Clyde Burke)

HOW LONG HAS THIS BEEN GOING ON? -Larry Clinton
(Mary Dugan); Ozzie Nelson (Vocal) and His Orchestra;
Tommy Tucker (Amy Arnell)
DAY DREAMS COME TRUE AT NIGHT -Dick Jurgens
(Eddy Howard) - Theme Song
SOUTH OF THE BORDER -Bing Crosby; Guy Lombardo
(Carmen Lombardo); Horace Heidt (Larry Cotton)
MY PRAYER -The Ink Spots; Glenn Miller (Ray Eberle);
Jimmy Dorsey (Bob Eberly); Sammy Kaye (Clyde Burke)
MELANCHOLY LULLABY -Glenn Miller (Ray Eberle); Hal
Kemp (Nan Wynn)
LILACS IN THE RAIN -Hal Kemp (Nan Wynn); Dick
Jurgens (Eddy Howard); Bob Crosby (Vocal) and His
Orchestra; Horace Heidt (Larry Cotton)
CIRIBIRIBIN -Harry James (Instrumental - Theme Song);
Bing Crosby and The Andrews Sisters
UNDER A BLANKET OF BLUE (From 1929) -Glen Gray
(Kenny Sargent)
SCATTER-BRAIN -Frankie Masters (Vocal) and His
Orchestra; Benny Goodman (Louise Tobin); Sammy Kaye
(Charlie Wilson); Freddy Martin (Glenn Hughes)
THE YODELIN' JIVE -Bing Crosby and The Andrews Sisters
(WHY COULDN'T IT LAST) LAST NIGHT -Glenn Miller
(Ray Eberle); Bob Crosby (Vocal) and His Orchestra; Hal
Kemp (Bob Allen); Horace Heidt (Larry Cotton)
CAN I HELP IT? -Glenn Miller (Ray Eberle); Larry Clinton
(Terry Allen); Bob Crosby (Vocal) and His Orchestra;
Horace Heidt (Larry Cotton)
I DIDN'T KNOW WHAT TIME IT WAS -Artie Shaw (Helen
Forrest); Benny Goodman (Louise Tobin); Jimmy Dorsey
(Bob Eberly); Hal Kemp (Bob Allen)

HOLY SMOKE! (CAN'T YA TAKE A JOKE?) -Kay Kyser
(Sully Mason); Frankie Masters (The Masters Voices)
BLUEBIRDS IN THE MOONLIGHT -Glenn Miller (Marion
Hutton); Benny Goodman (Mildred Bailey, Guest
Vocalist); Sammy Kaye (Jimmy Brown)
BLUE RAIN -Glenn Miller (Ray Eberle); Tommy Dorsey
(Jack Leonard)
DEEP NIGHT (From 1929) -Tommy Dorsey (Jack Leonard
and Band Chorus)
SPEAKING OF HEAVEN -Glenn Miller (Ray Eberle);
Sammy Kaye (Clyde Burke)
DARN THAT DREAM -Tommy Dorsey (Anita Boyer); Blue
Barron (Russ Carlyle)
OH! JOHNNY, OH! JOHNNY, OH! -Orrin Tucker (Bonnie
Baker)
CARELESS -Glenn Miller (Ray Eberle); Dick Jurgens (Eddy
Howard); Tommy Dorsey (Allan De Witt); Woody
Herman (Vocal) and His Orchestra
ADDRESS UNKNOWN -The Ink Spots; Horace Heidt (Larry
Cotton)
I THOUGHT ABOUT YOU -Benny Goodman (Mildred
Bailey, Guest Vocalist); Hal Kemp (Bob Allen); Bob
Crosby (Teddy Grace); Will Bradley (Carlotta Dale);
Dinah Shore
BETWEEN THE DEVIL AND THE DEEP BLUE SEA
(From 1931) -Frances Langford
ALL THE THINGS YOU ARE -Artie Shaw (Helen Forrest);
Tommy Dorsey (Jack Leonard); Mildred Bailey, with the
Alec Wilder Octet

AFTER ALL -Tommy Dorsey (Jack Leonard); Jan Savitt
(George "Bon-Bon"Tunnell); Bob Chester Dolores
O'Neill)
CHATTER BOX -Kay Kyser (Ginny Simms and Harry
Babbitt); Sammy Kaye (The Three Kaydettes and Band
Chorus)
720 IN THE BOOKS -Jan Savitt (Instrumental)

This year produced such an abundance of good songs that a
simple review of the "ten most popular" would in this instance
be a disservice rather than a help to the reader. From January
to December, there was one beautiful new ballad after another
and it seemed that Artie Shaw's Helen Forrest and Larry
Clinton's Bea Wain were singing all of them. However, as the
year progressed, Glenn Miller, Tommy Dorsey and Bob
Crosby added quite a few more. There were also big novelty
hits in JEEPERS CREEPERS, carrying over from 1938,
HOLD TIGHT; THREE LITTLE FISHIES; BEER BARREL
POLKA; SCATTER-BRAIN and OH! JOHNNY, as well as
the swing classics, LITTLE BROWN JUG; IN THE MOOD
and CHEROKEE.

From such a wealth of material, it has always seemed
surprising that few songs from 1939 were later recorded
enough to qualify as standards. Of these, probably none was
more loved than ALL THE THINGS YOU ARE, which was
always high on everyone's list of favorites from this era.

Instrumental "Collector's Items"

TIN ROOF BLUES	-Charlie Barnet
KNOCKIN' AT THE FAMOUS DOOR	-Charlie Barnet
JUMP SESSION	-Charlie Barnet
SWING STREET STRUT	-Charlie Barnet
SCOTCH AND SODA	-Charlie Barnet
I NEVER KNEW	-Charlie Barnet
LAMENT FOR A LOST LOVE	-Charlie Barnet
THE LAST JUMP	-Charlie Barnet
THE DUKE'S IDEA	-Charlie Barnet
THE COUNT'S IDEA	-Charlie Barnet
JIVE AT FIVE	-Count Basie
ROCK-A-BYE BASIE	-Count Basie
TAXI WAR DANCE	-Count Basie
JUMP FOR ME	-Count Basie
TWELFTH STREET RAG	-Count Basie
POUND CAKE	-Count Basie
THE APPLE JUMP	-Count Basie
IN A PERSIAN MARKET	-Larry Clinton
A STUDY IN GREEN	-Larry Clinton
A STUDY IN RED	-Larry Clinton
GOLDEN BANTAM	-Larry Clinton
SATAN IN SATIN	-Larry Clinton
BOOGIE WOOGIE MAXIXE	-Bob Crosby
AIR MAIL STOMP	-Bob Crosby
RIGAMAROLE	-Jimmy Dorsey
SWAMP FIRE	-Jimmy Dorsey
A MAN AND HIS DRUM	-Jimmy Dorsey
MAJOR AND MINOR STOMP	-Jimmy Dorsey
BY THE RIVER SAINTE MARIE	-Tommy Dorsey

MARCHETA	-Tommy Dorsey
SWING LOW SWEET CHARIOT	-Tommy Dorsey
LONESOME ROAD (1&2)	-Tommy Dorsey
MILENBERG JOYS (1&2)	-Tommy Dorsey
EASY DOES IT	-Tommy Dorsey
STOMP IT OFF	-Tommy Dorsey
BOY MEETS HORN	-Duke Ellington
JAZZ POTPOURRI	-Duke Ellington
BATTLE OF SWING	-Duke Ellington
BLUE LIGHT	-Duke Ellington
LADY IN BLUE	-Duke Ellington
SMORGASBORD AND SCHNAPPS	-Duke Ellington
PORTRAIT OF THE LION	-Duke Ellington
SOLID OLD MAN	-Duke Ellington
COTTON CLUB STOMP	-Duke Ellington
BOUNCING BUOYANCY	-Duke Ellington
ROSE OF WASHINGTON SQUARE	-Benny Goodman (Full Band)
THE SIREN'S SONG	-Benny Goodman (Full Band)
PIC-A-RIB	-Benny Goodman (Full Band)
JUMPIN' AT THE WOODSIDE	-Benny Goodman (Full Band)
STEALIN' APPLES	-Benny Goodman (Full Band)
BOY MEETS HORN	-Benny Goodman (Full Band)
ROSE ROOM	-Benny Goodman (Full Band)
FLYING HOME	-Benny Goodman (Full Band)
MEMORIES OF YOU	-Benny Goodman (Sextet)
HONEYSUCKLE ROSE	-Benny Goodman (Sextet)
SEVEN COME ELEVEN	-Benny Goodman (Sextet)

BLUE LOU	-Benny Goodman (All-Stars)
THE BLUES	-Benny Goodman (All-Stars)
RIVERBOAT SHUFFLE	-Glen Gray
BONEYARD SHUFFLE	-Glen Gray
WASHBOARD BLUES	-Glen Gray
TIPPIN' IN	-Erskine Hawkins
DO YOU WANNA JUMP CHILLUN?	-Erskine Hawkins
PALEFACE	-Woody Herman
THE SHEIK OF ARABY	-Woody Herman
CASBAH BLUES	-Woody Herman
FAREWELL BLUES	-Woody Herman
EAST SIDE KICK	-Woody Herman
MIDNIGHT ECHOES	-Woody Herman
BLUES UPSTAIRS	-Woody Herman
BLUES DOWNSTAIRS	-Woody Herman
FATHER STEPS IN	-Earl Hines
SWEET GEORGIA BROWN	-Harry James
INDIANA	-Harry James
KING PORTER STOMP	-Harry James
FANNY MAY	-Harry James
SUGAR DADDY	-Harry James
FEET DRAGGIN' BLUES	-Harry James
FLASH	-Harry James
CROSS COUNTRY JUMP	-Harry James
CONCERTO FOR TRUMPET	-Harry James
I'M IN THE MARKET FOR YOU	-Harry James
BACK BEAT BOOGIE	-Harry James
NIGHT SPECIAL	-Harry James
I FOUND A NEW BABY	-Harry James

AVALON	-Harry James
WILLOW WEEP FOR ME	-Harry James
HELL'S BELLS	-Art Kassel (Theme)
SOME LIKE IT HOT	-Gene Krupa
APURKSODY (Theme)	-Gene Krupa
QUIET AND ROLL 'EM	-Gene Krupa
THE MADAM SWINGS IT	-Gene Krupa
DRACULA	-Gene Krupa
FOO FOR TWO	-Gene Krupa
JUNGLE MADNESS	-Gene Krupa
ON THE BEAM	-Gene Krupa
SYMPHONY IN RIFFS	-Gene Krupa
THREE LITTLE WORDS	-Gene Krupa
RUNNIN' WILD	-Glenn Miller
SLIP HORN JIVE	-Glenn Miller
PAGAN LOVE SONG	-Glenn Miller
FAREWELL BLUES	-Glenn Miller
I WANT TO BE HAPPY	-Glenn Miller
JOHNSON RAG	-Glenn Miller
GLEN ISLAND SPECIAL	-Glenn Miller
GET HAPPY	-Jan Savitt
THAT'S A-PLENTY	-Jan Savitt
WHEN BUDDHA SMILES	-Jan Savitt
JUNGLE DRUMS	-Artie Shaw
IT HAD TO BE YOU	-Artie Shaw
LOVER COME BACK TO ME	-Artie Shaw
MY HEART STOOD STILL	-Artie Shaw
VILIA	-Artie Shaw
THE MAN I LOVE	-Artie Shaw
ZIGEUNER	-Artie Shaw
ROSE ROOM	-Artie Shaw

I'M COMING, VIRGINIA	-Artie Shaw
PASTEL BLUE	-Artie Shaw
ONE-NIGHT STAND	-Artie Shaw
ONE FOOT IN THE GROOVE	-Artie Shaw
OCTAROON	-Artie Shaw
OUT OF NOWHERE	-Artie Shaw
SERENADE TO A SAVAGE	-Artie Shaw
CARIOCA	-Artie Shaw
OH! LADY BE GOOD	-Artie Shaw
AT SUNDOWN	-Artie Shaw
SWEET SUE (JUST YOU)	-Artie Shaw
ST. LOUIS BLUES	-Artie Shaw
PERSIAN RUG	-Jack Teagarden

Developments This Year in Popular Music

- When one considers all the leading bands, swing and sweet and reviews how they were faring at different stages of the era, it is difficult to find a year when so many were doing as well as in 1939. Goodman, the Dorseys, Shaw, Crosby, Basie, Ellington, Lunceford, Kemp, Kyser, Gray and Lombardo were cruising along in their accustomed high rankings in the polls. Harry James' first band was struggling, but with good musicians and his talented young singers, Frank Sinatra and Connie Haines, it was still a very appealing band with much promise. Woody Herman and Gene Krupa were maintaining a solid level of performance, as were Charlie Barnet and Sammy Kaye. Then, there was Larry Clinton, coming off a spectacular 1938 and wafted gloriously into 1939 by DEEP PURPLE, latest in a seemingly never-ending succession of hits by singer Bea Wain, plus the novelty hit, JEEPERS CREEPERS.

- Finally, if we compare this year's large output of high quality songs and instrumentals with that of other years, we have to conclude that all things considered, America's cornucopia of musical pleasure was overflowing in 1939 as at no other time in the Big Band Era.

- Highlights of the year, however, had to be the meteoric rise of the Glenn Miller band and the emergence of The Ink Spots as recording stars. Miller's group, in particular, seemed to be taking the country by storm, as its distinctive sound attracted millions of followers. Should that phenomenon be difficult to comprehend, a big band fan who heard Glenn Miller's original and exclusive saxophone-clarinet combination for the first time, was usually struck by two definite impressions. First, it was a *different* sound from that produced by any other big band. Second, with all the saxophones, plus that all-important clarinet playing in unison and skillfully used, as they often were to carry portions of the melody, it was not only a more pleasing sound, it could be described as an exhilarating, thrilling, listening experience. The auditory sensation produced by the blending of these particular instruments - only certain clarinetists were able to achieve the special tone - was something that had apparently pleased Glenn Miller at some time during his already lengthy experience as a big band musician and arranger. Evidently, too, he believed that it would have the same effect on the general public and this belief proved even to be underestimated. That delicious flow of sound was never more evident than in the band's theme, MOONLIGHT

SERENADE, which might well qualify as the theme song for the big band years in their entirety. Some of the other early recordings in which the reed section carried a large part of the melody, thus enabling the listener to savor it to best advantage, included TO YOU, STAIRWAY TO THE STARS and THE LAMP IS LOW.

- Early into 1939, the band was recording one big hit after another and was in great demand everywhere, especially after its smashing successes at the renowned Meadowbrook and Glen Island Casino supper clubs. In this, its first full year of operation, it made a couple dozen popular recordings of which three became million-sellers: MOONLIGHT SERENADE, LITTLE BROWN JUG and IN THE MOOD.

- In *Downbeat's* popularity poll for 1939, Miller was voted second, both to Benny Goodman in the swing category and to Tommy Dorsey among sweet bands - an astonishingly rapid rise to prominence, but by year's end the band had risen to No. 1, as would be reflected by the mid-1940 polls.

- Another important characteristic of the Glenn Miller band's long-lasting impact upon a very large and devoted following was Glenn's uncanny ability to find and record songs and instrumentals, not only beautifully suited to his style, but which became identified with the Miller band and no others. A few are mentioned above, but over the years these would also include such numbers as PAVANNE, BLUE EVENING, PENNSYLVANIA 6-5000, A MILLION DREAMS AGO, YESTERTHOUGHTS, FALLING LEAVES, A NIGHTIN-GALE SANG IN BERKELEY SQUARE, ANVIL CHORUS,

SONG OF THE VOLGA BOATMEN, I KNOW WHY,
CHATTANOOGA CHOO CHOO, YOU AND I, ELMER'S
TUNE, A STRING OF PEARLS, MOONLIGHT COCK-
TAIL, AMERICAN PATROL, KALAMAZOO, SERENADE
IN BLUE and JUKE BOX SATURDAY NIGHT.

- The Ink Spots' recording of IF I DIDN'T CARE was their
first hit, appearing early in the year. It wasn't the song nearly
as much as it was their unusual, appealing style which captured
the public's fancy. They were not the typical harmonizing
group. Most of their songs consisted of solos with musical and
vocal accompaniment and would begin with the high tenor
voice of Bill Kenny, who sang softly and enunciated each word
almost exaggeratedly. They specialized in romantic ballads
and in the middle of each song, deep-voiced Orville "Hoppy"
Jones would deliver a talking chorus, departing somewhat from
the lyrics as interpreted by Kenny, but repeating much the
same message in an earnest appeal to an imaginary girl friend.
The contrast was intriguing and one found oneself listening just
a bit closer than to the standard vocal renditions. Ivory "Deek"
Watson and Charlie Fuqua, who also played guitar, rounded
out the quartet with pleasing vocal effects. The group's
accompaniment was embellished by a softly played piano. The
Ink Spots were unique for all time. In their crooning style,
they made persuasive romantic appeals and uttered timeless
declarations of love, with matchless clarity. A lyricist could
not wish for better articulation of his words. So it was that
throughout the Big Band Era, regardless of how much the
Millers, Jameses, Dorseys, et al, might have dominated the
juke boxes and despite the popularity of other singing groups
like the Andrews Sisters, the King Sisters and the Mills

Brothers, or solo stars such as Bing Crosby, Frank Sinatra, Perry Como, Peggy Lee and Dinah Shore, the latest Ink Spots recording would always be given its share of air time and juke box space, because they had become an "institution." Their uniqueness meant that whether their originals were "covered" (when an artist chooses to record a song currently having been made into a hit by another) by others, or whether it was they who were covering, their versions always received equal attention from disc jockeys and record-buyers - a distinction enjoyed by only a handful of top recording artists. Actually, the Ink Spots' many hits included very few such "shared" ones and in each instance their version was either the more popular one or ranked very close to the leader. Examples are: MY PRAYER, I'LL NEVER SMILE AGAIN, THE GYPSY and TO EACH HIS OWN. MY PRAYER was one of this year's hits, following IF I DIDN'T CARE, ADDRESS UNKNOWN, IT'S FUNNY TO EVERYONE BUT ME and COQUETTE. Having hit upon a winning formula after years of trying, the Ink Spots invariably chose songs which permitted them to repeat the same style. Different as it was, with its soothing tone it provided an often welcome change of pace for the music listener and assured the Ink Spots of many years of success despite occasional changes in personnel.

- Early in the year, a pretty, blonde singer with prominent dimples joined the Jimmy Dorsey band, making her first recording (ALL OF ME) a winning one in that it would stand up well over many years. Helen O'Connell also made a winning combination with Bob Eberly, as they became the most effective girl - boy vocal pairing boasted by any band in the entire era. They remained together with Jimmy Dorsey, turning out hit after hit for more than four years, with 1941 being their most outstanding year, hit-wise.

- Girl vocalists Bea Wain and Edythe Wright retired from the Larry Clinton and Tommy Dorsey bands, respectively, while the Four King Sisters, Alyce, Donna, Louise and Yvonne, joined Alvino Rey after two years with Horace Heidt.

- On October 6, the bands of Paul Whiteman, Fred Waring, Benny Goodman and Glenn Miller took part in a swing concert in Carnegie Hall.

- That same month, the Palomar Ballroom in Los Angeles, unoccupied at the time, but containing the music and instruments belonging to Charlie Barnet and his bandsmen, was destroyed by fire.

- Toward the end of the year, there were two unusual hit songs from unexpected sources. Making the biggest splash was OH! JOHNNY, OH! JOHNNY, OH! - a revival from 1917 sung by "Wee" Bonnie Baker with Orrin Tucker's orchestra. Miss Baker's youthful, cute-sounding voice and the lyrics of that light-hearted song were a perfect pairing, heard often over several weeks, delighting millions and giving the band unaccustomed national recognition. The other was a catchy bit of fluff called SCATTER-BRAIN, composed by little-known bandleader Frankie Masters, which thrust him and his band briefly into the limelight. It was also recorded by Benny Goodman and Sammy Kaye and the combined effort helped to keep it in first place on *Your Hit Parade* for six weeks.

- About the same time, a Broadway musical with the name *Very Warm For May* closed after only 59 performances. Such a non-event was only remembered afterward because of one outstanding hit song in its Jerome Kern - Oscar Hammerstein score. That was ALL THE THINGS YOU ARE, so beautiful that hardly anyone from that generation could name five all-time favorites without including it.

- In December, a vocal group calling itself "The Pied Pipers" was employed by the enterprising Tommy Dorsey. It proved to be one of the better singing groups in its own right, but was most effective when used in combination with lead singers such as Frank Sinatra and Connie Haines. On such occasions, when five or six vocalists were before the microphones out in front of the band, the song was converted into a "production number," an impressive display of vocal talent much admired by all and soon imitated by other bands. Few, however, approached the standard set by the Dorsey group.

- In addition to that of Harry James, getting started this year were the bands of Tommy Byrne, Tony Pastor and Jack Teagarden.

- Diminutive drummer/bandleader Chick Webb, who had long been in ill health as a result of a birth defect, passed away at age 30. His protege, singer Ella Fitzgerald, was only 21 but since her name already had marquee value, the band members elected her to replace him as leader. She filled that role admirably well for a few years, until finally embarking on her great career as a single.

1 9 4 0

The Most Popular Recordings

January - March

FAITHFUL FOREVER -Glenn Miller (Ray Eberle)

STOP, IT'S WONDERFUL -Orrin Tucker (Bonnie Baker)

ON A LITTLE STREET IN SINGAPORE -Jimmy Dorsey (Bob
    Eberly); Glenn Miller (Ray Eberle)

AT THE BALALAIKA -Nelson Eddy; Wayne King (Vocal, with
    Trio) and His Orchestra; Orrin Tucker (Gil Mershon)

INDIAN SUMMER -Glenn Miller (Ray Eberle); Tommy Dorsey
    (Jack Leonard)

GAUCHO SERENADE -Glenn Miller (Ray Eberle)

YOU'D BE SURPRISED -Orrin Tucker (Bonnie Baker)

BETWEEN 18TH AND 19TH ON CHESTNUT STREET -Bing
    Crosby and Connie Boswell; Bob Crosby (Nappy Lamare and
    Eddie Miller)

THE LITTLE RED FOX -Kay Kyser (Kay Kyser, Harry Babbitt,
    "Little Audrey," Pokey Carriere); Hal Kemp (The Smoothies)

IN AN OLD DUTCH GARDEN -Glenn Miller (Ray Eberle);
    Sammy Kaye (Charlie Wilson and Chorus); Dick Jurgens (Eddy
    Howard)

DO I LOVE YOU? -Artie Shaw (Helen Forrest); Dick Jurgens
    (Eddy Howard); Woody Herman (Vocal) and His Orchestra

SO LONG -Russ Morgan (Vocal) and His Orchestra; The
    Charioteers

TO YOU, SWEETHEART, ALOHA (From 1936) -Bing Crosby;
    Horace Heidt (Larry Cotton); Dick Todd

IT'S A BLUE WORLD -Glenn Miller (Ray Eberle); Tommy
    Dorsey (Anita Boyer); Woody Herman (Vocal) and His
    Orchestra
MA, HE'S MAKIN' EYES AT ME -Kay Kyser (Sully
    Mason); Dick Robertson
TUXEDO JUNCTION -Glenn Miller, Erskine Hawkins and
    Harry James Orchestras (Instrumentals)
GIVE A LITTLE WHISTLE -Glenn Miller (Marion Hutton);
    Woody Herman (Vocal) and His Orchestra; Dick Jurgens
    (Eddy Howard)
I'VE GOT MY EYES ON YOU -Artie Shaw (Helen Forrest);
    Tommy Dorsey (Allan DeWitt); Bob Crosby (Marion
    Mann); Les Brown (Herb Muse)
LITTLE GIRL (From 1931) -Mitchell Ayres (Tommy Taylor)
WHAT'S THE MATTER WITH ME? -Glenn Miller (Marion
    Hutton); Benny Goodman (Helen Forrest); Dick Jurgens
    (Ronnie Kemper)
THE STARLIT HOUR -Glenn Miller (Ray Eberle); Tommy
    Dorsey (Jack Leonard); Kay Kyser (Ginny Simms); Bob
    Crosby (Vocal) and His Orchestra
WHEN YOU WISH UPON A STAR (Academy Award-
    Winner from the full-length animated Disney cartoon,
    Pinocchio) -Glenn Miller (Ray Eberle); Frances Langford;
    Sammy Kaye (Tommy Ryan); Horace Heidt (Larry Cotton)
ON THE ISLE OF MAY -Kay Kyser (Harry Babbitt, Ginny
    Simms); Dick Jurgens (Eddy Howard); Woody Herman
    (Vocal) and His Orchestra; Frances Langford
SAY SI SI -Glenn Miller (Marion Hutton); The Andrews
    Sisters

WITH THE WIND AND THE RAIN IN YOUR HAIR -Bob
    Chester (Dolores O'Neill); Kay Kyser (Ginny Simms);
    Frances Langford; Sammy Kaye (Tommy Ryan)
LONDONDERRY AIR -Glenn Miller (Instrumental)

April - June

CECELIA -Dick Jurgens (Ronnie Kemper); Bob Crosby
    (Vocal) and His Orchestra
THE WOODPECKER SONG -Glenn Miller (Marion Hutton);
    The Andrews Sisters; Gene Krupa (Irene Daye); Sammy
    Kaye (Jimmy Brown)
I CONCENTRATE ON YOU -Tommy Dorsey (Anita Boyer);
    Glen Gray (Kenny Sargent); Dick Jurgens (Eddy Howard);
    Les Brown (Shirley Howard)
THE SINGING HILLS -Bing Crosby; Horace Heidt (Larry
    Cotton)
THE SKY FELL DOWN -Tommy Dorsey (Frank Sinatra);
    Benny Goodman (Helen Forrest)
LET THERE BE LOVE -Hal Kemp (Nan Wynn); Jimmy
    Dorsey (Bob Eberly); Kay Kyser (Harry Babbitt); Sammy
    Kaye (Tommy Ryan)
HOW HIGH THE MOON -Benny Goodman (Helen Forrest);
    Harry James (Dick Haymes); Larry Clinton (Terry Allen)
THIS IS THE BEGINNING OF THE END -Tommy Dorsey
    (Frank Sinatra); Bob Crosby (Vocal) and His Orchestra
TOO ROMANTIC -Bing Crosby; Tommy Dorsey (Frank
    Sinatra)
POLKA DOTS AND MOONBEAMS -Tommy Dorsey (Frank
    Sinatra); Glenn Miller (Ray Eberle)
ONLY A ROSE (From 1926) -Jimmy Dorsey (Bob Eberly)

SAY IT -Glenn Miller (Ray Eberle); Tommy Dorsey (Frank
   Sinatra)
PLAYMATES -Kay Kyser (Sully Mason, Band Chorus); Hal
   Kemp (The Smoothies)
NO NAME JIVE (1 & 2) -Glen Gray (Instrumental)
IMAGINATION -Glenn Miller (Ray Eberle); Tommy Dorsey
   (Frank Sinatra)
THE PESSIMISTIC CHARACTER WITH THE CRAB
   APPLE FACE -Bing Crosby; Kay Kyser (Sully Mason)
RHUMBOOGIE -The Andrews Sisters; Gene Krupa (Irene
   Daye); Bob Chester (Al Stuart); Woody Herman
   (Dillagene)
SHAKE DOWN THE STARS -Glenn Miller (Ray Eberle);
   Tommy Dorsey (Frank Sinatra); Bob Crosby (Vocal) and
   His Orchestra
MAKE BELIEVE ISLAND -Mitchell Ayres (Mary Ann
   Mercer); Dick Jurgens (Harry Cool); Sammy Kaye
   (Tommy Ryan); Gene Krupa (Howard Dulany)
I CAN'T LOVE YOU ANYMORE -Benny Goodman (Helen
   Forrest); Hal Kemp (Janet Blair)
EAST OF THE SUN (AND WEST OF THE MOON)
   (From 1935) -Tommy Dorsey (Frank Sinatra)
APRIL IN PARIS (From 1932) -Artie Shaw (Instrumental)
APRIL PLAYED THE FIDDLE -Bing Crosby; Glenn Miller
   (Ray Eberle); Tommy Dorsey (Frank Sinatra)
WHERE WAS I? -Charlie Barnet (Mary Ann McCall); Jan
   Savitt (Allan DeWitt); Sammy Kaye (Clyde Burke)
FRIENDSHIP -Kay Kyser (Ginny Simms, Harry Babbitt, Jack
   Martin, Merwyn Bogue); Tommy Dorsey (The Pied
   Pipers)

GIMME A LITTLE KISS, WILL YA, HUH? (From 1926) -
Tommy Tucker (Amy Arnell)

IT'S A WONDERFUL WORLD -Jan Savitt (George
"Bon-Bon" Tunnell) Theme Song

WHERE DO I GO FROM YOU? -Hal Kemp (Bob Allen);
Woody Herman (Vocal) and His Orchestra; Orrin Tucker
(Bonnie Baker)

I HAVEN'T TIME TO BE A MILLIONAIRE -Bing Crosby;
Kay Kyser (Harry Babbitt, with Band Chorus); Dick
Jurgens (Harry Cool)

DEVIL MAY CARE -Glenn Miller (Ray Eberle); Bing
Crosby; Tommy Dorsey (Frank Sinatra); Jimmy Dorsey
(Bob Eberly)

SIERRA SUE -Glenn Miller (Ray Eberle); Bing Crosby;
Sammy Kaye (Tommy Ryan)

THE BREEZE AND I -Jimmy Dorsey (Bob Eberly)

I'M STEPPING OUT WITH A MEMORY TONIGHT -Glenn
Miller (Ray Eberle); Jimmy Dorsey (Helen O'Connell)

YOU'RE LONELY AND I'M LONELY -Tommy Dorsey
(Frank Sinatra); Charlie Barnet (Mary Ann McCall); Tony
Martin

July - September

BLUE (AND BROKEN-HEARTED) (From 1923) -Jimmy
Dorsey (Bob Eberly and Helen O'Connell); Mildred Bailey

HEAR MY SONG VIOLETTA -Glenn Miller (Ray Eberle);
Tommy Dorsey (Frank Sinatra); Jimmy Dorsey (Bob
Eberly)

PENNSYLVANIA 6-5000 -Glenn Miller (Instrumental)

I'LL NEVER SMILE AGAIN -Tommy Dorsey (Frank Sinatra
and The Pied Pipers); The Ink Spots; Glenn Miller (Ray
Eberle)

GOODBYE, LITTLE DARLIN', GOODBYE -Glenn Miller
(Ray Eberle); Gene Autry; Dick Robertson

MISTER MEADOWLARK -Bing Crosby and Johnny Mercer;
Benny Goodman (Helen Forrest); Harry James (Dick
Haymes)

I FOUND A MILLION DOLLAR BABY (From 1927) -Bing
Crosby

I'M NOBODY'S BABY (From 1921) -Judy Garland; Benny
Goodman (Helen Forrest); Tommy Dorsey (Connie
Haines); Tommy Tucker (Amy Arnell)

SIX LESSONS FROM MADAME LA ZONGA -Jimmy
Dorsey (Helen O'Connell); The King Sisters; Charlie
Barnet (Mary Ann McCall); Gene Krupa (Irene Daye)

WHEN THE SWALLOWS COME BACK TO CAPISTRANO
-The Ink Spots; Glenn Miller (Ray Eberle); Gene Krupa
(Irene Daye)

BEAT ME DADDY, EIGHT TO THE BAR -Will Bradley
(Ray McKinley); The Andrews Sisters

ALL THIS AND HEAVEN TOO -Tommy Dorsey (Frank
Sinatra); Jimmy Dorsey (Bob Eberly); Gene Krupa
(Howard Dulany)

I WANT MY MAMA -Xavier Cugat (Carmen Castillo); The
Andrews Sisters; Kay Kyser (Harry Babbitt and Jack
Martin)

WHISPERING GRASS -The Ink Spots

FOOLS RUSH IN -Glenn Miller (Ray Eberle); Tommy
Dorsey (Frank Sinatra); Harry James (Dick Haymes); Kay
Kyser (Ginny Simms)

THE ONE I LOVE BELONGS TO SOMEBODY ELSE -
    Tommy Dorsey (Frank Sinatra and The Pied Pipers)
THE NEARNESS OF YOU -Glenn Miller (Ray Eberle);
    Harry James (Dick Haymes); Kay Kyser (Harry Babbitt)
ORCHIDS FOR REMEMBRANCE -Harry James (Dick
    Haymes); Gene Krupa (Howard Dulany); Bob Chester
    (Dolores O'Neill); Eddy Howard (Vocal) and His
    Orchestra
BLUEBERRY HILL -Glenn Miller (Ray Eberle); Gene Krupa
    (Howard Dulany); Sammy Kaye (Tommy Ryan)
DO YOU EVER THINK OF ME? -Bing Crosby and The
    Merry Macs
PRACTICE MAKES PERFECT -Bob Chester (Al Stuart)
THAT'S FOR ME -Bing Crosby; Tommy Dorsey (Connie
    Haines)
MAYBE (Written in 1935) -The Ink Spots
TRADE WINDS -Bing Crosby
OUR LOVE AFFAIR -Judy Garland; Glenn Miller (Ray
    Eberle); Tommy Dorsey (Frank Sinatra); Glen Gray
    (Kenny Sargent)

October - December

ONLY FOREVER -Bing Crosby
TEMPTATION (From 1933) -Artie Shaw (Instrumental)
CALL OF THE CANYON -Glenn Miller (Ray Eberle)
I COULD MAKE YOU CARE -Tommy Dorsey (Frank
    Sinatra); The Ink Spots
A MILLION DREAMS AGO -Glenn Miller (Ray Eberle)
FALLING LEAVES -Glenn Miller (Instrumental)

WE THREE (MY ECHO, MY SHADOW AND ME) -The
Ink Spots; Tommy Dorsey (Frank Sinatra); Bob Chester
(Dolores O'Neill)

POMPTON TURNPIKE -Charlie Barnet (Instrumental)

A FERRYBOAT SERENADE -The Andrews Sisters; Kay
Kyser (Harry Babbitt, with Band Chorus); The King
Sisters

MY GREATEST MISTAKE -The Ink Spots; Harry James
(Dick Haymes)

HIT THE ROAD -The Andrews Sisters

THERE I GO -Vaughn Monroe (Vocal) and His Orchestra;
Woody Herman (Vocal) and His Orchestra; Tommy
Tucker (Amy Arnell)

THE FIVE O'CLOCK WHISTLE -Glenn Miller (Marion
Hutton)

YOU FORGOT ABOUT ME -Bob Crosby (Vocal, with The
Bob-O-Links) and His Orchestra; Gene Krupa (Howard
Dulany and Irene Daye); Artie Shaw (Anita Boyer)

SCRUB ME MAMA WITH A BOOGIE BEAT -Will Bradley
(Ray McKinley); The Andrews Sisters

CELERY STALKS AT MIDNIGHT -Will Bradley
(Instrumental)

A NIGHTINGALE SANG IN BERKELEY SQUARE -Glenn
Miller (Ray Eberle)

A HANDFUL OF STARS -Glenn Miller (Ray Eberle)

YESTERTHOUGHTS -Glenn Miller (Ray Eberle)

ALONG THE SANTA FE TRAIL -Glenn Miller (Ray
Eberle); Bing Crosby

DOWN ARGENTINA WAY -Dinah Shore; Gene Krupa
(Irene Daye); Bob Crosby (Bonnie King)

DO YOU KNOW WHY? -Glenn Miller (Ray Eberle); Tommy
    Dorsey (Frank Sinatra); Bob Crosby (Bonnie King)
ISN'T THAT JUST LIKE LOVE? -Glenn Miller (Jack
    Lathrop); Tommy Dorsey (The Pied Pipers); Gene Krupa
    (Irene Daye)
JAVA JIVE -The Ink Spots
CABIN IN THE SKY -Benny Goodman (Helen Forrest);
    Vaughn Monroe (Vocal) and His Orchestra
A STONE'S THROW FROM HEAVEN -Glenn Miller (Ray
    Eberle)
FRENESI -Artie Shaw (Instrumental)
AND SO DO I -Jimmy Dorsey (Bob Eberly); Frances
    Langford; Tommy Dorsey (Connie Haines)
I GIVE YOU MY WORD -Mitchell Ayres (Tommy Taylor);
    Jack Leonard
I'D KNOW YOU ANYWHERE -Glenn Miller (Ray Eberle);
    Bing Crosby; Gene Krupa (Irene Daye); Bob Crosby
    (Bonnie King)
BIG NOISE FROM WINNETKA -Bob Haggart (string bass)
    and Ray Beauduc (drums) from the Bob Crosby Orchestra,
    in an instrumental duet
DOWN THE ROAD A PIECE -Will Bradley Trio (Freddy
    Slack, piano; Doc Goldberg, string bass; Ray McKinley,
    drums and vocal)
REDSKIN RHUMBA -Charlie Barnet (Instrumental signature
    tune)

Of all this year's hits, the following proved most popular,
according to results of the weekly radio survey, *Your Hit
Parade*: I'LL NEVER SMILE AGAIN; THE WOODPECKER

SONG; THERE I GO; CARELESS (introduced late in 1939); WHEN YOU WISH UPON A STAR; PRACTICE MAKES PERFECT; IMAGINATION; MAYBE; ONLY FOREVER; TRADE WINDS.

Greatest longevity was probably achieved by: WHEN YOU WISH UPON A STAR; THE NEARNESS OF YOU; FOOLS RUSH IN and IMAGINATION.

Instrumental "Collector's Items

CLAP HANDS HERE COMES CHARLIE	-Charlie Barnet
TAPPIN' AT THE TAPPA	-Charlie Barnet
COMANCHE WAR DANCE	-Charlie Barnet
SOUTHLAND SHUFFLE	-Charlie Barnet
LEAPIN' AT THE LINCOLN	-Charlie Barnet
ROCKIN' IN RHYTHM	-Charlie Barnet
RING DEM BELLS	-Charlie Barnet
SOUTHERN FRIED	-Charlie Barnet
NO NAME JIVE (1& 2)	-Charlie Barnet
BLOW TOP	-Count Basie
EASY DOES IT	-Count Basie
LOUISIANA	-Count Basie
SUPER CHIEF	-Count Basie
THE WORLD IS MAD (1& 2)	-Count Basie
MOTEN SWING	-Count Basie
STAMPEDE IN G MINOR	-Count Basie
ROCKIN' THE BLUES	-Count Basie
LONESOME ROAD	-Will Bradley
EASY DOES IT	-Bob Chester

THE OCTAVE JUMP	-Bob Chester
CHESTER'S CHOICE	-Bob Chester
OFF THE RECORD	-Bob Chester
FLINGIN' A WHING DING	-Bob Chester
BUZZ, BUZZ, BUZZ	-Bob Chester
STUDY IN SURREALISM	-Larry Clinton
LIMEHOUSE BLUES	-Larry Clinton
A STUDY IN MODERNISM	-Larry Clinton
TEN MILE HOP	-Larry Clinton
MISSOURI SCRAMBLER	-Larry Clinton
CARNIVAL OF VENICE	-Larry Clinton
QUIET PLEASE	-Tommy Dorsey
SO WHAT?	-Tommy Dorsey
SWING HIGH	-Tommy Dorsey
SWANEE RIVER	-Tommy Dorsey
JACK THE BEAR	-Duke Ellington
CONGA BRAVA	-Duke Ellington
SOPHISTICATED LADY	-Duke Ellington
KO-KO	-Duke Ellington
CONCERTO FOR COOTIE	-Duke Ellington
COTTON TAIL	-Duke Ellington
NEVER NO LAMENT	-Duke Ellington
DUSK	-Duke Ellington
BOJANGLES	-Duke Ellington
BLUE GOOSE	-Duke Ellington
SEPIA PANORAMA	-Duke Ellington
IN A MELLOTONE	-Duke Ellington
WARM VALLEY	-Duke Ellington
THE FLAMING SWORD	-Duke Ellington
OPUS LOCAL 802	-Benny Goodman (Full Band)
BUSY AS A BEE	-Benny Goodman (Full Band)

BOARD MEETING	-Benny Goodman (Full Band)
ZAGGIN' WITH ZIG	-Benny Goodman (Full Band)
CRAZY RHYTHM	-Benny Goodman (Full Band)
HENDERSON STOMP	-Benny Goodman (Full Band)
BENNY RIDES AGAIN	-Benny Goodman (Full Band)
TILL TOM SPECIAL	-Benny Goodman (Sextet)
GONE WITH WHAT WIND?	-Benny Goodman (Sextet)
COCOANUT GROVE	-Benny Goodman (Sextet)
THE SHEIK	-Benny Goodman (Sextet)
I SURRENDER DEAR	-Benny Goodman (Sextet)
GRAND SLAM	-Benny Goodman (Sextet)
SIX APPEAL	-Benny Goodman (Sextet)
ROYAL GARDEN BLUES	-Benny Goodman (Sextet)
WHOLLY CATS	-Benny Goodman (Sextet)
ROCK ISLAND FLAG STOP	-Glen Gray
WHEN BUDDHA SMILES	-Glen Gray
BODY AND SOUL	-Coleman Hawkins
AFTER HOURS	-Erskine Hawkins
BLUES ON PARADE	-Woody Herman
BLUE INK	-Woody Herman
WHISTLE STOP	-Woody Herman
HERMAN AT THE SHERMAN	-Woody Herman
JUKIN'	-Woody Herman
GET YOUR BOOTS LACED PAPA	-Woody Herman
DEEP NIGHT	-Woody Herman
ST. LOUIS BLUES BOOGIE WOOGIE	-Earl Hines
HODGE PODGE	-Harry James
HEADIN' FOR HALLELUJAH	-Harry James

COME AND GET IT	-Harry James
THE SHEIK OF ARABY	-Harry James
SUPERCHIEF	-Harry James
TEMPO DE LUXE	-Harry James
EXACTLY LIKE YOU	-Harry James
MARCHETA	-Gene Krupa
BLUE RHYTHM FANTASY	-Gene Krupa
BLUES KRIEG	-Gene Krupa
WASHINGTON AND LEE SWING	-Gene Krupa
SWEET GEORGIA BROWN	-Gene Krupa
FULL DRESS HOP	-Gene Krupa
RUG CUTTER'S SWING	-Glenn Miller
BUGLE CALL RAG	-Glenn Miller
SLOW FREIGHT	-Glenn Miller
MY BLUE HEAVEN	-Glenn Miller
CHANTEZ-LES BAS	-Artie Shaw
MARINELA	-Artie Shaw
DANZA LUCUMI	-Artie Shaw
CROSS YOUR HEART	-Artie Shaw Gramercy Five
SMOKE GETS IN YOUR EYES	-Artie Shaw Gramercy Five
KEEPIN' MYSELF FOR YOU	-Artie Shaw Gramercy Five
SPECIAL DELIVERY STOMP	-Artie Shaw Gramercy Five
DOCTOR LIVINGSTONE, I PRESUME	-Artie Shaw Gramercy Five
WHEN THE QUAIL COME BACK TO SAN QUENTIN	-Artie Shaw Gramercy Five

Developments This Year in Popular Music

- The song of the year, by all accounts, was I'LL NEVER SMILE AGAIN. It was written by Ruth Lowe, pianist with Ina Ray Hutton's all-girl orchestra, in the days following the loss of her newlywed husband. It was offered to Tommy Dorsey and after some hesitation, he decided not only to record it, but to make it a production number by featuring his newly-acquired complement of singers, Frank Sinatra and the Pied Pipers. The great popularity of this recording did much to establish Frank Sinatra as a band singer and contributed greatly to the employment of vocal groups by many of the big bands. Between the Tommy Dorsey recording and the Ink Spots and Glenn Miller versions, this song was heard frequently during the summer and fall and remained on *Your Hit Parade* for sixteen weeks, seven of them in first place.

- For the reader scanning this year's list of popular songs and recording artists, it may be confusing to see some of the vocalists listed with more than one orchestra. The reason is that many changes occurred at the end of 1939 and early in 1940. For example, Jack Leonard, although he had left Tommy Dorsey, had some important holdover hits in ALL THE THINGS YOU ARE, STARLIT HOUR and INDIAN SUMMER. Allan De Witt, who replaced Leonard and was in turn replaced by Frank Sinatra, was heard on CARELESS and I'VE GOT MY EYES ON YOU. At the same time, new Dorsey recordings featuring Frank Sinatra were also appearing, so that momentarily, to the casual listener, the identity of the current Tommy Dorsey boy singer was a bit uncertain. However, by the time I'LL NEVER SMILE AGAIN hit its peak in late summer, everyone knew Tommy's rising star.

Other moves were these:

- Allan De Witt landed with Jan Savitt.
- Helen Forrest, left without work when Artie Shaw disbanded, was hired by Benny Goodman, since Benny had been unable to find a steady replacement for Martha Tilton.
- Anita Boyer, who had been with Tommy Dorsey in the latter half of 1939, caught on with Artie Shaw's new band.
- Connie Haines, like Frank Sinatra, moved from Harry James to Tommy Dorsey, early this year.
- Harry James made another remarkable find in the person of young Dick Haymes, possessor of one of the most pleasing voices of any singer ever. Dick was trying to sell some songs he had written, when Harry said, "Never mind the songs, how about singing with my band?" And so another career was begun.
- Harry Cool succeeded Eddy Howard with Dick Jurgens.
- Bonnie King replaced Marion Mann with Bob Crosby, who at this time also added a singing trio he called "The Bob-O-Links," one of whose members was Johnny Desmond, who would later become the singing star of Glenn Miller's Air Force Band.
- Janet Blair, a future movie star, succeeded Nan Wynn with Hal Kemp.

- Frank Sinatra evidently had a quality to his singing which had attracted first Harry James' attention and then that of Tommy Dorsey. Although he was already in his mid-twenties, he appeared several years younger and his voice had a youthful sound as well. Going with the Dorsey band proved a big break for him, as Tommy provided him with the kind of material which enabled Frank to establish himself as the preeminent crooner of romantic songs. His voice, while not the rich baritone-type that was most admired during this era, nevertheless had an appealing tone, which, paired with his technique of extending and "bending" notes, served to impart a plaintive sound to romantic ballads. This was what seemed to have a special effect on the teenaged girls among his fans, who flocked to his theater performances and tried to outdo each other in demonstrating how much the Sinatra voice and persona affected them.

- According to this year's polls, Glenn Miller had marched to the head of the class, while the Dorseys, Artie Shaw and Kay Kyser continued as very strong figures in the big band scheme of things. The Benny Goodman band suffered through most of the year as Benny took a great deal of time off following a serious throat infection. The Kay Kyser entourage may well have looked back years later and concluded that 1940 was possibly their best year, with the radio show at the height of its popularity and the band having turned out some twenty popular recordings. While many of these suffered from being titles also recorded by the likes of Glenn Miller and Bing Crosby, they were competitive and this was a large number of hit recordings for any unit to have to its credit in one year during the Big Band Era.

- The Ink Spots also surely looked back fondly at 1940, for it seemed that their fans barely had time to savor WHEN THE SWALLOWS COME BACK TO CAPISTRANO when along came MAYBE. Next, it was WE THREE together with JAVA JIVE. Soon after these came I'LL NEVER SMILE AGAIN, DO I WORRY? and WHISPERING GRASS. With such momentum having been created, these smooth balladeers closed out the year with a flurry of good recordings in their inimitable style, including: I COULD MAKE YOU CARE; MY GREATEST MISTAKE; RING, TELEPHONE, RING and I'D CLIMB THE HIGHEST MOUNTAIN.

The remarkable feature of the Ink Spots' recordings to this point was that nearly all of them were their exclusives (one notable exception was I'LL NEVER SMILE AGAIN) and once one of their records was played on the air, it was as if the song belonged to them. This was at a time when musicians were not usually performing their own compositions, but rather those of independent songwriters and several artists would often record the same songs. The Ink Spots' records were heard so often on radio and juke boxes this year that it not only may have been their biggest year, but it found them competing very closely in those two areas with the biggest names in music.

- After his long rest and rehabilitation in Mexico during the winter of 1939-1940, Artie Shaw returned to form a large new band which included a dozen violins. One of its first recordings was the upbeat, Latin-flavored hit, FRENESI, which was on the charts for seven months starting in July. In the fall, the band recorded Hoagy Carmichael's classic STAR DUST with an arrangement by Lennie Hayton. One postwar poll of disc jockeys rated it the best recording of the Big Band Era. Artie also created the "Gamercy Five" this year, a jazz group formed from band members for special appearances and occasional recording. He gave it a distinctive sound through the inclusion of a harpsichord. It recorded eight sides, including the memorable SUMMIT RIDGE DRIVE; SMOKE GETS IN YOUR EYES and MY BLUE HEAVEN. Two more sides were long-remembered and no doubt sold extra copies simply because of clever titles: DR. LIVINGSTONE, I PRESUME and WHEN THE QUAIL COME BACK TO SAN QUENTIN, a sly takeoff on this year's hit, WHEN THE SWALLOWS COME BACK TO CAPISTRANO.

- New bands getting started this year were those of Lionel Hampton, Eddy Howard, Vaughn Monroe and Charlie Spivak.

- Another significant move took place when former Jimmie Lunceford arranger Sy Oliver joined Tommy Dorsey.

- On a sad note, Hal Kemp, the well-liked leader of one of the era's best bands, lost his life toward the end of the year in an auto accident. Several colleagues took turns at trying to keep the band operating, but to no avail.

1 9 4 1

The Most Popular Recordings

January - March

I HEAR A RHAPSODY -Jimmy Dorsey (Bob Eberly);
  Charlie Barnet (Bob Carroll); Dinah Shore
THE LAST TIME I SAW PARIS (Academy Award-winner
  from the film, *Lady Be Good)* -Vaughn Monroe (Vocal)
  and His Orchestra; Dick Jurgens (Buddy Moreno); Kate
  Smith
THE SAME OLD STORY - Frankie Masters (Vocal) and His
  Orchestra; Eddy Duchin (Johnny Drake)
YOU WALK BY -Tommy Tucker (Amy Arnell and Don
  Brown); Blue Barron (Russ Carlyle); Eddy Duchin
  (Johnny Drake)
PERFIDIA -Glenn Miller (Dorothy Claire and The
  Modernaires); Instrumental versions by Xavier Cugat and
  Jimmy Dorsey
ANVIL CHORUS (1 & 2) -Glenn Miller (Instrumental)
SUMMIT RIDGE DRIVE -Artie Shaw Gramercy Five
  (Instrumental)
MAY I NEVER LOVE AGAIN -Bob Chester (Dolores
  O'Neill)
STAR DUST (From 1929) -Artie Shaw (Instrumental); Glenn
  Miller (Instrumental); Tommy Dorsey (Frank Sinatra and
  The Pied Pipers)

IT ALL COMES BACK TO ME NOW -Gene Krupa (Howard
Dulany); Hal Kemp (Bob Allen)

PLEASE (From 1932) -A Bing Crosby remake of a prior hit.

YOU'VE GOT ME THIS WAY -Glenn Miller (Marion
Hutton); Kay Kyser (Harry Babbitt); Tommy Dorsey (The
Pied Pipers); Jimmy Dorsey (Helen O'Connell)

THERE'LL BE SOME CHANGES MADE (From 1921) -
Repopularized by a revival of the 1939 recording by Benny
Goodman (Louise Tobin) and recordings by Gene Krupa
(Irene Daye) and Vaughn Monroe (Marilyn Duke)

YOU'RE MY THRILL (From 1933) -Charlie Barnet (Lena
Horne)

HIGH ON A WINDY HILL -Jimmy Dorsey (Bob Eberly);
Vaughn Monroe (Vocal) and His Orchestra; Gene Krupa
(Howard Dulany)

FOR YOU (From 1930) -Tommy Dorsey (Jo Stafford)

SO YOU'RE THE ONE -Vaughn Monroe (Vocal) and His
Orchestra; Hal Kemp (Janet Blair); Eddy Duchin (June
Robbins)

MY BLUE HEAVEN (From 1927) -Artie Shaw Gramercy
Five (Instrumental)

YES MY DARLING DAUGHTER -Glenn Miller (Marion
Hutton, Band Chorus); Dinah Shore; The Andrews Sisters

NEW SAN ANTONIO ROSE -Bing Crosby; Bob Wills and
His Texas Playboys

SONG OF THE VOLGA BOATMEN -Glenn Miller
(Instrumental)

BOOGIE WOOGIE BUGLE BOY -The Andrews Sisters

BEWITCHED (BOTHERED AND BEWILDERED) -Benny
Goodman (Helen Forrest); Bob Chester (Anita Bradley);
Leo Reisman (Anita Boyer)

DANCING IN THE DARK (From 1931) -Artie Shaw
  (Instrumental)
AMAPOLA (From 1924) -Jimmy Dorsey (Bob Eberly and
  Helen O'Connell); Benny Goodman (Helen Forrest)
YOU STEPPED OUT OF A DREAM -Glenn Miller (Ray
  Eberle and The Modernaires); Kay Kyser (Harry Babbitt);
  Dick Jurgens (Harry Cool)
THE WISE OLD OWL -Al Donahue (Dee Keating); Kay
  Kyser (Harry Babbitt); Teddy Powell (Ruth Gaylor)
OH! LOOK AT ME NOW -Tommy Dorsey (Frank Sinatra,
  Connie Haines and The Pied Pipers); Woody Herman
  (Vocal) and His Orchestra

April - June

DRUM BOOGIE -Gene Krupa (Irene Daye)
MUSIC MAKERS -Harry James (Instrumental)
DOLORES -Tommy Dorsey (Frank Sinatra and The Pied
  Pipers); Bing Crosby, with The Merry Macs; Harry James
  (Dick Haymes)
WALKIN' BY THE RIVER -Harry James (Dick Haymes);
  Hal Kemp (Janet Blair)
UNTIL TOMORROW -Sammy Kaye (The Kaydettes); Woody
  Herman (Vocal) and His Orchestra; Bob Chester (Bill
  Reynolds)
I'LL BE WITH YOU IN APPLE BLOSSOM TIME (From
  1920) -The Andrews Sisters
WITHOUT A SONG (From 1929) -Tommy Dorsey (Frank
  Sinatra)

WE'LL MEET AGAIN -The Ink Spots; Kay Kyser (Harry
Babbitt, Ginny Simms and Band Chorus); Guy Lombardo
(Carmen Lombardo); 1942 additions: Benny Goodman
(Peggy Lee); Woody Herman (Billie Rogers)

RACING WITH THE MOON -Vaughn Monroe (Vocal) and
His Orchestra (Theme Song)

I, YI, YI, YI, YI (I LIKE YOU VERY MUCH) -The
Andrews Sisters; Kay Kyser (Ginny Simms, Harry
Babbitt, Merwyn Bogue)

THE BAND PLAYED ON -Guy Lombardo (Kenny Gardner
and Lombardo Trio)

I UNDERSTAND -Jimmy Dorsey (Bob Eberly); The Four
King Sisters

EVERYTHING HAPPENS TO ME -Tommy Dorsey (Frank
Sinatra); Kay Kyser (Harry Babbitt); Alvino Rey (Alyce
King); Woody Herman (Vocal) & Orchestra

NUMBER TEN LULLABY LANE -Eddy Duchin (June
Robbins)

DO I WORRY? -The Ink Spots; Tommy Dorsey (Frank
Sinatra)

I COULD WRITE A BOOK -Bob Chester (Bill Darnell);
Eddy Duchin (Tony Leonard)

NIGHTY NIGHT -Alvino Rey (Yvonne King, with Band
Chorus)

IT'S ALWAYS YOU -Glenn Miller (Ray Eberle); Bing
Crosby; Tommy Dorsey (Frank Sinatra)

MARIA ELENA -Jimmy Dorsey (Bob Eberly)

LET'S GET AWAY FROM IT ALL -Tommy Dorsey (Frank
Sinatra, with Connie Haines and The Pied Pipers); Gene
Krupa (Anita O'Day)

WILL YOU STILL BE MINE? -Tommy Dorsey (Connie Haines)

INTERMEZZO (A LOVE STORY) -Freddy Martin (Clyde Rogers); Benny Goodman, Wayne King, Guy Lombardo and Charlie Spivak recorded instrumental versions.

MY SISTER AND I -Jimmy Dorsey (Bob Eberly); Bob Chester (Bill Darnell); The Four King Sisters

WHEN THE LILACS BLOOM AGAIN -Claude Thornhill (Dick Harding)

THE THINGS I LOVE -Jan Savitt (Allan DeWitt); Jimmy Dorsey (Bob Eberly)

IDA, SWEET AS APPLE CIDER (From 1903) -Glenn Miller (Tex Beneke)

G'BYE NOW -Horace Heidt (Ronnie Kemper); Vaughn Monroe (Marilyn Duke)

MY SILENT LOVE -Harry James (Dick Haymes)

BIRTH OF THE BLUES (From 1926) -Bing Crosby; Benny Goodman (Instrumental)

AURORA -The Andrews Sisters; Jimmy Dorsey (Helen O'Connell)

THE HUT SUT SONG -Freddy Martin (Eddie Stone, with Band Chorus); Horace Heidt (Donna and Her Don Juans); The Four King Sisters

FLAMINGO -Duke Ellington (Herb Jeffries)

BLESS 'EM ALL -The Four King Sisters and Barry Wood

JUST A LITTLE BIT SOUTH OF NORTH CAROLINA - Gene Krupa (Anita O'Day)

SWEETER THAN THE SWEETEST -Glenn Miller (Paula Kelly and The Modernaires)

DADDY -Sammy Kaye (The Kaye Choir)

GEORGIA ON MY MIND (From 1930) -Gene Krupa (Anita O'Day)

July - September

BLUE CHAMPAGNE -Jimmy Dorsey (Bob Eberly)

THE ANGELS CAME THRU -Glenn Miller (Ray Eberle); Charlie Spivak (Garry Stevens)

TAKE THE A TRAIN -Duke Ellington (Instrumental)

GREEN EYES -Jimmy Dorsey (Bob Eberly and Helen O'Connell)

ALL ALONE AND LONELY -Jimmy Dorsey (Bob Eberly)

BOOGLIE WOOGLIE PIGGY -Glenn Miller (Paula Kelly, Tex Beneke and The Modernaires); Les Brown (Doris Day)

UNDER BLUE CANADIAN SKIES -Glenn Miller (Ray Eberle)

YOURS (From 1931) -Jimmy Dorsey (Bob Eberly and Helen O'Connell)

LET ME OFF UPTOWN -Gene Krupa (Anita O'Day and Roy Eldridge)

BLUE SKIES (From 1927) -Tommy Dorsey (Frank Sinatra, with Band Chorus)

'TIL REVEILLE -Kay Kyser (Harry Babbitt, with Band Chorus); Bing Crosby; Freddy Martin (Clyde Rogers)

PIANO CONCERTO No. 1 IN B-FLAT MINOR (Tchaikovsky, 1875); -Freddy Martin (Instrumental)

SWINGIN' ON NOTHIN' -Tommy Dorsey (Jo Stafford and Sy Oliver)

WHY DON'T WE DO THIS MORE OFTEN -Freddy Martin
(Eddie Stone); Kay Kyser (Harry Babbitt, Ginny Simms
and Band Chorus)

DO YOU CARE? -Bing Crosby; Les Brown (Betty Bonney);
Bob Crosby (Vocal, with The Bob-O-Links) and His
Orchestra

KISS THE BOYS GOODBYE -Alvino Rey (Yvonne King);
Tommy Dorsey (Connie Haines); Bea Wain

YOU ARE MY SUNSHINE -Bing Crosby; Wayne King
(Vocal) and His Orchestra; Gene Autry

ADIOS -Glenn Miller (Instrumental)

JOLTIN' JOE DIMAGGIO -Les Brown (Betty Bonney); Bob
Chester (Himself, Betty Bradley, Bob Haymes and Band
Chorus)

EMBRACEABLE YOU (From 1929) -Jimmy Dorsey (Helen
O'Connell); Tommy Dorsey (Jo Stafford and The Pied
Pipers)

TIME WAS -Jimmy Dorsey Bob Eberly and Helen
O'Connell); Charlie Spivak (Garry Stevens); Kate Smith

IT'S SO PEACEFUL IN THE COUNTRY -Charlie Spivak
(Garry Stevens); Jan Savitt (Allan DeWitt); Bob Chester
(Betty Bradley); Mildred Bailey

JIM -Jimmy Dorsey (Bob Eberly and Helen O'Connell);
Tommy Tucker (Amy Arnell); Dinah Shore; Claude
Thornhill (Kay Doyle)

BUCKLE DOWN WINSOCKI -Benny Goodman (Tommy
Taylor, with Band Chorus)

I SEE A MILLION PEOPLE -Benny Goodman (Peggy Lee);
Jan Savitt (Allan DeWitt); Cab Calloway (Vocal) and His
Orchestra

DELILAH -Glenn Miller (Tex Beneke, Paula Kelly and The
   Modernaires)
YOU AND I -Glenn Miller (Ray Eberle); Bing Crosby; Dinah
   Shore
I DON'T WANT TO SET THE WORLD ON FIRE -The Ink
   Spots; Tommy Tucker (Amy Arnell and The Voices
   Three); Horace Heidt (Larry Cotton, with Donna and Her
   Don Juans)

October - December

I KNOW WHY -Glenn Miller (Paula Kelly and The
   Modernaires)
I GUESS I'LL HAVE TO DREAM THE REST -Glenn Miller
   (Ray Eberle and The Modernaires); Tommy Dorsey (Frank
   Sinatra and The Pied Pipers)
THIS TIME THE DREAM'S ON ME -Glenn Miller (Ray
   Eberle); Gene Krupa (Johnny Desmond); Woody Herman
   (Vocal) and His Orchestra)
TRUMPET RHAPSODY -Harry James (Instrumental)
SOMEONE'S ROCKING MY DREAMBOAT -The Ink Spots
YES, INDEED -Tommy Dorsey (Jo Stafford and Sy Oliver);
   Bing Crosby and Connie Boswell); Harry James (Dick
   Haymes, with Band Chorus)
I GOT IT BAD AND THAT AIN'T GOOD -Duke Ellington
   (Ivie Anderson); Benny Goodman (Peggy Lee); Jimmy
   Dorsey (Helen O'Connell); Dinah Shore

TONIGHT WE LOVE (Based on Tchaikovsky's Piano
    Concerto No. 1 in B-Flat Minor) -Freddy Martin (Clyde
    Rogers).   The instrumental version was far and away
    Freddy Martin's most popular recording. This vocal
    version served to further identify the melody with his
    band, to the extent that he made it his theme song.
DON'T TAKE YOUR LOVE FROM ME -Artie Shaw (Lena
    Horne); Alvino Rey (Yvonne King); Mildred Bailey
VIOLETS FOR YOUR FURS -Tommy Dorsey (Frank
    Sinatra)
SHEPHERD SERENADE -Bing Crosby; Horace Heidt
    (Larry Cotton, Gordon MacRae, Fred Lowery)
IT HAPPENED IN SUN VALLEY -Glenn Miller (Ray
    Eberle, Paula Kelly, Tex Beneke, The Modernaires and
    Band Chorus)
YOU MADE ME LOVE YOU (From 1913) -Harry James
    (Instrumental)
JEALOUS -Alvino Rey (Yvonne King, with Band Chorus)
LET'S DO IT (From 1928) -Benny Goodman (Peggy Lee)
CHATTANOOGA CHOO CHOO -Glenn Miller (Tex
    Beneke, Paula Kelly and The Modernaires)
PAPA NICCOLINI -Glenn Miller (Ray Eberle, Tex Beneke
    and The Modernaires)
YOU'VE CHANGED -Harry James (Dick Haymes)
THIS LOVE OF MINE -Tommy Dorsey (Frank Sinatra)
ELMER'S TUNE -Glenn Miller (Ray Eberle and The
    Modernaires)
I'M THRILLED -Glenn Miller (Ray Eberle); Claude
    Thornhill (Dick Harding)

A SINNER KISSED AN ANGEL -Harry James (Dick
   Haymes); Vaughn Monroe (vocal) and His Orchestra;
   Tommy Dorsey (Frank Sinatra)
DREAMSVILLE OHIO -Glenn Miller (Ray Eberle, with The
   Modernaires); Charlie Spivak (June Hutton)
HE'S 1-A IN THE ARMY AND HE'S A-1IN MY HEART -
   Harry James (Helen Forrest); Les Brown (Betty Bradley)
ORANGE BLOSSOM LANE -Glenn Miller (Ray Eberle);
   Claude Thornhill (Dick Harding)
YOU DON'T KNOW WHAT LOVE IS -Harry James (Dick
   Haymes); Benny Goodman (Art Lund); Jan Savitt (George
   "Bon-Bon" Tunnell)
THE BELLS OF SAN RAQUEL -Claude Thornhill (Dick
   Harding); Dick Jurgens (Harry Cool)

Of this year's large number of hit songs, the following
achieved the greatest popularity, according to results of the
weekly radio survey, *Your Hit Parade* : I HEAR A RHAP-
SODY; AMAPOLA; YOU AND I; DADDY; MARIA
ELENA; FRENESI; I DON'T WANT TO SET THE WORLD
ON FIRE; TONIGHT WE LOVE; INTERMEZZO; YOURS
and THE HUT SUT SONG.

Be that as it may, from May to July, one could not listen to
a disc jockey or pass a juke box without hearing either Jimmy
Dorsey's GREEN EYES or the Andrews Sisters' IN APPLE
BLOSSOM TIME. The records of *Billboard 's* charts bear
this out, showing 24 weeks for GREEN EYES and 17 weeks
for IN APPLE BLOSSOM TIME during this period. While
Your Hit Parade, usually reliable for determining what was
really popular, played GREEN EYES for 13 weeks, it failed to

recognize the popularity of IN APPLE BLOSSOM TIME in any of its broadcasts this year!

The longest-lasting popularity of any of this year's new songs was probably obtained by: THE LAST TIME I SAW PARIS and BEWITCHED (BOTHERED AND BEWIL-DERED). BLUE SKIES and EMBRACEABLE YOU, already standards when repopularized this year, continued as such for many more years.

Instrumental "Collector's Items"

BLUE JUICE	-Charlie Barnet
CHARLESTON ALLEY	-Charlie Barnet
LITTLE JOHN ORDINARY	-Charlie Barnet
MERRY-GO-ROUND	-Charlie Barnet
BIRMINGHAM BREAKDOWN	-Charlie Barnet
LITTLE DIP	-Charlie Barnet
PONCE DE LEON	-Charlie Barnet
SPANISH KICK	-Charlie Barnet
MURDER AT PEYTON HALL	-Charlie Barnet
MACUMBA	-Charlie Barnet
IT'S SQUARE BUT IT ROCKS	-Count Basie
WIGGLE WOOGIE	-Count Basie
BEAU BRUMMEL	-Count Basie
JUMP THE BLUES AWAY	-Count Basie
DEEP IN THE BLUES	-Count Basie
THE JITTERS	-Count Basie
FEEDIN' THE BEAN	-Count Basie
GOIN' TO CHICAGO BLUES	-Count Basie

TUNE TOWN SHUFFLE	-Count Basie
BASIE BOOGIE	-Count Basie
FIESTA IN BLUE	-Count Basie
DOWN FOR DOUBLE	-Count Basie
COMING OUT PARTY	-Count Basie
BIZET HAS HIS DAY	-Les Brown
MEXICAN HAT DANCE	-Les Brown
MARCHE SLAV (Tchaikovsky)	-Les Brown
JAZZ ME BLUES	-Larry Clinton
BACH TO BOOGIE	-Larry Clinton
DEEP RIVER	-Tommy Dorsey
SWING LOW SWEET CHARIOT	-Tommy Dorsey
SERENADE TO THE SPOT	-Tommy Dorsey
LOOSE LID SPECIAL	-Tommy Dorsey
BACK STAGE AT THE BALLET	-Tommy Dorsey
HALLELUJAH	-Tommy Dorsey
ON THE ALAMO	-Tommy Dorsey
JUMPIN' PUNKINS	-Duke Ellington
JOHN HARDY	-Duke Ellington
BLUE SERGE	-Duke Ellington
AFTER ALL	-Duke Ellington
BAKIFF	-Duke Ellington
ARE YOU STICKING?	-Duke Ellington
THE GIDDYBUG GALLOP	-Duke Ellington
MOON OVER CUBA	-Duke Ellington
FIVE O'CLOCK DRAG	-Duke Ellington
CHELSEA BRIDGE	-Duke Ellington
RAINCHECK	-Duke Ellington
MOONLIGHT ON THE GANGES	-Benny Goodman
TIME ON MY HANDS	-Benny Goodman
SCARECROW	-Benny Goodman

SOLO FLIGHT	-Benny Goodman
FIESTA IN BLUE	-Benny Goodman
CHERRY	-Benny Goodman
AIR MAIL SPECIAL	-Benny Goodman
LA ROSITA	-Benny Goodman
THE COUNT	-Benny Goodman
THE EARL	-Benny Goodman
POUND RIDGE	-Benny Goodman
CLARINET A LA KING	-Benny Goodman
I CAN'T GIVE YOU ANYTHING BUT LOVE	-Benny Goodman (Sextet)
ON THE ALAMO	-Benny Goodman (Sextet)
A SMO-O-O-OTH ONE	-Benny Goodman (Sextet)
IF I HAD YOU	-Benny Goodman (Sextet)
LIMEHOUSE BLUES	-Benny Goodman (Sextet)
I FOUND A NEW BABY	-Benny Goodman (Sextet)
SWING TONIC	-Glen Gray
THE GOLDEN WEDDING	-Woody Herman
FUR TRAPPERS' BALL	-Woody Herman
LAZY RHAPSODY	-Woody Herman
NIGHT WATCHMAN	-Woody Herman
BISHOP'S BLUES	-Woody Herman
WOODSHEDDIN' WITH WOODY	-Woody Herman
THREE WAYS TO SMOKE A PIPE	-Woody Herman
TEN DAY FURLOUGH	-Woody Herman
HOT CHESTNUTS	-Woody Herman
LAS CHIAPANECAS	-Woody Herman
SOUTH	-The Woodchoppers
FAN IT	-The Woodchoppers

THE EARL	-Earl "Fatha" Hines
SWINGIN' ON C	-Earl "Fatha" Hines
LA PALOMA	-Harry James
A LITTLE BIT OF HEAVEN	-Harry James
ANSWER MAN	-Harry James
ELI-ELI	-Harry James
LAMENT TO LOVE	-Harry James
LOST IN LOVE	-Harry James
NOTHIN'	-Harry James
MISIRLOU	-Harry James
NOBODY KNOWS THE TROUBLE I'VE SEEN	-Harry James
FLATBUSH FLANAGAN	-Harry James
FLIGHT OF THE BUMBLE BEE	-Harry James
CARNIVAL OF VENICE	-Harry James
DUKE'S MIXTURE	-Harry James
JEFFRIES' BLUES	-Harry James
SHARP AS A TACK	-Harry James
JUGHEAD	-Harry James
DODGERS' FAN DANCE	-Harry James
MY MELANCHOLY BABY	-Harry James
RECORD SESSION	-Harry James
AFTER YOU'VE GONE	-Gene Krupa
KICK IT	-Gene Krupa
TUNIN' UP	-Gene Krupa
BALL OF FIRE	-Gene Krupa
SIREN SERENADE	-Gene Krupa
BATTLE AXE	-Jimmie Lunceford
CHOCOLATE	-Jimmie Lunceford
HI SPOOK	-Jimmie Lunceford
YARD DOG MAZURKA	-Jimmie Lunceford

GONE	-Jimmie Lunceford
IMPROMPTU	-Jimmie Lunceford
BOULDER BUFF	-Glenn Miller
SUN VALLEY JUMP	-Glenn Miller
LONG TALL MAMA	-Glenn Miller
I DREAMT I DWELT IN HARLEM	-Glenn Miller
GREEN GOON JIVE	-Jan Savitt
MEADOWBROOK SHUFFLE	-Jan Savitt
SUGARFOOT STRUT	-Jan Savitt
BLUES (1&2)	-Artie Shaw
PRELUDE IN C MAJOR	-Artie Shaw
PYRAMID	-Artie Shaw
WHAT IS THERE TO SAY?	-Artie Shaw
CONCERTO FOR CLARINET	-Artie Shaw
I COVER THE WATERFRONT	-Artie Shaw
MOON GLOW	-Artie Shaw
IF I HAD YOU	-Artie Shaw
GEORGIA ON MY MIND	-Artie Shaw
WHY SHOULDN'T I?	-Artie Shaw
IT HAD TO BE YOU	-Artie Shaw
CONFESSIN'	-Artie Shaw
NOCTURNE	-Artie Shaw
BEYOND THE BLUE HORIZON	-Artie Shaw
ST. JAMES INFIRMARY (1&2)	-Artie Shaw

Developments This Year in Popular Music

This was the last of the pre-war Big Band Years. It was a bountiful year in general and for a few of the bands in particular. Through this seventh consecutive year of big band growth, their future had appeared limitless. Then came December 7th, the day that President Roosevelt said would "live in infamy," to markedly alter that future.

However, it is again pertinent to review how the leading bands were faring as the year drew to a close. First, it was obvious that the Glenn Miller juggernaut was now in high gear, as that band was fast becoming the country's consensus favorite. *Metronome* discontinued its polls after 1940. At that time, its readers had voted Miller second in both sweet and swing categories. Both in 1940 and 1941, the *Downbeat* poll listed Miller first among sweet bands and fourth in the swing group. For *Downbeat's* readers, Benny Goodman, Duke Ellington and Woody Herman were the leaders in swing in 1940, while Goodman, Tommy Dorsey and Ellington led in 1941.

Polls aside, the Glenn Miller band was greatly in demand and was breaking attendance records everywhere. Its numerous recordings were being snapped up by ardent fans, converted into instant hits by disc jockeys and taking up most of the space in juke boxes. Millions tuned in each night to its "prime time" Chesterfield broadcasts.

In January, 1941, The Modernaires, a talented and experienced male vocal quartet, joined the band. They had sung with Fred Waring, Charlie Barnet and Paul Whiteman. The previous October, by special request from New York's leading disc jickey, Martin Block, they had re-recorded with the Miller band Block's theme song, MAKE BELIEVE BALLROOM, which they had done a few years earlier with Charlie Barnet.

This contact with the group evidently gave Miller the idea to employ the Modernaires, giving the band an added dimension with regard to its vocal presentations. Glenn was proving himself to be, like his colleague Tommy Dorsey, an astute businessman, as well as an outstanding musician, judge of talent, organizer, leader and expert on the public's musical tastes.

In March, the Miller band began two months of work on its first movie, *Sun Valley Serenade* , which, unlike most films in which orchestras appeared, made the band prominent in the story. It featured ice skating star Sonja Henie and popular screen figures John Payne and Lynn Bari, these two playing the parts of band vocalists. With the advantage of a beautiful ski resort as a setting and just enough skating and skiing sequences interwoven with music from the country's current favorite dance band, the film's success was predictable and another with the band was planned for the following year (*Orchestra Wives*). These movies both did well at the boxofice and each in turn gave the band another boost in popularity.

But, although it had become a dominant force among the big bands, the Miller group by no means had the field to itself. The polls, as mentioned, also had the names of Tommy Dorsey, Goodman, Ellington, Kyser and Herman near the top in popularity. Another band enjoying perhaps its greatest year in 1941, was that of Jimmy Dorsey, thanks to an incredibly long series of first-rate recordings by singers Bob Eberly and Helen O'Connell, separately and together. The list is impressive enough to be recalled here.

Popular recordings of 1941 by Jimmy Dorsey, featuring singers Bob Eberly and Helen O'Connell:

I HEAR A RHAPSODY (Bob Eberly)
I UNDERSTAND (Bob Eberly)
HIGH ON A WINDY HILL (Bob Eberly)
AMAPOLA (Bob Eberly and Helen O'Connell)
YOURS (Bob Eberly and Helen O'Connell)
THE THINGS I LOVE (Bob Eberly)
MY SISTER AND I (Bob Eberly)
MARIA ELENA (Bob Eberly - a million-seller)
GREEN EYES (Bob Eberly and Helen O'Connell - a
    million-seller)
BLUE CHAMPAGNE (Bob Eberly)
AURORA (Helen O'Connell)
ALL ALONE AND LONELY (Bob Eberly)
TIME WAS (Bob Eberly and Helen O'Connell)
EMBRACEABLE YOU (Helen O'Connell)
JIM (Bob Eberly and Helen O'Connell)
THIS IS NO LAUGHING MATTER (Bob Eberly)
THE WHITE CLIFFS OF DOVER (Bob Eberly)
I GOT IT BAD AND THAT AIN'T GOOD (Helen
    O'Connell)
I SAID NO (Bob Eberly and Helen O'Connell)
I REMEMBER YOU (Bob Eberly)
NOT MINE (Bob Eberly and Helen O'Connell)
ARTHUR MURRAY TAUGHT ME DANCING IN A
    HURRY (Helen O'Connell)
TANGERINE (Bob Eberly and Helen O'Connell)

Admittedly, Bob and Helen were provided with an unusual number of good songs in 1941, or at least, songs with potential. But with inspired arrangements on some by Tutti Camaratta and their exceptional abilities, they were able to do the best that could be done with their material. The result was that if any discerning fan of popular music was later asked what was most memorable, what it was that most distinguished 1941from the other years, he or she would probably have cited the large number of popular hits by Bob Eberly and Helen O'Connell, with Jimmy Dorsey's orchestra.

Like 1939, this was an exceptionally prolific year, when new hit records crowded each other off the charts each week, from January to December. Quality-wise, those of 1939 generally had the edge. The difference was that in 1939 the many excellent songs consisted, for the most part, of straightforward, well-structured romantic poetry, superimposed on some of the loveliest compositions of the entire era. Some of 1939's adaptations in particular were quite beautiful, such as THE LAMP IS LOW; MOON LOVE; MY PRAYER and OUR LOVE. On the other hand, a great many of the hits of 1941 seemed to be divided between songs with a more simplistic Latin, or exotic flavor (AMAPOLA, AURORA, DOLORES, MARIA ELENA, GREEN EYES, FLAMINGO) and novelty numbers (DADDY, THE HUT SUT SONG, CHAT-TANOOGA CHOO CHOO, ELMER'S TUNE). Nevertheless, it was a musically diverse and entertaining year and one more example of how each year acquired its own distinct musical personality.

- With FLAMINGO, I GOT IT BAD AND THAT AIN'T

GOOD and TAKE THE "A" TRAIN enjoying great popularity, Duke Ellington and his fine vocalists, Herb Jeffries and Ivie Anderson, entered a long overdue period of wider appreciation of their respective talents.

- In August, Helen Forrest left Benny Goodman to join Harry James, for what would prove to be a winning combination, resulting in some of the most memorable hits of the war years. Helen and the Harry James band would benefit a few months later from the great success of Harry's "hunch" recording of YOU MADE ME LOVE YOU as an instrumental. It was a prime example of the way that a good recording, with the help of disc jockeys, could focus attention on a band and greatly improve its fortunes. In this instance, unexpected crowds lined up early in the morning around the Paramount Theater for the first appearance in New York of Harry James following two weeks' steady playing of YOU MADE ME LOVE YOU by disc jockey Martin Block, on his *Make Believe Ballroom* show. At that point the James band was poised to take full advantage of the series of good ballads by Helen Forrest and equally good instrumentals which would propel it into the position of leading band in the country before the end of 1942.

- In Chicago, Benny discovered a replacement for Helen Forrest in young Peggy Lee, just getting started on a long, fruitful career of her own.

After an altogether too-brief stay among the leading big bands, during which time his contributions were considerable, Larry Clinton disbanded late this year to enter military service, where he became an Army Air Corps pilot-instructor.

   - Making their debuts this year were the bands of Stan Kenton, Hal McIntyre and Freddy Slack. Kenton scored a great initial impact during a summer-long engagement at the Balboa (California) Ballroom, following which he was able to set an attendance record at the new Hollywood Palladium.

1 9 4 2

The Most Popular Recordings

January - March

BLUES IN THE NIGHT -Woody Herman (Vocal) and His
  Orchestra; Dinah Shore; Jimmie Lunceford (Willie
  Smith); Harry James (Instrumental); Artie Shaw (Hot Lips
  Page); Benny Goodman (Peggy Lee); Bing Crosby;
  Tommy Dorsey (Jo Stafford)

AUTUMN NOCTURNE -Harry James, Charlie Spivak and
  Claude Thornhill (Instrumentals)

ROSE O'DAY -Kate Smith; The Four King Sisters; Freddy
  Martin (Eddie Stone and Band Chorus); Woody Herman
  (Vocal with Carolyn Grey) and His Orchestra

WINTER WEATHER -Benny Goodman (Peggy Lee and Art
  Lund); Bob Chester (Betty Bradley); Tommy Dorsey (The
  Pied Pipers)

ANNIVERSARY WALTZ -Bing Crosby; Freddy Martin
  (Clyde Rogers and The Martin Men)

A STRING OF PEARLS -Glenn Miller (Instrumental)

'TIS AUTUMN -Woody Herman (Vocal, with Carolyn Grey,
  Chorus) and His Orchestra; Les Brown (Ralph Young);
  Freddy Martin (Clyde Rogers); Alvino Rey (The Four
  King Sisters); Jan Savitt (Allan DeWitt)

EV'RYTHING I LOVE -Glenn Miller (Ray Eberle and
  Choir); Jimmy Dorsey (Bob Eberly); Benny Goodman
  (Peggy Lee)

HOW ABOUT YOU? -Tommy Dorsey (Frank Sinatra)

I SAID NO -Alvino Rey (Yvonne King); Jimmy Dorsey
(Helen O'Connell and Bob Eberly); Claude Thornhill
(Lillian Lane)

THE SHRINE OF ST. CECILIA -Vaughn Monroe (Vocal)
and His Orchestra The Andrews Sisters; Sammy Kaye
(Allan Foster)

I'M GLAD THERE IS YOU -Jimmy Dorsey (Bob Eberly);
Alvino Rey (Alyce King)

THIS IS NO LAUGHING MATTER -Glenn Miller (Ray
Eberle); Jimmy Dorsey (Bob Eberly); Charlie Spivak
(Garry Stevens)

HUMPTY DUMPTY HEART -Glenn Miller (Ray Eberle);
Bing Crosby

MOONLIGHT COCKTAIL -Glenn Miller (Ray Eberle and
The Modernaires)

DEEP IN THE HEART OF TEXAS -Horace Heidt (Band
Chorus); Alvino Rey (Skeets Herfurt, Bill Schallen); Bing
Crosby, accompanied by Woody Herman's Woodchoppers

REMEMBER PEARL HARBOR -Sammy Kaye (The Glee
Club); Charlie Spivak (Garry Stevens and The Stardusters)

THE DEVIL SAT DOWN AND CRIED -Harry James
(Harry James, Dick Haymes and Helen Forrest)

THE WHITE CLIFFS OF DOVER -Glenn Miller (Ray
Eberle); Jimmy Dorsey (Bob Eberly); Kay Kyser (Harry
Babbitt, with Band Chorus)

GRIEG PIANO CONCERTO -Freddy Martin and Claude
Thornhill (Instrumentals)

I DON'T WANT TO WALK WITHOUT YOU -Harry James
(Helen Forrest)

DAY DREAMING -Glenn Miller (Ray Eberle and The
    Modernaires)
DEAR MOM -Glenn Miller (Ray Eberle and The
    Modernaires)
A ZOOT SUIT -Kay Kyser (Sully Mason, Trudy Erwin, Jack
    Martin and Max Williams); Benny Goodman (Art Lund);
    Bob Crosby (Nappy Lamare)
MISS YOU -Freddy Martin (Clyde Rogers); Bing Crosby;
    Dinah Shore; Eddy Howard (Vocal) and His Orchestra;
    Sammy Kaye (Allan Foster)
WHEN JOHNNY COMES MARCHING HOME -Glenn
    Miller (Tex Beneke, Marion Hutton and The Modernaires)
SOMEBODY ELSE IS TAKING MY PLACE (From 1937) -
    Benny Goodman (Peggy Lee); Russ Morgan (The
    Morganaires)
SNOOTIE LITTLE CUTIE -Tommy Dorsey (Frank Sinatra,
    Connie Haines and The Pied Pipers)
I'LL REMEMBER APRIL -Charlie Spivak (Garry Stevens);
    Charlie Barnet (Bob Carroll); Woody Herman (Vocal) and
    His Orchestra
ARTHUR MURRAY TAUGHT ME DANCING IN A
    HURRY -Jimmy Dorsey (Helen O'Connell); The Four
    King Sisters; Charlie Spivak (June Hutton)
WHAT IS THIS THING CALLED LOVE? (From 1930) -
    Tommy Dorsey (Connie Haines)
TANGERINE -Jimmy Dorsey (Bob Eberly and Helen
    O'Connell); Vaughn Monroe (Vocal) and His Orchestra
BY THE LIGHT OF THE SILV'RY MOON (From 1909) -
    Ray Noble (Snooky Lanson)

April - June

EASTER PARADE (From 1933) -Harry James (Instrumental)
I REMEMBER YOU -Jimmy Dorsey (Bob Eberly); Harry
    James (Helen Forrest); Charlie Spivak (Garry Stevens,
    June Hutton and The Stardusters); Freddy Martin (Clyde
    Rogers)
NIGHT AND DAY (From 1932) -Frank Sinatra
SHE'LL ALWAYS REMEMBER -Glenn Miller (Ray Eberle
    and The Modernaires); Woody Herman (Carolyn Grey);
    Dinah Shore; Claude Thornhill (Dick Harding)
ALWAYS IN MY HEART -Jimmy Dorsey (Bob Eberly);
    Glenn Miller (Ray Eberle)
THE LAMPLIGHTER'S SERENADE -Glenn Miller (Ray
    Eberle and The Modernaires); Bing Crosby; Woody
    Herman (Vocal) and His Orchestra
WHEN THE ROSES BLOOM AGAIN -Glenn Miller (Ray
    Eberle); Jimmy Dorsey (Bob Eberly); Kay Kyser (Harry
    Babbitt); Benny Goodman (Art Lund); Hal McIntyre (Carl
    Denny)
NOT MINE -Jimmy Dorsey (Bob Eberly and Helen
    O'Connell); Benny Goodman (Peggy Lee); Artie Shaw
    (Georgia Gibbs); Dinah Shore
THE STORY OF A STARRY NIGHT - Glenn Miller (Ray
    Eberle); Charlie Spivak (Garry Stevens, June Hutton and
    The Stardusters)
TRUMPET BLUES -Harry James (Instrumental)
WHEN YOU'RE A LONG, LONG WAY FROM HOME -
    Harry James (Jimmy Saunders); Russ Morgan (Vocal) and
    His Orchestra

SKYLARK -Bing Crosby; Glenn Miller (Ray Eberle); Harry
    James (Helen Forrest); Gene Krupa (Anita O'Day)
JERSEY BOUNCE -Benny Goodman (Instrumental)
DON'T SIT UNDER THE APPLE TREE -Glenn Miller
    (Marion Hutton, Tex Beneke and The Modernaires); The
    Andrews Sisters
JOHNNY DOUGHBOY FOUND A ROSE IN IRELAND -
    Kay Kyser (The Glee Club); Freddy Martin (Clyde
    Rogers); Sammy Kaye (Tommy Ryan)
ONE DOZEN ROSES -Dinah Shore; Harry James (Jimmy
    Saunders); Dick Jurgens (Buddy Moreno); Glen Gray (Pee
    Wee Hunt)
SLEEPY LAGOON   (From 1930) -Harry James
    (Instrumental)
ALL I NEED IS YOU -Benny Goodman (Peggy Lee); Dinah
    Shore; Claude Thornhill (Dick Harding)
JUST PLAIN LONESOME -Kay Kyser (Harry Babbitt); Bing
    Crosby; Freddy Martin (Stuart Wade); Woody Herman
    (Vocal) and His Orchestra)
WONDER WHEN MY BABY'S COMING HOME Jimmy
    Dorsey (Helen O'Connell); Sammy Kaye (Nancy Norman)
WHO WOULDN'T LOVE YOU? -Kay Kyser (Harry Babbitt
    and Trudy Erwin)
THREE LITTLE SISTERS -The Andrews Sisters; Vaughn
    Monroe (The Four V's); Dinah Shore
LAST CALL FOR LOVE -Tommy Dorsey (Frank Sinatra and
    The Pied Pipers)
HAWAIIAN WAR CHANT (From 1938, re-recorded) -
    Tommy Dorsey (Instrumental)
IDAHO -Benny Goodman (Dick Haymes); Alvino Rey
    (Yvonne King and Chorus)

AMEN -Woody Herman (Vocal) and His Orchestra

IF YOU ARE BUT A DREAM -Jimmy Dorsey (Bob Eberly)

THIS IS WORTH FIGHTING FOR -Vaughn Monroe (Vocal)
    and His Orchestra

I CAN'T GIVE YOU ANYTHING BUT LOVE (From 1928)
    -Tommy Dorsey (Jo Stafford)

THE NIGHT WE CALLED IT A DAY -Tommy Dorsey (Jo
    Stafford)

July - September

SWEET ELOISE -Glenn Miller (Ray Eberle and The
    Modernaires)

JINGLE, JANGLE, JINGLE -Kay Kyser (Harry Babbitt, Julie
    Conway and Band Chorus)

MAD ABOUT HIM, SAD WITHOUT HIM, HOW CAN I
    BE GLAD WITHOUT HIM BLUES -Dinah Shore

AMERICAN PATROL (From 1885) -Glenn Miller
    (Instrumental)

STRICTLY INSTRUMENTAL -Harry James (Instrumental)

YOU WERE NEVER LOVELIER -Woody Herman (Vocal)
    and His Orchestra; Vaughn Monroe (Marilyn Duke)

HE WEARS A PAIR OF SILVER WINGS -Alvino Rey
    (Alyce King); Kay Kyser (Harry Babbitt); Dinah Shore

THAT SOLDIER OF MINE -Harry James (Helen Forrest)

JUST AS THOUGH YOU WERE HERE -Tommy Dorsey
    (Frank Sinatra and The Pied Pipers) ; The Ink Spots

STREET OF DREAMS -Tommy Dorsey (Frank Sinatra and
    The Pied Pipers); The Ink Spots

FOR ME AND MY GAL (From 1917) -Judy Garland and
    Gene Kelly

PENNSYLVANIA POLKA -The Andrews Sisters
BUT NOT FOR ME -Harry James (Helen Forrest)
I LEFT MY HEART AT THE STAGEDOOR CANTEEN -
    Sammy Kaye (Don Cornell); Charlie Spivak (Garry
    Stevens); Russ Morgan (Vocal) and His Orchestra
IT MUST BE JELLY ('CAUSE JAM DON'T SHAKE LIKE
    THAT) -Glenn Miller (The Modernaires)
TAKE ME -Tommy Dorsey (Frank Sinatra); Jimmy Dorsey
    (Helen O'Connell); Benny Goodman (Dick Haymes)
MY DEVOTION -Jimmy Dorsey (Bob Eberly); Vaughn
    Monroe (Vocal) and His Orchestra; Charlie Spivak (Garry
    Stevens); The Four King Sisters
BE CAREFUL IT'S MY HEART -Bing Crosby; Tommy
    Dorsey (Frank Sinatra); Dinah Shore; Claude Thornhill
    (Lillian Lane)
I'M OLD FASHIONED -Alvino Rey (Alyce King); Glenn
    Miller (Skip Nelson); Glen Gray (Kenny Sargent)
MASSACHUSETTS -Gene Krupa (Anita O'Day)
"MURDER" HE SAYS -Gene Krupa (Anita O'Day); Jimmy
    Dorsey (Helen O'Connell); Dinah Shore
AT LAST -Glenn Miller (Ray Eberle); Charlie Spivak (Garry
    Stevens and The Stardusters)
I CRIED FOR YOU -Harry James (Helen Forrest)
(I'VE GOT A GAL IN) KALAMAZOO -Glenn Miller (Tex
    Beneke and The Modernaires)
DEARLY BELOVED -Glenn Miller (Skip Nelson, with Band
    Chorus); Alvino Rey (Bill Schallen); Glen Gray (Kenny
    Sargent and The Le Brun Sisters); Dinah Shore
VELVET MOON -Harry James (Instrumental)
DER FUEHRER'S FACE -Spike Jones and His "City
    Slickers" (Carl Grayson and Willie Spicer)

YESTERDAY'S GARDENIAS -Glenn Miller (Ray Eberle and
 The Modernaires); Charlie Spivak (Garry Stevens); Bob
 Chester (Gene Howard); Glen Gray (Kenny Sargent and
 The Le Brun Sisters)
SERENADE IN BLUE -Glenn Miller (Ray Eberle and The
 Modernaires)

October - December

MANHATTAN SERENADE (From 1928) -Harry James
 (Helen Forrest); Jimmy Dorsey (Bob Eberly); Tommy
 Dorsey (Jo Stafford)
STRIP POLKA -Kay Kyser (Jack Martin); Johnny Mercer;
 Alvino Rey (The Four King Sisters and Chorus); The
 Andrews Sisters
WHY DON'T YOU DO RIGHT? -Benny Goodman (Peggy
 Lee)
AT THE CROSSROADS -Jimmy Dorsey (Bob Eberly);
 Vaughn Monroe (Vocal) and His Orchestra
YOU CAN DEPEND ON ME (From 1932) -Tommy Dorsey
 (Jo Stafford)
THERE WILL NEVER BE ANOTHER YOU -Gordon
 Jenkins (Bob Carroll); Woody Herman (Vocal) and His
 Orchestra; Sammy Kaye (Nancy Norman)
WHEN THE LIGHTS GO ON AGAIN (ALL OVER THE
 WORLD) -Vaughn Monroe (Vocal) and His Orchestra
EVERY NIGHT ABOUT THIS TIME -Jimmy Dorsey (Bob
 Eberly); The Ink Spots
PRAISE THE LORD AND PASS THE AMMUNITION -Kay
 Kyser (Band Chorus)

THE SONG IS YOU (From 1932) -Tommy Dorsey (Frank
   Sinatra)
HE'S MY GUY -Harry James (Helen Forrest); Dinah Shore
CHERRY -Harry James (Instrumental)
WHITE CHRISTMAS (Academy Award-winner, from the
   film, *Holiday Inn*) -Bing Crosby
HAPPY HOLIDAY -Bing Crosby
THERE ARE SUCH THINGS -Tommy Dorsey (Frank Sinatra
   and The Pied Pipers)
(AS LONG AS YOU'RE NOT IN LOVE WITH
   SOMEBODY ELSE) WHY DON'T YOU FALL IN
   LOVE WITH ME? -Dinah Shore; Dick Jurgens (Harry
   Cool); Hal McIntyre (Jerry Stuart)
DAYBREAK -Tommy Dorsey (Frank Sinatra); also: Tommy
   Dorsey (Dick Haymes); Jimmy Dorsey (Bob Eberly);
   Harry James (Johnny McAfee)
I CAME HERE TO TALK FOR JOE -Kay Kyser (Harry
   Babbitt); Sammy Kaye (Don Cornell); Glen Gray (Kenny
   Sargent and The Le Brun Sisters)
MISTER FIVE BY FIVE -Freddy Slack (Ella Mae Morse);
   Harry James (Helen Forrest); The Andrews Sisters
JUKE BOX SATURDAY NIGHT -Glenn Miller (Marion
   Hutton, Tex Beneke and The Modernaires)
I HAD THE CRAZIEST DREAM -Harry James (Helen
   Forrest)
MOONLIGHT BECOMES YOU -Bing Crosby; Harry James
   (Johnny McAfee); Glenn Miller (Skip Nelson and The
   Modernaires)

Of this year's favorite songs, the following achieved the greatest popularity, according to results of the weekly radio survey, *Your Hit Parade:* THE WHITE CLIFFS OF DOVER; JINGLE JANGLE JINGLE; SLEEPY LAGOON; MY DEVOTION; HE WEARS A PAIR OF SILVER WINGS; DEEP IN THE HEART OF TEXAS; DON'T SIT UNDER THE APPLE TREE; ELMER'S TUNE; SOMEBODY ELSE IS TAKING MY PLACE and ONE DOZEN ROSES.

There wasn't time for WHITE CHRISTMAS to score enough points to qualify this year, but it more than made up for it by returning year after year, for many years, with the Bing Crosby version ultimately becoming the biggest-selling record in history. Among this year's non-holiday songs, only a few have been favored by singers having chosen to perform them over the years, such as THERE WILL NEVER BE ANOTHER YOU; BUT NOT FOR ME and I'M GLAD THERE IS YOU.

Instrumental "Collector's Items"

SHADY LADY	-Charlie Barnet
WASHINGTON WHIRLIGIG	-Charlie Barnet
BASIE BLUES	-Count Basie
HOW LONG BLUES	-Count Basie
ROYAL GARDEN BLUES	-Count Basie
BUGLE BLUES	-Count Basie
SUGAR BLUES	-Count Basie
FAREWELL BLUES	-Count Basie
CAFE SOCIETY BLUES	-Count Basie

WAY BACK BLUES	-Count Basie
ORIGINAL DIXIELAND ONE-STEP	-Bob Crosby
BRASS BOOGIE (1&2)	-Bob Crosby
SUGARFOOT STOMP	-Bob Crosby
KING PORTER STOMP	-Bob Crosby
JIMTOWN BLUES	-Bob Crosby
ECCENTRIC	-Bob Crosby
MILENBERG JOYS	-Bob Crosby
BLACK ZEPHYR	-Bob Crosby
BLUE SURREAL	-Bob Crosby
CHAIN GANG	-Bob Crosby
EC-STACY	-Bob Crosby
SORGHUM SWITCH	-Jimmy Dorsey
QUIET PLEASE (re-recorded)	-Tommy Dorsey
NOT SO QUIET PLEASE	-Tommy Dorsey
MOONLIGHT ON THE GANGES	-Tommy Dorsey
WELL GIT IT	-Tommy Dorsey
BLUE BLAZES	-Tommy Dorsey
ZONKY	-Tommy Dorsey
BLUES NO MORE	-Tommy Dorsey
PERDIDO	-Duke Ellington
THE C-JAM BLUES	-Duke Ellington
MOON MIST	-Duke Ellington
WHAT AM I HERE FOR?	-Duke Ellington
SOMEONE	-Duke Ellington
MY LITTLE BROWN BOOK	-Duke Ellington
MAIN STEM	-Duke Ellington
JOHNNY COME LATELY	-Duke Ellington
SENTIMENTAL LADY	-Duke Ellington
I DIDN'T KNOW ABOUT YOU	-Duke Ellington
SHERMAN SHUFFLE	-Duke Ellington

ROYAL FLUSH	-Benny Goodman
DEAR OLD SOUTHLAND	-Benny Goodman
AT THE DARKTOWN STRUTTERS' BALL	-Benny Goodman
A STRING OF PEARLS	-Benny Goodman
RAMONA	-Benny Goodman
SIX FLATS UNFURNISHED	-Benny Goodman
AFTER YOU'VE GONE	-Benny Goodman
MISSION TO MOSCOW	-Benny Goodman
THE WANG WANG BLUES	-Benny Goodman (Sextet)
ST. LOUIS BLUES	-Benny Goodman (Sextet)
FLYING HOME	-Lionel Hampton
BEAR MASH BLUES	-Erskine Hawkins
A STRING OF PEARLS	-Woody Herman
DOWN UNDER	-Woody Herman
PLEASE BE THERE	-Woody Herman
GOTTA GET TO ST. JOE	-Woody Herman
THE SINGING SANDS OF ALAMOSA	-Woody Herman
CRAZY RHYTHM	-Harry James
THE CLIPPER	-Harry James
LET ME UP	-Harry James
B-19	-Harry James
THE MOLE	-Harry James
ESTRELLITA	-Harry James
JAMES SESSION	-Harry James
JUMP TOWN	-Harry James
MEMPHIS BLUES	-Harry James
PRINCE CHARMING	-Harry James
THAT DRUMMER'S BAND	-Gene Krupa
PUSHIN' SAND	-Kay Kyser

CARIBBEAN CLIPPER	-Glenn Miller
RAINBOW RHAPSODY	-Glenn Miller
SLEEPY TOWN TRAIN	-Glenn Miller
DUSK	-Artie Shaw
SUITE No. 8	-Artie Shaw
ABSENT-MINDED MOON	-Artie Shaw
HINDUSTAN	-Artie Shaw
CARNIVAL	-Artie Shaw
NEEDLENOSE	-Artie Shaw
TWO-IN-ONE BLUES	-Artie Shaw
ELKS PARADE	-Bobby Sherwood

Developments This Year in Popular Music

- Building on their strong performances in 1941, the leading bands gave every indication, as 1942 progressed, that they were heading toward a peak year, both for their collective popularity and the quality of their numerous recordings. Millions of Americans were now either entering military service or employed in the production of war materials. Whether the bands and all those who were personally involved in the war effort realized it or not, they needed each other. The bands provided invaluable moral support just by being there - to be heard on radio and juke box through their recordings and to appear in person where service personnel and defense workers could attend dances. The bands included military bases in their itineraries and placed emphasis on songs whose themes were either inspirational, such as REMEMBER PEARL HARBOR; PRAISE THE LORD AND PASS THE AMMUNITION; AMERICAN PATROL; (THERE'LL BE BLUEBIRDS

OVER) THE WHITE CLIFFS OF DOVER and WHEN THE LIGHTS GO ON AGAIN (ALL OVER THE WORLD) or which provided light-hearted diversion, such as JINGLE JANGLE JINGLE; COW COW BOOGIE; ELMER'S TUNE; JUKE BOX SATURDAY NIGHT; (I'VE GOT A GAL IN) KALAMAZOO and WHO WOULDN'T LOVE YOU. Others reflected the heartache of young lovers separated by a call to duty, as exemplified by ALWAYS IN MY HEART; MISS YOU; I DON'T WANT TO WALK WITHOUT YOU and WONDER WHEN MY BABY'S COMING HOME.

The men and women in service, wherever they were stationed, often had access to a radio at some time during the day and invariably, radio enabled them to hear the currently popular recordings. Armed Forces Radio Service provided music for personnel stationed overseas and moving around the world on naval or merchant vessels. New bars, snack and coffee shops and bowling alleys opened near military bases and war plants. They, as well as post exchanges on the bases themselves, installed juke boxes, almost without exception. The result of all this was a sudden and enormous expansion of the audience for big band music, which was reflected by increased record sales (at least until the recording ban) and larger crowds in attendance wherever the bands played.

- Once again comparing the leading bands according to their numbers of hit records, we find that Glenn Miller had nearly thirty to repeat as leader in this regard. Harry James had twenty-three hits, while Tommy and Jimmy Dorsey had nineteen each. Following these, Charlie Spivak, Benny Goodman, Kay Kyser and Woody Herman were at, or close to a dozen each, with Alvino Rey, Freddy Martin, Vaughn Monroe and Sammy Kaye close behind to round out the dozen most-heard bands on radio and juke box at this peak juncture of the era. Add to these the names of Bing Crosby, Dinah Shore, The Four King Sisters, (both with and without the Alvino Rey Orchestra) and the Andrews Sisters and the chief hitmakers at this particular time will have been identified.

Totals of twenty to thirty hit records for the leaders were particularly impressive, considering that the recording strike went into effect on August 1. This meant that they achieved more in only seven months than they had been able to accomplish in twelve months in 1941.

Much of the success of the Tommy Dorsey and Harry James bands in 1942 was due to singers Frank Sinatra and Helen Forrest, who each had the kind of year which Bob Eberly and Helen O'Connell had enjoyed a year earlier. They were beneficiaries of great material and being the accomplished professionals they were, made the most of it. Listed in the approximate order in which they became hits are the fabulous songs which these two could claim as their memorable contributions to an exciting year:

Frank Sinatra
    THIS LOVE OF MINE
    VIOLETS FOR YOUR FURS
    HOW ABOUT YOU?
    JUST AS THOUGH YOU WERE HERE*
    STREET OF DREAMS*
    TAKE ME
    BE CAREFUL, IT'S MY HEART
    IN THE BLUE OF EVENING
    THERE ARE SUCH THINGS*
    DAYBREAK
    IT STARTED ALL OVER AGAIN*
    THE SONG IS YOU
    *With The Pied Pipers

Helen Forrest
    I DON'T WANT TO WALK WITHOUT YOU
    BUT NOT FOR ME
    I REMEMBER YOU
    SKYLARK
    I CRIED FOR YOU
    THAT SOLDIER OF MINE
    MISTER FIVE BY FIVE
    MANHATTAN SERENADE
    HE'S MY GUY
    I HAD THE CRAZIEST DREAM
    I'VE HEARD THAT SONG BEFORE

- In other news, Artie Shaw entered the Navy early this year, where he led a service band until late 1943, being discharged early in 1944.

- Ray McKinley and Bobby Sherwood formed bands this year.

- In May, Dick Haymes moved from Harry James to Benny Goodman, replacing Art Lund. However, he stayed with Benny only four months, as he received a lucrative offer from Tommy Dorsey to replace Frank Sinatra, who was leaving to go on his own.

- In July, as the result of a falling-out, Glenn Miller and singer Ray Eberle parted company after an association of four years, four months, covering almost all of the band's existence.

Ray Eberle, at age 19, had not sought employment as a singer, but as soon as Glenn Miller saw him and noted his resemblance to his brother Bob, Jimmy Dorsey's much-admired vocalist, he offered him a chance to audition with his band and then hired him.

During his long tenure with the band, Ray made approximately 125 recordings, representing nearly half of the band's total and nearly all of the romantic ballads. Tex Beneke and Glenn's girl singers were utilized for the most part on novelty tunes. Ray's name had become synonymous with the Glenn Miller Orchestra and his work was consistently good. In fan polls, he was twice voted most popular male band vocalist, although talent-wise, critics never regarded him in the same light as his brother, or Dick Haymes or Frank Sinatra. His voice blended well with the sound of the Miller band, perhaps better than would have those of the few more highly-regarded singers.

Glenn Miller replaced Ray Eberle with 20 year-old "Skip" Nelson. "Skip" had been born "Scipione Mirabella," but wisely opted for a name which rolled off the American tongue more easily, as had many others before him, including Artie Shaw (Arthur Arshawsky); Peggy Lee (Norma Deloris Egstrom) and Doris Day (Doris Kappelhoff).

- The year would boast several of the most famous swing instrumentals of the Big Band Era, including Glenn Miller's A STRING OF PEARLS, Benny Goodman's JERSEY BOUNCE and Harry James' STRICTLY INSTRUMENTAL and TRUMPET BLUES.

- Sunday evening, September 27 marked the last appearance of Glenn Miller's civilian band. The event took place at the Central Theater in Passaic, New Jersey and it was reported that as the last notes faded, musicians and audience alike were overcome with emotion at the breakup of a fabulously successful and much-loved musical organization. Little did anyone, present at the Central Theater that evening or not, suspect the fates which would ultimately befall both Glenn Miller personally and the big bands as a whole.

- Musicians and fans also mourned the loss this year of a great and popular figure, trumpeter/bandleader Bunny Berigan.

1 9 4 3

The Most Popular Recordings

January - March

YOU'D BE SO NICE TO COME HOME TO -Dinah Shore;
   Dick Jurgens (Harry Cool); Six Hits and a Miss
ROSE ANN OF CHARING CROSS -Peter Piper and His
   Orchestra; The Four Vagabonds
BRAZIL -Xavier Cugat (Band Chorus); Jimmy Dorsey (Bob
   Eberly)
CAN'T GET OUT OF THIS MOOD -Kay Kyser (Harry
   Babbitt, Julie Conway and Trio); Freddy Martin (Bob
   Haymes and The Martin Men); Johnny Long (The Four
   Teens)
I LOST MY SUGAR IN SALT LAKE CITY -Freddy Slack
   (Johnny Mercer)
MOONLIGHT MOOD -Glenn Miller (Skip Nelson and The
   Modernaires); Kay Kyser (Harry Babbitt, Julie Conway
   and Trio)
IT STARTED ALL OVER AGAIN -Tommy Dorsey (Frank
   Sinatra and The Pied Pipers)
I'VE HEARD THAT SONG BEFORE -Harry James (Helen
   Forrest)
THAT OLD BLACK MAGIC -Glenn Miller (Skip Nelson);
   Charlie Barnet (Frances Wayne); Freddy Slack (Margaret
   Whiting)

179

HIT THE ROAD TO DREAMLAND -Freddy Slack (The
    Mellowaires)
TAKING A CHANCE ON LOVE (Recorded 1940, but far
    more popular this year.) -Benny Goodman (Helen
    Forrest); Sammy Kaye (The Three Kaydettes)
AS TIME GOES BY (From 1931) -Rudy Vallee (Vocal) and
    His Orchestra; Jacques Renard (Paul Small) -Both reissues
    of 1931 recordings.
DON'T GET AROUND MUCH ANY MORE -Originally a
    Duke Ellington instrumental called NEVER NO
    LAMENT, when first recorded in 1940. Ellington's new
    version remained an instrumental, but there were now also
    lyrics developed around the new title. The Ink Spots found
    them suited to their style, making a recording which
    remained for several weeks on the popularity charts.
A PINK COCKTAIL FOR A BLUE LADY -Glenn Miller
    (Skip Nelson)
FOR ME AND MY GAL (From 1917, repopularized 1942,
    1943) -Judy Garland and Gene Kelly; Guy Lombardo
    (Kenny Gardner)

April - June

GOBS OF LOVE -The Four King Sisters
IT CAN'T BE WRONG -Dick Haymes and The Song
    Spinners
SOMETHING TO REMEMBER YOU BY (From 1931) -
    Dinah Shore
LET'S GET LOST -Kay Kyser (Harry Babbitt, Julie Conway
    and Trio); Vaughn Monroe (Vocal, with The Four Lee
    Sister); Jimmy Dorsey (Bob Eberly)

YOU'LL NEVER KNOW -Academy Award-winning song from the movie, *Hello, Frisco, Hello* -Dick Haymes and The Song Spinners; Frank Sinatra and The Bobby Tucker Singers

COMIN' IN ON A WING AND A PRAYER -The Four Vagabonds; The Song Spinners

IT'S ALWAYS YOU (From 1941) -Glenn Miller (Ray Eberle); Tommy Dorsey (Frank Sinatra)

IN THE BLUE OF EVENING -Tommy Dorsey (Frank Sinatra)

ST. LOUIS BLUES MARCH -Glenn Miller Army Air Corps Band

CABIN IN THE SKY (From 1940) -Benny Goodman (Helen Forrest)

HOLIDAY FOR STRINGS -David Rose (Instrumental)

July - September

ALL OR NOTHING AT ALL (From 1939) -Harry James (Frank Sinatra)

PEOPLE WILL SAY WE'RE IN LOVE -Bing Crosby, with Trudy Erwin and The Sportsmen Glee Club; Frank Sinatra and The Bobby Tucker Singers

IN MY ARMS -Dick Haymes and The Song Spinners

PUT YOUR ARMS AROUND ME, HONEY - Dick Haymes and The Song Spinners

SUNDAY, MONDAY OR ALWAYS -Bing Crosby and The Ken Darby Singers; Frank Sinatra and The Bobby Tucker Singers

I HEARD YOU CRIED LAST NIGHT -Harry James (Helen Forrest); Dick Haymes and The Song Spinners

(Theme from) THE WARSAW CONCERTO -Freddy Martin
    (Instrumental)
CLOSE TO YOU -Frank Sinatra and The Bobby Tucker
    Singers
STORMY WEATHER (From 1933) -Lena Horne
PAPER DOLL -The Mills Brothers
IF YOU PLEASE -Bing Crosby

October - December

PISTOL PACKIN' MAMA - Bing Crosby and The Andrews
    Sisters; Al Dexter (Vocal) and His "Troopers" country-
    western band
THEY'RE EITHER TOO YOUNG OR TOO OLD -Jimmy
    Dorsey (Kitty Kallen)
FOR THE FIRST TIME -Dick Haymes and The Song
    Spinners
I'LL BE AROUND -The Mills Brothers
MY HEART TELLS ME -Glen Gray (Eugenie Baird)
VICTORY POLKA -Bing Crosby and The Andrews Sisters
SURREY WITH THE FRINGE ON TOP -Alfred Drake, of
    the cast of the Broadway musical, *Oklahoma!*
OH! WHAT A BEAUTIFUL MORNING -Bing Crosby, with
    Trudy Erwin and The Sportsmen Glee Club
THE DREAMER -Kay Armen and The Balladiers
SHOO, SHOO, BABY -Ella Mae Morse; The Andrews Sisters
I'LL BE HOME FOR CHRISTMAS -Bing Crosby
SPEAK LOW -Guy Lombardo (Billy Leach)
CUDDLE UP A LITTLE CLOSER -Kay Armen and The
    Balladiers

MY IDEAL (From 1930) -Jimmy Dorsey (Bob Eberly); Billy
   Butterfield (Margaret Whiting)
DARLING, JE VOUS AIME BEAUCOUP -Hildegarde's
   theme song
JINGLE BELLS (From 1857) -Bing Crosby and The Andrews
   Sisters

Of this year's favorite songs, the following achieved the
greatest popularity, according to results of the weekly radio
survey, *Your Hit Parade*:   YOU'LL NEVER KNOW;
PEOPLE WILL SAY WE'RE IN LOVE; THERE ARE SUCH
THINGS; SUNDAY, MONDAY OR ALWAYS; AS TIME
GOES BY; PAPER DOLL; BRAZIL; COMIN' IN ON A WING
AND A PRAYER; I'VE HEARD THAT SONG
BEFORE and DON'T GET AROUND MUCH ANYMORE.

Songs from 1943 which continued to be played and sung by
artists over many years were: BRAZIL; THAT OLD BLACK
MAGIC; PEOPLE WILL SAY WE'RE IN LOVE and especially, AS TIME GOES BY.

Each year to this point, some song or group of songs had
put their stamp on the year, making it memorable in part
because of the association. For example, 1939 brings to mind
the beautiful adaptations of the classics and ALL THE
THINGS YOU ARE; 1940 recalls I'LL NEVER SMILE
AGAIN and also all the Ink Spots' hits; 1941, as we mentioned, was dominated by all the Bob Eberly-Helen O'Connell
hits. Despite its limitations, 1943 also would be remembered
for a trio of outstanding songs. Early in the year, the classic
movie *Casablanca* brought us the equally-classic song, AS

TIME GOES BY. About the same time, *Oklahoma!* opened
on Broadway, bringing us PEOPLE WILL SAY WE'RE IN
LOVE, as part of its memorable score. In the fall, the Mills
Brothers' PAPER DOLL, recorded the year before, made its
impact as the biggest-selling record of the Big Band Era,
except for holiday songs which were reintroduced every year.

Instrumental "Collector's Items"

In this year of the recording ban, for recorded music by the
big bands, civilian and military disc jockeys had to make do
with much older material.   Under those conditions, many
"collector's items" from previous years were reissued for
additional spins on the country's turntables.   Among those
frequently heard were the following:

WASHINGTON WHIRLIGIG	-Charlie Barnet
RUSTY DUSTY BLUES	-Count Basie
BLUE SURREAL	-Bob Crosby
WEARY BLUES	-Tommy Dorsey
MANDY MAKE UP YOUR MIND	-Tommy Dorsey
BOOGIE WOOGIE	-Tommy Dorsey
SONG OF INDIA	-Tommy Dorsey
PERDIDO	-Duke Ellington
BOJANGLES	-Duke Ellington
SENTIMENTAL LADY	-Duke Ellington
TAKE THE "A" TRAIN	-Duke Ellington
MISSION TO MOSCOW	-Benny Goodman
THE WORLD IS WAITING FOR THE SUNRISE	-Benny Goodman

(AT THE) WOODCHOPPERS	
BALL	-Woody Herman
PLEASE BE THERE	-Woody Herman
PRINCE CHARMING	-Harry James
FLASH	-Harry James
JUMP TOWN	-Harry James
TWO O'CLOCK JUMP	-Harry James
CROSS YOUR HEART	-Artie Shaw Gramercy Five
FURLOUGH FLING	-Freddy Slack
RIFFETTE	-Freddy Slack

Developments This Year in Popular Music

Each in his own way, the music-loving public was more concerned with the war than with the bands' inability to make new recordings because of the musicians' strike against the record companies. After all, the bands were playing everywhere as usual and one could still tune the radio to music and hear new songs there as well as on juke boxes. However, any records played now on which orchestras were heard, had to have been recorded prior to August 1, 1942. This meant that many of the "new" songs were already several months old and simply late being introduced. Another portion of the record fare containing orchestra music consisted of last year's hits being carried forward for an extended time on radio and juke box. Next, were the really new recordings made by singers without instrumental accompaniment: Bing Crosby with The Ken Darby Singers; Frank Sinatra and The Bobby Tucker Singers; Dick Haymes and The Song Spinners, etc.

The Mills Brothers' PAPER DOLL, unable to catch on a year earlier, found these circumstances ideal and once it appeared on *Your Hit Parade* (September 11) was not displaced until mid-February of 1944. It was on the charts for 36 weeks and sold six million copies to lead all non-holiday recordings in popularity. The brothers, Herbert, Harry and Donald, accompanied by their father, John Sr., had been turning out pleasing performances for many years before scoring with this blockbuster. With song sensations of the past, such as THE MUSIC GOES 'ROUND AND AROUND, BIE MIR BIST DU SCHOEN and OH! JOHNNY, artists other than those with the hit record had made cover recordings. Not so with PAPER DOLL. It was as though everyone either conceded that they could not top the Mills Brothers, or possibly thought that they deserved exclusivity on this one. In any case, it was all theirs.

Suffice to say that there was enough popular music available so that the lack of continuity in the bands' production of new recordings wasn't immediately apparent. In retrospect, however, that break in continuity and everyone's failure to make much of it, could have been the beginning of the end. And the subtleness of this year's slippage may have contributed to the deceptive manner in which the end would finally overtake us a few years later.

Band personnel continued to be affected by members entering military service, changing jobs and going into business for themselves.

- Peggy Lee left Benny Goodman in March to marry former Goodman guitarist Dave Barbour.

- Singer Kenny Sargent, long a fixture with Glen Gray, left to take a radio job and was replaced by Eugenie Baird, the first girl singer ever employed by the band.

- Ella Mae Morse left Freddy Slack about mid-year to begin working as a single.

- Dick Haymes followed the trend, leaving Tommy Dorsey to begin what developed into a very successful career on his own, including major film roles.

- Doris Day, who had started with Bob Crosby in 1940, then moved to Les Brown, left that band in 1941 to have a baby. Now she returned to Les for a more lengthy and productive stay.

- This was the year of the Harry James-Betty Grable romance, leading to their marriage. She was then a top star of Hollywood musicals and a favorite "pin-up girl" of service-men. Meanwhile, the James band was enjoying its status as the new public favorite.

- Late in the year, Helen Forrest left Harry James to go on her own. Helen, the quintessential girl band singer, who made every performance a work of art, with Artie Shaw, Benny Goodman and Harry James, thus ended her most productive association. Her voice and phrasing, together with Harry's incomparable playing - his trumpet almost seemed to "sing" on those lovely compositions - resulted in some unforgettable wartime classics, such as I DON'T WANT TO WALK WITH OUT YOU, I HAD THE CRAZIEST DREAM and I'VE

HEARD THAT SONG BEFORE.

- After legal problems forced him to give up his band, Gene Krupa was first re-hired by Benny Goodman, then moved as a matter of convenience to Tommy Dorsey's band, simply because it was not touring at the time, thus allowing him to remain in New York. Gene would later have his own band once again.

- Captain Glenn Miller was extremely busy with his Army Air Corps Band. He had obtained the services of former Krupa singer Johnny Desmond, who had a superb voice, worked beautifully with the band and remained with it until it disbanded at the end of the war. The band also had a fine vocal group, called The Crew Chiefs, a first-class string section recruited from among former symphony orchestra players and stars from various big bands, such as drummer and novelty singer Ray McKinley, pianist Mel Powell, clarinetist "Peanuts" Hucko, bass player "Trigger" Alpert and arranger Jerry Gray. The band's most important work at this time was on a weekly radio series called *I Sustain the Wings*, which used dramatic episodes to glamorize the air service and aid recruiting.

- At the same time, somewhere in the Pacific, Artie Shaw was also working very hard, in fact, to the point of exhaustion as he led a band for the Navy. His unit featured such big band luminaries as trumpeters Johnny Best and Max Kaminsky, pianist and former leader Claude Thornhill and tenor saxophonist Sam Donahue, who replaced Artie when he had to give it up.

The Miller and Shaw service bands may have been the best known, but there were large and small dance bands throughout the armed forces, testimony both to the popularity of the music of the period and to the number of musicians doing a tour of duty. In years gone by, a military band would have been a marching band only, but now, while there were still occasions to use marching bands, the Big Band Era had changed the focus. Additionally, the scheduling of regular dances on the military bases and occasional concert-type appearances by name bands was considered an important and desirable type of recreation for American military personnel of the 1940s. The Saturday night dances held at bases throughout the U. S. and overseas did wonders for the morale of service people.

1 9 4 4

The Most Popular Recordings

January - March

NO LOVE, NO NOTHIN' Ella Mae Morse, with Dick
 Walters' Orchestra; Johnny Long (Patti Dugan)
STAR EYES -Jimmy Dorsey (Bob Eberly and Kitty Kallen)
RATION BLUES -Louis Jordan and His Tympany Five
MY SHINING HOUR -Glen Gray (Eugenie Baird)
DO NOTHIN' TILL YOU HEAR FROM ME -Duke
 Ellington (Instrumental) It was called CONCERTO FOR
 COOTIE when first recorded in 1940. Now given
 appropriate lyrics, it was also recorded by Woody Herman
 (Vocal) and His Orchestra and Stan Kenton (Red Dorris)
I COULDN'T SLEEP A WINK LAST NIGHT -Frank Sinatra
 and The Bobby Tucker Singers
WHEN THEY ASK ABOUT YOU -Jimmy Dorsey (Kitty
 Kallen)
MAIRZY DOATS -The Merry Macs; The Four King Sisters;
 The Pied Pipers
BESAME MUCHO -Jimmy Dorsey (Bob Eberly and Kitty
 Kallen); Andy Russell
A LOVELY WAY TO SPEND AN EVENING -Frank Sinatra
 and The Bobby Tucker Singers); The Ink Spots
THE MUSIC STOPPED -Frank Sinatra and The Bobby
 Tucker Singers; Woody Herman (Frances Wayne)

190

POINCIANA -(From 1936) -Bing Crosby; David Rose
(Instrumental)
I LOVE YOU ("...hums the April breeze," etc.) -Bing
Crosby; Perry Como; Jo Stafford
IT'S LOVE, LOVE, LOVE -The Four King Sisters; Guy
Lombardo (Skip Nelson)

April - June

I'LL GET BY (From 1928) -A 1941 recording by Harry
James (Dick Haymes) was reissued and new ones by The
Ink Spots and The Four King Sisters helped this song gain
renewed popularity.
LONG AGO AND FAR AWAY -Bing Crosby; Dick Haymes
and Helen Forrest; Perry Como; Jo Stafford
SAN FERNANDO VALLEY -Bing Crosby; Johnny Mercer
GOODNIGHT, WHEREVER YOU ARE -Russ Morgan
(Vocal) and His Orchestra
SUDDENLY IT'S SPRING -Glen Gray (Eugenie Baird);
Hildegarde
STRAIGHTEN UP AND FLY RIGHT -The King Cole Trio
(Nat "King" Cole, piano and vocalist); The Andrews
Sisters
I'LL BE SEEING YOU (From 1938) -Bing Crosby (new
recording); Tommy Dorsey (a 1940 recording with Frank
Sinatra)
THE G. I. JIVE -Louis Jordan (Vocal) and His Tympany
Five; Johnny Mercer
AMOR -Bing Crosby; Andy Russell
YOU ALWAYS HURT THE ONE YOU LOVE -The Mills
Brothers

LILI MARLENE (Popular war song of German origin) -Perry
    Como; Hildegarde. German language version played on
    Nazi propaganda broadcasts beamed to Allied forces was
    sung by Lale Anderson.
LIKE SOMEONE IN LOVE -Bing Crosby
SWINGING ON A STAR -Bing Crosby
TIME WAITS FOR NO ONE -Helen Forrest; Johnny Long
    (Patti Dugan)
TILL THEN -The Mills Brothers
HOW BLUE THE NIGHT -Dick Haymes

July - September

MILKMAN, KEEP THOSE BOTTLES QUIET -Woody
    Herman (Vocal) and His Orchestra; Ella Mae Morse; The
    Four King Sisters
IT COULD HAPPEN TO YOU -Bing Crosby; Jo Stafford
SLEEPY TIME GAL (From 1925) -Harry James
    (Instrumental-reissue)
I'LL WALK ALONE -Louis Prima (Lily Ann Carol); Dinah
    Shore; Martha Tilton
IS YOU IS OR IS YOU AIN'T MY BABY? -Bing Crosby and
    The Andrews Sisters; Louis Jordan (Vocal) and His
    Tympany Five
IT HAD TO BE YOU (From 1924) -Dick Haymes and Helen
    Forrest; Artie Shaw (Instrumental); Betty Hutton
GOING MY WAY -Bing Crosby
AND HER TEARS FLOWED LIKE WINE -Stan Kenton
    (Anita O'Day, with Band Chorus)
ESTRELLITA (From 1915) -Harry James' instrumental, a
    "Collector's Item" in 1942, received wider play this year.

HOW MANY HEARTS HAVE YOU BROKEN? -Stan
   Kenton (Gene Howard); The Three Suns
A HOT TIME IN THE TOWN OF BERLIN -Bing Crosby
   and The Andrews Sisters
THE DAY AFTER FOREVER -Bing Crosby
TOGETHER (From 1928) -Dick Haymes and Helen Forrest;
   Guy Lombardo (Tony Craig)

October - December

LET ME LOVE YOU TONIGHT -Woody Herman (Vocal)
   and His Orchestra
DON'T TAKE YOUR LOVE FROM ME (From 1940) -Glen
   Gray (Eugenie Baird)
DANCE WITH A DOLLY (Based on a dance tune from early
   American frontier days: BUFFALO GALS, WON'T YOU
   COME OUT TONIGHT?) -Russ Morgan (Al Jennings)
TOO-RA-LOO-RA-LOO-RAL (From 1914) -Bing Crosby
I'M MAKING BELIEVE -Ella Fitzgerald and The Ink Spots
SPRING WILL BE A LITTLE LATE THIS YEAR -Morton
   Downey
ALWAYS (From 1926) -Guy Lombardo (Tony Craig);
   Sammy Kaye (Tony Alamo); Gordon Jenkins
   (Instrumental)
IT'S FUNNY TO EVERYONE BUT ME (From 1939) -1939
   recordings by The Ink Spots and Harry James (Frank
   Sinatra) were repopularized
THE TROLLEY SONG -Judy Garland; Vaughn Monroe
   (Vocal, with Marilyn Duke) and His Orchestra; The Four
   King Sisters; The Pied Pipers
SWEET AND LOVELY (From 1931) -Bing Crosby (reissue)

STRANGE MUSIC -Bing Crosby

TWILIGHT TIME -The Three Suns (Instrumental Theme);
Les Brown (Instrumental)

INTO EACH LIFE SOME RAIN MUST FALL -Ella
Fitzgerald and The Ink Spots

WHAT A DIFF'RENCE A DAY MADE (From 1934) -Andy
Russell

THE VERY THOUGHT OF YOU -Vaughn Monroe (Vocal)
and His Orchestra

TICO-TICO -Ethel Smith (organ) with the Banda Carioca);
The Andrew Sisters

WILL YOU STILL BE MINE? (From 1941) -Tommy Dorsey
(Connie Haines) The 1941 recording was repopularized.

DON'T FENCE ME IN -Bing Crosby and The Andrews
Sisters

CONFESSIN' (THAT I LOVE YOU) (From 1930) -Perry
Como

THERE GOES THAT SONG AGAIN -Kay Kyser (Georgia
Carroll); Sammy Kaye (Nancy Norman); Russ Morgan
(Vocal) and His Orchestra

THE BOY NEXT DOOR -Judy Garland

HAVE YOURSELF A MERRY LITTLE CHRISTMAS -Judy
Garland

MEET ME IN ST. LOUIS, LOUIS -Judy Garland

Of this year's favorite songs, the following achieved the greatest popularity, according to results of the weekly radio survey, *Your Hit Parade*: I'LL BE SEEING YOU; I'LL WALK ALONE; LONG AGO AND FAR AWAY; THE TROLLEY SONG; I'LL GET BY; I LOVE YOU; AMOR; SWINGING ON A STAR; BESAME MUCHO and IT'S

LOVE, LOVE, LOVE.

In contrast to most other of the big band years, 1944 did not see great new songs crowding each other off the charts. There were instead a few nice new ones, several nice old ones being repopularized and many mediocre ones - all receiving extended play because of a lack of good new material.

Song of the year was I'LL BE SEEING YOU, which we discuss in detail below. It originated in 1938, was completely ignored then, but fit perfectly in 1944. Other very nice songs belonging to this year were I'LL WALK ALONE, IT COULD HAPPEN TO YOU and a trio introduced by Frank Sinatra in the movie *Higher and Higher*: I COULDN'T SLEEP A WINK LAST NIGHT; THIS IS A LOVELY WAY TO SPEND AN EVENING and THE MUSIC STOPPED.

Instrumental "Collector's Items"

The recording strike having been settled with one of the three companies, Decca Records, but continuing for most of the year against RCA Victor and Columbia, there was still a scarcity of new instrumentals. Following are some of the year's most-heard recordings of this type, which of course continued to include a number of reissues:

BIZET HAS HIS DAY	-Les Brown
BODY AND SOUL	-Jimmy Dorsey
SOLO FLIGHT	-Benny Goodman Quintet
OVERTIME	-Lionel Hampton
LOOSE WIG	-Lionel Hampton

HAMP'S BOOGIE WOOGIE	-Lionel Hampton
I ONLY HAVE EYES FOR YOU	-Coleman Hawkins
'SWONDERFUL	-Coleman Hawkins
I'M IN THE MOOD FOR LOVE	-Coleman Hawkins
BEAN AT THE MET	-Coleman Hawkins
FLAME THROWER	-Coleman Hawkins
NIGHT AND DAY	-Coleman Hawkins
I GET A KICK OUT OF YOU	-Woody Herman
PERDIDO	-Woody Herman
BACK BEAT BOOGIE	-Harry James
MEMPHIS BLUES	-Harry James
EAGER BEAVER	-Stan Kenton
ARTISTRY IN RHYTHM	-Stan Kenton
HUMORESQUE	-Guy Lombardo
JEEP RHYTHM	-Jimmie Lunceford
BACK DOOR STUFF	-Jimmie Lunceford
RUSSIAN LULLABY	-Red Norvo
SUBTLE SEXTOLOGY	-Red Norvo
SEVEN COME ELEVEN	-Red Norvo
THE MAN I LOVE	-Red Norvo
DANCING IN THE DARK	-Artie Shaw
IT HAD TO BE YOU	-Artie Shaw
TEMPTATION	-Artie Shaw
SUMMIT RIDGE DRIVE	-Artie Shaw (Gramercy Five)
CUBAN SUGAR MILL	-Freddie Slack

Developments This Year in Popular Music

- Former band singers Dick Haymes and Helen Forrest were making hit records, separately and together at this time.

- The Merry Macs singing group gained more prominence this year with the top recording of the novelty hit, MAIRZY DOATS. They were not newcomers, having begun in the early thirties with a trio of brothers named McMichael. Later joined by a girl named MacKay, they adopted the name, "Merry Macs." Although their personnel underwent changes through the years, they kept the name and the format of three boys and a girl, as well as their smooth, upbeat singing style.

- With hits this year of RATION BLUES; G. I. JIVE and IS YOU IS OR IS YOU AIN'T MY BABY? another veteran, Louis Jordan, gained a sizeable share of the musical spotlight. Louis sang and played alto sax with his "Tympany Five." The group appeared in two movies this year: *Follow the Boys* and *Meet Miss Bobby Socks*.

- The Stan Kenton Orchestra, of "progressive jazz" fame, was three years into its existence and only now had begun to have some recordings on the popularity charts. These consisted of : DO NOTHIN' 'TIL YOU HEAR FROM ME (Red Dorris); AND HER TEARS FLOWED LIKE WINE (Anita O'Day) and HOW MANY HEARTS HAVE YOU BROKEN? (Gene Howard) Also getting some air time was the swinging EAGER BEAVER and Stan's theme song, ARTISTRY IN RHYTHM, which sounded very much like a swing version of SOFTLY, AS IN A MORNING SUNRISE.

- November 22nd saw the end of the differences between the musicians' union and the last remaining companies, RCA Victor and Columbia Records, so that the bands once again were free to record with all companies.

- When he volunteered for military service in 1942, Glenn Miller was already beyond the age limit established for draftees, so he had to plead to be allowed to join. Again, when he wanted to take his service band overseas, he had to argue with the generals, because the band was doing such an effective job on the Army Air Corps promotional radio program, *I Sustain the Wings*. Once again getting his way, Glenn then left it up to each band member to decide whether he wanted to go overseas or not - even offering to arrange transfers for any preferring to remain. Almost to a man they elected to accompany Glenn, although he had cautioned them that his plans entailed a very heavy work schedule. The band arrived in England early this year and as promised, immediately was plunged into a back-breaking schedule of in-person appearances, radio broadcasts on both the U. S. Armed Forces Radio Network and the BBC, as well as recording sessions. So, while the Glenn Miller civilian band was now missing from its former venues in America, his Army Air Corps band, which many thought artistically superior, was carrying on for the enjoyment of many thousands of Americans in uniform, as well as making new admirers among the British.

England was still a German target, now of flying bombs, which picked up where the piloted bombers had left off. Air-raid warnings frequently interrupted the band's work and once, while the band was away from its billet just outside

London, one of the "buzz-bombs" struck in the area, causing much damage, injuries and loss of life in the immediate vicinity.

Toward the end of the year, with the Allied advance into Europe going reasonably well and with vast numbers of the armed forces having moved from England to France, Glenn began making plans to move the band's base of operations to the continent. When the time arrived for the band to move to Paris, the ever-conscientious and protective Glenn Miller was concerned and anxious to see that all the men's living and working arrangements were satisfactory and ready for them. He desperately wanted to get to Paris in advance of the band, but some of the worst possible weather was keeping even combat aircraft grounded. Evidently, in one of those situations where someone is extremely anxious to arrive at his destination and someone else wants to do all he can to help, an ill-advised decision was made. A pilot of one of the small, liaison-type planes thought that he could fly Glenn Miller the relatively short distance from a spot near the east coast of England across the channel to Paris, despite the weather. It proved a tragic error in judgement and no trace of the plane was ever found.

- Singer Andy Russell (AMOR; BESAME MUCHO; I DREAM OF YOU; WHAT A DIFFERENCE A DAY MADE) was heard frequently on Armed Forces Radio at this time.

- The movie, *A Guy Named Joe* , starring Spencer Tracy and Irene Dunne in a story of wartime romance, resurrected the old song, I'LL GET BY (1928). Since there was a continuing shortage of new recordings, disc jockeys took advantage of the film's popularity to revive a 1941 recording by Harry James (Dick Haymes' vocal). The Ink Spots and The Four King Sisters also made popular versions.

- However, during this year when the global conflict was reaching a peak of intensity on all fronts, two songs especially applicable to lovers separated by calls to duty, firmly established themselves among the songs most closely associated with World War II.

First, I'LL BE SEEING YOU, (music by Sammy Fain, lyrics by Irving Kahal) captivated the American public at home and service personnel away from home. It remained on radio's *Your Hit Parade* for 24 weeks, ten of those in first place. It was first heard in an obscure Broadway musical called *Right This Way* in 1938. Next, it was selected by Tommy Dorsey as one of the first recordings to be made with his new singer, Frank Sinatra, in 1940. However, it wasn't until this year's reintroduction that the beautiful sentiments it expressed caught on with a public tormented by separations from loved ones. Mr. Kahal's choice of "that small cafe," "the park across the way" and "the children's carousel" as some of "the old familiar places," gave this song a charming "old world" character which no doubt tugged at many a heartstring, helping to endow it with its special, enduring appeal. A leading young singer of the 1980s described it to a national television audience as "the perfect song."

A well-acted movie with the same name, starring Joseph Cotten, Ginger Rogers and 17 year-old Shirley Temple, released in 1944 and with the song as a recurrent theme, unquestionably helped in its revival that year, as did a new recording by Bing Crosby. Movie-makers through the years have often chosen this one as the most appropriate song to be playing in the background during the most sentimental moments of their films about the war years. *Yanks; Swing Shift* and *Shining Through* are a few which come immediately to mind.

The other song was particularly related to the combatants who faced each other in North Africa and Europe, for it was a song of German origin, dealing with the love of an imaginary German soldier for his LILI MARLENE, the girl who would wait for him "underneath the lamplight, by the barrack gate." It started as a favorite of German soldiers in the Afrika Korps, who would play and sing it during moments of relaxation. Sometimes, on quiet evenings, its strains would be wafted by desert breezes across the sands to the British encampments, where they fell on appreciative ears. Before long, the song was adopted and shared by friend and foe alike. Soon, the widely-heard German radio propagandist, "Axis Sally," was using it as her theme song and Allied troops throughout the European Theater of Operations would tune in just to hear it, although they also enjoyed chuckling at "Sally's" rantings at a time when it was obvious that her days on radio were numbered. Many thousands of veterans of that campaign - on both sides - would forevermore feel a twinge of nostalgia at the sound of the music, or merely the name, LILI MARLENE, representing as she did, in those lonely, apprehensive moments of long ago, every fighting man's "girl he left behind," - for many, their inspiration to get it over with, quickly.

Most never knew the identity of the girl who sang on the recording used by "Axis Sally." She was a Danish-German girl named Lale Andersen and her recording understandably sold over a million copies. In 1960, she had another hit with a recording in German of NEVER ON SUNDAY. A popular postwar recording of LILI MARLENE was made by the movie star with a husky-voiced German accent, Marlene Dietrich. In 1944, the popular American recordings were by Perry Como and Hildegarde.

1945

January - March

I DREAM OF YOU -Tommy Dorsey (Freddy Stuart); Andy
    Russell; Frank Sinatra; Perry Como
SWEET DREAMS, SWEETHEART -Ray Noble (Larry
    Stewart)
AC-CENT-TCHU-ATE THE POSITIVE -Johnny Mercer and
    The Pied Pipers; Bing Crosby and The Andrews Sisters;
    Kay Kyser (Dolly Mitchell)
I DIDN'T KNOW ABOUT YOU -Jo Stafford; Woody
    Herman (Vocal) and His Orchestra
COCKTAILS FOR TWO (From 1934) -Spike Jones and His
    "City Slickers"
EVELINA -Bing Crosby; Frankie Carle (Paul Small)
SLEIGH RIDE IN JULY -Bing Crosby; Dinah Shore; Tommy
    Dorsey (Bonnie Lou Williams); Les Brown (Gordon
    Drake)
THREE CABALLEROS -Bing Crosby and The Andrews
    Sisters
MY DREAMS ARE GETTING BETTER ALL THE TIME -
    Les Brown (Doris Day); Johnny Long (Dick Robertson)
A LITTLE ON THE LONELY SIDE -Guy Lombardo (Jimmy
    Brown); Frankie Carle (Paul Allen)

EV'RY TIME WE SAY GOODBYE -Charlie Spivak (Irene
    Daye); Benny Goodman (Peggy Mann)
MOONLIGHT IN VERMONT -Margaret Whiting
SATURDAY NIGHT (IS THE LONELIEST NIGHT IN THE
    WEEK) -Frank Sinatra; Woody Herman (Frances Wayne);
    Sammy Kaye (Nancy Norman); The Four King Sisters
RUM AND COCA COLA -The Andrews Sisters; Vaughn
    Monroe (Vocal with The Norton Sisters) and His
    Orchestra
ONE MEAT BALL -The Andrews Sisters
ROBIN HOOD -Les Brown (Butch Stone); Louis Prima
    (Vocal) and His Orchestra
MY FUNNY VALENTINE (From 1937) -Hal McIntyre (Ruth
    Gaylor)
OPUS No. 1 -Tommy Dorsey (Instrumental)
I'M BEGINNING TO SEE THE LIGHT -Harry James (Kitty
    Kallen)
ONE FOR MY BABY (AND ONE MORE FOR THE ROAD)
    -Lena Horne
MORE AND MORE -Bing Crosby; Tommy Dorsey (Bonnie
    Lou Williams)
CANDY -Johnny Mercer, with Jo Stafford and The Pied
    Pipers; The Four King Sisters; Dinah Shore

April - June

LET'S TAKE THE LONG WAY HOME -Bing Crosby; Jo
    Stafford
ALL OF MY LIFE -Bing Crosby
GUESS I'LL HANG MY TEARS OUT TO DRY -Harry
    James (Kitty Kallen)

LAURA -Dick Haymes; Woody Herman (Vocal) and His Orchestra

JUST A PRAYER AWAY -Bing Crosby

BEGIN THE BEGUINE (From 1935) -Eddie Heywood, piano solo

THERE MUST BE A WAY -Charlie Spivak (Jimmy Saunders)

CHLOE (From 1928) -Spike Jones and His "City Slickers" Orchestra (Red Ingle)

CALDONIA -Louis Jordan (Vocal) and His Tympany Five; Woody Herman (Vocal) and His Orchestra

YAH-TA-TA, YAH-TA-TA (TALK, TALK, TALK) -Bing Crosby and Judy Garland; Harry James (Kitty Kallen)

LOVER MAN (OH WHERE CAN YOU BE?) -Billie Holiday

DREAM -The Pied Pipers; Frank Sinatra; Jimmy Dorsey (Teddy Walters)

CLOSE AS PAGES IN A BOOK -Bing Crosby; Benny Goodman (Jane Harvey); Frances Langford

SENTIMENTAL JOURNEY -Les Brown (Doris Day)

THERE, I'VE SAID IT AGAIN -Vaughn Monroe (Vocal, with The Norton Sisters) and His Orchestra; Jimmy Dorsey (Teddy Walters)

THE MORE I SEE YOU -Dick Haymes; Harry James (Buddy DeVito)

YOU BELONG TO MY HEART -Bing Crosby; Charlie Spivak (Jimmy Saunders)

BELL BOTTOM TROUSERS -Kay Kyser ("Ferdie and Slim"); Tony Pastor (Vocal with Ruth McCullough) and His Orchestra; Louis Prima (Lily Ann Carol)

ON THE SUNNY SIDE OF THE STREET (From 1930) -
    Tommy Dorsey (The Sentimentalists); Jo Stafford and The
    Pied Pipers
TEMPTATION (From 1933) -Perry Como; Bing Crosby
I WISH I KNEW -Harry James (Kitty Kallen); Dick Haymes
I SHOULD CARE -Frank Sinatra; Martha Tilton; Tommy
    Dorsey (Bonnie Lou Williams and The Sentimentalists);
    Jimmy Dorsey (Teddy Walters)
CHOPIN'S POLONAISE -Carmen Cavallaro, His piano and
    Orchestra (Instrumental)

July - September

OUT OF THIS WORLD -Bing Crosby; Tommy Dorsey
    (Stuart Foster); Jo Stafford
IF I LOVED YOU -Perry Como; Harry James (Buddy De
    Vito); Bing Crosby; Frank Sinatra
A KISS GOODNIGHT -Woody Herman (Vocal) and His
    Orchestra; Freddy Slack (Liza Morrow)
GOTTA BE THIS OR THAT -Benny Goodman (Vocal) and
    His Orchestra
CAN'T YOU READ BETWEEN THE LINES -Kay Kyser
    (Dolly Mitchell); Jimmy Dorsey (Jean Cromwell)
A STRANGER IN TOWN -Martha Tilton; Mel Torme
TAMPICO -Stan Kenton (June Christy)
I DON'T CARE WHO KNOWS IT -Harry James (Kitty
    Kallen)
ON THE ATCHISON, TOPEKA AND THE SANTA FE -
    Johnny Mercer and The Pied Pipers
TILL THE END OF TIME (Based on Chopin's Polonaise in
    A-Flat Major) -Perry Como

ALONG THE NAVAJO TRAIL -Bing Crosby and The
  Andrews Sisters; Gene Krupa (Buddy Stewart); Dinah
  Shore
I CAN'T BELIEVE THAT YOU'RE IN LOVE WITH ME
  (From 1927) -Bing Crosby
I'M GONNA LOVE THAT GAL/GUY -Perry Como; Benny
  Goodman (Dottie Reid); Ginny Simms
11;60 PM -Harry James (Kitty Kallen)
JUNE IS BUSTIN' OUT ALL OVER -Benny Goodman (Kay
  Penton)
THERE'S NO YOU -Jo Stafford; Frank Sinatra
BOOGIE WOOGIE (From 1938) -Tommy Dorsey
  (Instrumental - Reissue)
HAPPINESS IS JUST A THING CALLED JOE -Woody
  Herman (Frances Wayne)
I'LL BUY THAT DREAM -Harry James (Kitty Kallen); Dick
  Haymes and Helen Forrest
IT'S BEEN A LONG, LONG TIME -Harry James (Kitty
  Kallen); Bing Crosby, with The Les Paul Trio; Stan
  Kenton (June Christy); Charlie Spivak (Irene Daye)
THAT'S FOR ME (From 1940) -Dick Haymes; Jo Stafford;
  Kay Kyser (Mike Douglas and The Campus Kids)
CHICAGO (From 1922) -Tommy Dorsey (Sy Oliver and The
  Sentimentalists)

October - December

COTTAGE FOR SALE -Billy Eckstine
WAITIN' FOR THE TRAIN TO COME IN -Peggy Lee;
  Harry James (Kitty Kallen)
HOMESICK, THAT'S ALL -Frank Sinatra

AUTUMN SERENADE -Harry James (Instrumental)

I FALL IN LOVE TOO EASILY -Frank Sinatra; Eugenie
Baird and Mel Torme's Mel Tones

LOVE LETTERS (STRAIGHT FROM MY HEART) -Dick
Haymes

CHICKERY CHICK -Sammy Kaye (Nancy Norman, Billy
Williams and Chorus; Gene Krupa (Anita O'Day)

IT MIGHT AS WELL BE SPRING (Academy Award-winning
song from the film, *State Fair*) -Dick Haymes; Sammy
Kaye (Billy Williams); Margaret Whiting

(DID YOU EVER GET) THAT FEELING IN THE MOON-
LIGHT? -Perry Como

I CAN'T BEGIN TO TELL YOU -Bing Crosby; Andy
Russell; Harry James (Betty Grable, under the pseudonym,
"Ruth Haag.")

IT'S ONLY A PAPER MOON (From 1933) -Benny Goodman
(Dottie Reid); Ella Fitzgerald and The Delta Rhythm Boys;
The King Cole Trio (Nat "King" Cole)

MY GUY'S COME BACK -Benny Goodman (Liza Morrow);
Dinah Shore

NANCY -Frank Sinatra

JUST A LITTLE FOND AFFECTION -Gene Krupa (Buddy
Stewart)

Of this year's popular songs, the following achieved the
greatest popularity, according to results of the weekly radio
survey, *Your Hit Parade*: TILL THE END OF TIME; DON'T
FENCE ME IN; IF I LOVED YOU; IT'S BEEN A LONG,
LONG TIME; SENTIMENTAL JOURNEY; AC-CENT-
TCHUATE THE POSITIVE; MY DREAMS ARE GETTING

BETTER ALL THE TIME; CANDY and I CAN'T BEGIN TO TELL YOU.

The number of hit songs did not approach totals reached in some of the other years, but there was a lot of quality on this year's list. If there was one song which could be said to most remind people of the life and times of 1945, it would be SENTIMENTAL JOURNEY. However, TILL THE END OF TIME; IF I LOVED YOU; LAURA; THERE'S NO YOU; DREAM and LOVE LETTERS were all beautiful, romantic songs, each combining timeless kinds of words and music which might have entitled them to a measure of longevity. Of these, only LAURA seemed to attract repeat performances for a long period. The revival from 1937, MY FUNNY VALEN-TINE also enjoyed some favoritism over the years, while THERE MUST BE A WAY and THE MORE I SEE YOU were repopularized by young singers in the 1980s.

Instrumental "Collector's Items"

Freedom to once again make recordings helped to improve the supply of instrumentals. The following were among those given air time this year:

SKYLINER	-Charlie Barnet
WEST END BLUES	-Charlie Barnet
DAYBREAK SERENADE	-Les Brown
CLARINADE	-Benny Goodman
LOVE WALKED IN	-Benny Goodman
JUST YOU JUST ME	-Benny Goodman

BABY WON'T YOU PLEASE COME HOME	-Benny Goodman
FASCINATING RHYTHM	-Benny Goodman
RACHEL'S DREAM	-Benny Goodman
SHINE	-Benny Goodman
JUST ONE OF THOSE THINGS	-Benny Goodman
TIGER RAG	-Benny Goodman
AIN'T MISBEHAVIN'	-Benny Goodman
I GOT RHYTHM	-Benny Goodman
CHINA BOY	-Benny Goodman
SLIPPED DISC	-Benny Goodman
OOMPH FAH FAH	-Benny Goodman
LIZA	-Benny Goodman
AFTER YOU'VE GONE	-Benny Goodman
HEY BA-BA-RE-BOP	-Lionel Hampton
IT'S THE TALK OF THE TOWN	-Coleman Hawkins
STUFFY	-Coleman Hawkins
TIPPIN' IN	-Erskine Hawkins
REMEMBER	-Erskine Hawkins
APPLE HONEY	-Woody Herman
NORTHWEST PASSAGE	-Woody Herman
BIJOU	-Woody Herman
GOOSEY GANDER	-Woody Herman
9:20 SPECIAL	-Harry James
AIN'T MISBEHAVIN'	-Harry James
SOUTHERN SCANDAL	-Stan Kenton
LEAVE US LEAP	-Gene Krupa
'SWONDERFUL	-Artie Shaw
I'LL NEVER BE THE SAME	-Artie Shaw
SEPTEMBER SONG	-Artie Shaw
LITTLE JAZZ	-Artie Shaw

TIME ON MY HANDS   -Artie Shaw

Developments This Year in Popular Music

- Many of those who were fortunate enough to hear it claimed that the Army Air Corps (later "Air Force") Band put together by Glenn Miller and playing in France this year under the direction of arranger Jerry Gray and drummer Ray McKinley, was producing some of the best, if not the best music of the Big Band Era. Building on the original Miller sound, which emphasized the reed section, it was enhanced by the addition and discreet use of a 22-piece string section and French horn, which brought the number of musicians to forty. Singer Johnny Desmond, who never sounded better than he did with this fine orchestra, was backed by the (5) "Crew Chiefs" vocal group.

- Benny Goodman returned to the recording studios with a vengeance and with good material. Fans were so pleased to hear him swinging as of old, that even his *singing* on GOTTA BE THIS OR THAT was forgiven.

- Likewise, Harry James made up for two years of nothing but reissues with a great series of recordings. Provided with such appealing and swinging ballads as I'M BEGINNING TO SEE THE LIGHT; IT'S BEEN A LONG, LONG TIME and 11:60 P. M., singer Kitty Kallen responded superbly to the challenge of replacing Helen Forrest and the band continued to ride the crest of popularity.

- Another band at its peak was that of Les Brown. It

attracted more attention this year, because of Doris Day's super hit, SENTIMENTAL JOURNEY. But it also demonstrated its versatility with different kinds of well-played and well-received numbers such as ROBIN HOOD; DAYBREAK SERENADE and TWILIGHT TIME and so it occurred to increasing numbers of fans that this was an excellent band which could play any kind of music well, including swing.

- Woody Herman (SATURDAY NIGHT; LAURA; CALDONIA; A KISS GOODNIGHT; HAPPINESS IS JUST A THING CALLED JOE; APPLE HONEY and NORTHWEST PASSAGE) needed no discovery, as his band this year continued to rate among the best swing bands as it had throughout the era. Singer Frances Wayne was helping Woody with vocals.

- Gene Krupa wasn't missing any beats in 1945. After a stint with Stan Kenton, the swinging Miss Anita O'Day was back with Gene, aided now on vocals by Buddy Stewart.

- The bands of Tommy and Jimmy Dorsey, while not producing hit records with the frequency of old, were nevertheless making as many appearances as ever. But there was no question that Tommy never quite reached the same heights after Frank Sinatra left and now Jimmy was also feeling the absence of Bob Eberly and Helen O'Connell.

- On the other hand, among the non-swinging bands, Vaughn Monroe, Kay Kyser, Freddy Martin, Sammy Kaye, Charlie Spivak and the indefatigable Guy Lombardo were leading examples of the greater ease with which the sweet bands maintained their equilibrium through adverse changes of fortune.

- As though it weren't enough to be an incredibly talented lyricist and to have appeared in some movies as well as on radio, Johnny Mercer had now also become a singing star, with hits such as G. I. JIVE; SAN FERNANDO VALLEY; AC-CENT-TCHUATE THE POSITIVE; CANDY and ON THE ATCHISON, TOPEKA AND THE SANTA FE, the latter three with Jo Stafford and/or The Pied Pipers. Perhaps taking a leaf from Johnny, fellow songwriter Hoagy Carmichael was also demonstrating singing and acting talents. After a very well-played role in *To Have and Have Not* , with Humphrey Bogart and Lauren Bacall, Hoagy this year had a popular recording of HONG KONG BLUES, followed soon thereafter by DOCTOR, LAWYER, INDIAN CHIEF and OLE BUTTERMILK SKY.

- However, Bing Crosby, with fifteen popular recordings this year and Frank Sinatra, Perry Como and Jo Stafford, with seven or eight each, led all except the Harry James and Benny Goodman bands in this regard. The trend which saw some big bands recording less and independent singers recording more had already set in.

- The King Cole Trio, first formed in 1939, was beginning to become known nationally. It consisted of Nat "King" Cole on piano, Oscar Moore on guitar and Wesley Prince on bass, later replaced by Johnny Miller. The trio both played and sang, with occasional vocal solos by Nat, until his singing became so popular that it was decided he should be the featured vocalist.

1 9 4 6

The Most Popular Recordings

January - March

LET IT SNOW! LET IT SNOW! LET IT SNOW! -Vaughn
  Monroe (Vocal, with The Norton Sisters) and His
  Orchestra; Woody Herman (Vocal) and His Orchestra
THE FRIM FRAM SAUCE -The King Cole Trio (Nat "King"
  Cole)
DIG YOU LATER (A-HUBBA-HUBBA-HUBBA) -Perry
  Como
SYMPHONY -Freddy Martin (Clyde Rogers); Bing Crosby;
  Benny Goodman (Liza Morrow); Jo Stafford
COME TO BABY DO -Les Brown (Doris Day)
AREN'T YOU GLAD YOU'RE YOU? -Bing Crosby;
  Tommy Dorsey (Stuart Foster); Les Brown (Doris Day)
I'M ALWAYS CHASING RAINBOWS (From 1918);Perry
  Como; Harry James (Buddy DeVito); Dick Haymes and
  Helen Forrest
YOU'RE NOBODY 'TIL SOMEBODY LOVES YOU -Russ
  Morgan (Vocal) and His Orchestra
IT'S A GRAND NIGHT FOR SINGING -Dick Haymes
DAY BY DAY -Frank Sinatra; Bing Crosby, with Mel Torme
  and The Mel Tones; Les Brown (Doris Day); Jo Stafford

OH! WHAT IT SEEMED TO BE -Frankie Carle (Marjorie Hughes); Frank Sinatra; Dick Haymes and Helen Forrest; Charlie Spivak (Jimmy Saunders)

DOCTOR, LAWYER, INDIAN CHIEF -Betty Hutton; Hoagy Carmichael; Les Brown (Butch Stone)

JUST A-SITTIN' AND A-ROCKIN' -Stan Kenton (June Christy)

PERSONALITY -Johnny Mercer and The Pied Pipers; Bing Crosby; Dinah Shore

THE BELLS OF ST. MARY'S (From 1917) -Bing Crosby

ATLANTA, GA -Sammy Kaye (Billy Williams); Woody Herman (Vocal) and His Orchestra

GIVE ME THE SIMPLE LIFE -Benny Goodman (Liza Morrow); Bing Crosby

McNAMARA'S BAND (From 1940) -Bing Crosby and The King's Jesters

DEAR OLD DONEGAL -Bing Crosby

I'M A BIG GIRL NOW -Sammy Kaye (Betty Barclay)

THE DARKTOWN POKER CLUB -Phil Harris (Vocal) and His Orchestra

YOU WON'T BE SATISFIED (UNTIL YOU BREAK MY HEART) -Les Brown (Doris Day); Perry Como; Louis Armstrong and Ella Fitzgerald

I'M GLAD I WAITED FOR YOU -Peggy Lee

IT'S A PITY TO SAY GOODNIGHT -Stan Kenton (June Christy)

April - June

ONE-ZY, TWO-ZY -Phil Harris (Vocal) and His Orchestra; Kay Kyser (The Moonbeams)

ALL THROUGH THE DAY -Frank Sinatra; Perry Como;
    Margaret Whiting
SHOO FLY PIE AND APPLE PAN DOWDY -Stan Kenton
    (June Christy); Dinah Shore
SIOUX CITY SUE -Bing Crosby and The King's Jesters;
    Tony Pastor (Vocal) and his Orchestra
LAUGHING ON THE OUTSIDE (CRYING ON THE
    INSIDE) -Dinah Shore; Andy Russell; Sammy Kaye (Billy
    Williams)
I DON'T KNOW ENOUGH ABOUT YOU -Peggy Lee
BUMBLE BOOGIE -Freddy Martin (Instrumental)
THE GYPSY -The Ink Spots; Dinah Shore
SEEMS LIKE OLD TIMES -Vaughn Monroe (Vocal, with
    The Norton Sisters) and His Orchestra; Guy Lombardo
    (Don Rodney)
PRISONER OF LOVE (From 1931) -Perry Como; Billy
    Eckstine
BEWARE, BROTHER, BEWARE -Louis Jordan (Vocal) and
    His Tympany Five
THE HOUSE OF BLUE LIGHTS -Freddy Slack (Ella Mae
    Morse)
IN LOVE IN VAIN -Dick Haymes and Helen Forrest;
    Margaret Whiting; Les Brown (Jack Haskell)
FULL MOON AND EMPTY ARMS (Adapted from
    Rachmaninoff's Piano Concerto No. 2 in C-Minor) -Frank
    Sinatra; Ray Noble (Snooky Lanson)
CEMENT MIXER (PUT-TI, PUT-TI) -The Slim Gaillard
    Trio; Horace Heidt (Rocky Coluccio)
THEY SAY IT'S WONDERFUL -Perry Como; Frank
    Sinatra; Bing Crosby; Andy Russell

DON'T BE A BABY, BABY -Benny Goodman (Art Lund);
   The Mills Brothers
THE GIRL THAT I MARRY -Frank Sinatra
IF YOU WERE THE ONLY GIRL IN THE WORLD (From
   1919) -Perry Como
OH, BUT I DO -Bing Crosby; Harry James (Buddy DeVito)
COME RAIN OR COME SHINE -Dick Haymes and Helen
   Forrest; Margaret Whiting

July - September

I GOT THE SUN IN THE MORNING -Les Brown (Doris
   Day)
BOOGIE BLUES -Gene Krupa (Anita O'Day)
STONE COLD DEAD IN THE MARKET -Ella Fitzgerald
   and Louis Jordan
DOIN' WHAT COMES NATUR'LLY -Dinah Shore; Freddy
   Martin (Glen Hughes)
ALL BY MYSELF (From 1921) -Bing Crosby
SURRENDER -Perry Como; Woody Herman (Vocal) and His
   Orchestra
HAWAIIAN WAR CHANT (From 1938) -Spike Jones and
   His "City Slickers"
PUT YOUR DREAMS AWAY -Frank Sinatra
TO EACH HIS OWN -The Ink Spots; Eddy Howard (Vocal)
   and His Orchestra; Freddy Martin (Stuart Wade); Tony
   Martin
(GET YOUR KICKS ON) ROUTE 66 -The King Cole Trio
   (Nat "King" Cole); Bing Crosby and The Andrews Sisters
MY SUGAR IS SO REFINED -Johnny Mercer

BLUE SKIES (From 1927) -Benny Goodman (Art Lund);
  Bing Crosby
ON THE ALAMO (From 1922) -Benny Goodman (Art Lund)
FIVE MINUTES MORE -Frank Sinatra; Tex Beneke (Vocal)
  and The Glenn Miller Orchestra
CHOO CHOO CH'BOOGIE -Louis Jordan (Vocal) and His
  Tympany Five
SOUTH AMERICA, TAKE IT AWAY -Bing Crosby and The
  Andrews Sisters; Xavier Cugat (Buddy Clark)
YOU CALL IT MADNESS (BUT I CALL IT LOVE) -Billy
  Eckstine; The King Cole Trio (Nat "King" Cole)
I GUESS I'LL GET THE PAPERS AND GO HOME -The
  Mills Brothers; Les Brown (Jack Haskell)
THE COFFEE SONG -Frank Sinatra
THIS IS ALWAYS -Harry James (Buddy DeVito); Jo Stafford
NIGHT AND DAY (From 1932) -Bing Crosby

October - December

RUMORS ARE FLYING -Frankie Carle (Marjorie Hughes);
  The Andrews Sisters, with accompaniment by Les Paul,
  electric guitar; Tony Martin; The Three Suns
YOU KEEP COMING BACK LIKE A SONG -Bing Crosby;
  Dinah Shore; Jo Stafford
THE THINGS WE DID LAST SUMMER -Jo Stafford;
  Vaughn Monroe (Vocal) and His Orchestra
IN A SHANTY IN OLD SHANTY TOWN (From 1932) -
  Johnny Long (Band Chorus)
OLE BUTTERMILK SKY -Hoagy Carmichael; Kay Kyser
  (Jack Martin and The Campus Kids)

THE WHOLE WORLD IS SINGING MY SONG -Les Brown
(Doris Day)
YOU MAKE ME FEEL SO YOUNG -Dick Haymes
(I LOVE YOU) FOR SENTIMENTAL REASONS -The King
Cole Trio (Nat "King" Cole); Ella Fitzgerald and The
Delta Rhythm Boys; Eddy Howard Vocal) and His
Orchestra; Charlie Spivak (Jimmy Saunders); Dinah Shore
ZIP-A-DEE-DOO-DAH (Academy Award-winner from the
film, *Song of the South*) -Johnny Mercer and The Pied
Pipers
THE BEST MAN -The King Cole Trio (Nat "King" Cole);
Les Brown (Butch Stone)
HUGGIN' AND CHALKIN' -Hoagy Carmichael; Kay Kyser
(Mike Douglas and The Campus Kids)
THE OLD LAMPLIGHTER -Sammy Kaye (Billy Williams);
Kay Kyser (Mike Douglas and The Campus Kids)
FOR YOU, FOR ME, FOREVERMORE -Dick Haymes and
Judy Garland
THE CHRISTMAS SONG -The King Cole Trio (Nat "King"
Cole)
A GAL IN CALICO -Bing Crosby; Johnny Mercer and The
Pied Pipers; Tex Beneke (Vocal, with The Crew
Chiefs) and The Glenn Miller Orchestra
WINTER WONDERLAND (From 1934) -The Andrews
Sisters, with The Guy Lombardo Orchestra; Johnny
Mercer and The Pied Pipers; Perry Como and The
Satisfiers

Of this year's favorite songs, the following achieved the
greatest popularity, according to results of the weekly radio

survey, *Your Hit Parade*: THE GYPSY; TO EACH HIS OWN; OH! WHAT IT SEEMED TO BE; SYMPHONY; THEY SAY IT'S WONDERFUL; FIVE MINUTES MORE; ALL THROUGH THE DAY; IT MIGHT AS WELL BE SPRING; RUMORS ARE FLYING; LET IT SNOW! LET IT SNOW! LET IT SNOW! and SURRENDER.

With regard to longevity, THE CHRISTMAS SONG and YOU'RE NOBODY 'TIL SOMEBODY LOVES YOU outlasted all other songs which were new this year.

Instrumental "Collector's Items"

With a growing emphasis in the recording studios on independent singers and ballads, the bands were recording less and devoting less of their recording time to the once-popular instrumentals. The year's short supply included the following:

THE KING	-Count Basie
BLUE SKIES	-Count Basie
JIVIN' JOE JACKSON	-Count Basie
MAD BOOGIE	-Count Basie
HEY! BA-BA-RE-BOP	-Tex Beneke
THEN I'LL BE HAPPY	-Tommy Dorsey
THERE'S GOOD BLUES TONIGHT	-Tommy Dorsey
SWAMP FIRE	-Duke Ellington
OH! BABY (1&2)	-Benny Goodman
AIR MAIL SPECIAL (1&2)	-Lionel Hampton
BLOWIN' UP A STORM	-Woody Herman
SIDEWALKS OF CUBA	-Woody Herman

SOME DAY SWEETHEART	-Woody Herman
I SURRENDER DEAR	-Woodchoppers
FAN IT	-Woodchoppers
WHO'S SORRY NOW	-Harry James
INTERMISSION RIFF	-Stan Kenton
CONCERTO TO END ALL CONCERTOS	-Stan Kenton
ARTISTRY JUMPS	-Stan Kenton
SHERWOOD'S FOREST	-Bobby Sherwood

Developments This Year in Popular Music

- On January 17, the postwar version of the Glenn Miller Orchestra, under the direction of Tex Beneke, opened at the Capitol Theater in New York. It was made up mostly of Air Force Band alumni, with a major absentee being singer Johnny Desmond - unfortunate, since he had become such an integral part of the service unit, singing so well and becoming a major attraction, similar to the featured vocalist of any leading civilian band. The band included twelve violinists, although economics would soon dictate elimination of the strings.

- From the start, the year proved to be a high-water mark for Frankie Carle, his orchestra and his girl singer, daughter Marjorie Hughes. Their recording of OH! WHAT IT SEEMED TO BE became a hit early and they scored again toward the end of the year with RUMORS ARE FLYING.

- It was an important year in the career of singer Perry Como, as he had several hits, led by the million-selling

PRISONER OF LOVE and I'M ALWAYS CHASING RAIN-
BOWS.

- The Ink Spots, still going strong seven years after their
first hit, IF I DIDN'T CARE, made them nationally known,
crowned their great career with million-sellers of the year's
two biggest hits, TO EACH HIS OWN and THE GYPSY.

- Oddly, TO EACH HIS OWN was not heard in the film of
that name, for which Olivia DeHavilland won an "Oscar" as
Best Actress. It should be noted that Eddy Howard's and
Freddy Martin's records of this top hit also exceeded a million
copies sold.

- A million copies were also sold of Bing Crosby's McNA-
MARA'S BAND and SOUTH AMERICA, TAKE IT AWAY.
Actually, Bing teamed with The King's Jesters vocal trio on
"McNamara" (It was originally their number.) and with The
Andrews Sisters on "South America." Those girls had another
million-seller in WINTER WONDERLAND, recorded with
Guy Lombardo, further proof of their versatility, as well as
their continuing appeal.

- Louis Jordan and His Tympany Five achieved the magic
number twice this year, with BEWARE, BROTHER,
BEWARE and CHOO CHOO CH'BOOGIE.

- Stan Kenton, with June Christy singing SHOO FLY PIE
AND APPLE PAN DOWDY also reached that mark, as did
Spike Jones and His City Slickers for their GLOW WORM.

- In a recording session on September 16, Les Brown made

one of the best records of his long career: I'VE GOT MY LOVE TO KEEP ME WARM. In one of the finest examples of skillful arranging, Skip Martin took this otherwise quite average 1937 ballad and crafted it into one of the best swing instrumentals ever. However, the work of genius was temporarily nullified when this recording was lost in the vaults of Columbia Records until the winter of 1948-1949, when it was finally found at Les Brown's continued urging and finally issued to become the big hit it was destined to be.

- Nat "King" Cole and his Trio further established themselves with GET YOUR KICKS ON ROUTE 66; (I LOVE YOU) FOR SENTIMENTAL REASONS; THE FRIM FRAM SAUCE; YOU CALL IT MADNESS, BUT I CALL IT LOVE and THE CHRISTMAS SONG.

- A SUNDAY KIND OF LOVE, sung by Fran Warren with Claude Thornhill's orchestra, was one of those "dark horse" recordings of the big band years. While somewhat overshadowed during its year of release, it gained more stature with the passing of time.

- As this year wore on, it became noticeable that it was different, musically, from preceding years. With the sharp reduction in band recordings, offset by increased recording by independent singers, the listener to radio music sensed that something was lacking. For one thing, the majority of songs being heard, including those which sold millions of copies, did not compare in quality with those heard in the peak years, 1939-1942. It also seems, in retrospect, that the occasional record contributions of a handful of bands this year, were just

enough to deceive their longtime followers into believing that
it was only a matter of the pace having slowed somewhat,
concealing the fact that this was really the "last gasp." The
music-loving public, no doubt preoccupied with the many
aspects of transition from war to peacetime activities, was
caught unaware. Even the breakup of several of the leading
bands at year-end went practically unnoticed and only the
passage of time would make it increasingly clear that this was
the year which marked the end of an era.

Author's Epilogue

The big bands and the kind of music that was prevalent during their reign were sorely missed. To paraphrase what a lyricist once wrote about the lingering effect after a song had ended, although the music had stopped, the songs kept playing in our heads. While each month's and each year's favorite songs were continually replaced by others during that period, they were all filed away in people's memories, so that at least parts of the words and music would be remembered for years. In many instances, hearing an old song is reminiscent of a particular time, an event which took place and people with whom we were associated. The writer's experience was that he could also remember specific moments when he heard certain songs, the room he was in, and even the location of the radio, phonograph or juke box in that room - and that included a great many cities, towns and military bases.

It can't be stressed too much how so many people of different ages loved the recordings we have listed in this book. The strength of that love was so durable that many of the songs were converted into popular classics, being rerecorded time and time again by others over the years. But it usually proved difficult to improve on the original versions. Relatively few of these were later made available to collectors and the rest have faded from memory, as leaves fall from trees. Most unhelpful, in terms of their being remembered, was the fact that there was no written record of these twelve years of music which filled the lives of millions with pleasure - a gross injustice to all concerned, particularly the musicians, the bandleaders and

225

singers, all those talented artists who were responsible for so much happiness.

It is hoped that this accounting will help to fill the void, as well as give deserved recognition to those artists named herein who have received precious little since making their highly esteemed and deeply appreciated contributions.

Bibliography

Connor, D. Russell and Hicks, Warren W.: *BG On the Record, A Bio-Discography of Benny Goodman*; Arlington House, New Rochelle, New York, NY, 1969

Crowther, Bruce & Pinfold, Mike: *The Big Band Years*; Facts On File Publications, New York, NY, 1988

Ewen, David: *American Popular Songs, From the Revolutionary War to the Present*; Random House, New York, NY, 1984

Flower, John: *Moonlight Serenade,* (A Glenn Miller Discography); Arlington House, Inc., New Rochelle, NY, 1972

Fernett, Gene: *A Thousand Golden Horns*; Pendell Publications, Midland, MI, 1966

Jacobs, Dick: *Who Wrote That Song?* ; Betterway Publications, Inc., White Hall, VA, 1988

Kinkle, Roger D.: *The Complete Encyclopedia of Popular Music and Jazz 1900-1950* Volumes (I-IV); Arlington House, New Rochelle, NY, 1974

Lax, Roger and Smith, Frederick: *The Great Song Thesaurus*; Oxford University Press, New York, NY, 1984

McCarthy, Albert: *The Dance Band Era*; Chilton Book Co., Philadelphia, PA, 1971

Murells, Joseph: *Million Selling Records From the 1900s to the 1980s*; Arco Publishing Company, Inc., New York, NY, 1985

Rust, Brian: *The American Dance Band Discography 1917-1942 (Volumes I&II)*; Arlington House, New Rochelle, NY, 1975

Rust, Brian, with DeBus, Allen G.: *The Complete Entertainment Discography, From the Mid-1890s to 1942*; Arlington House, New Rochelle, NY, 1973

Shapiro, Nat: *Popular Music, 1920-1979*; Volume 2, 1940-1949, Volume 4, 1930-1939; Adrian Press, New York, NY, 1965 & 1968

Simon, George T.: *The Big Bands*, (4th Edition); Schirmer Books, a Division of MacMillan Publishing Co., Inc., New York, NY, 1981

Whitburn, Joel: *Pop Memories 1890-1954*; Record Research, Inc., Menomonee Falls, WI, 1986

Williams, John R.: *This Was Your Hit Parade*; Printed by Courier-Gazette, Inc., Portland, ME, 1973

Index of Songs and Instrumentals

The index lists three types of songs:

1. Titles of popular "Hit Parade"-type songs. These are followed by the trimester and year in which they became popular. (See: About a Quarter to Nine, below) The reader may then turn to the year and trimester to learn the names of the recording artists.

2. Titles of pre-Big Band Era songs which continued to be heard between 1935 and 1946. These are followed only by the years in which they were written - unless they were repopularized, in which case they are also followed by the trimester and year of new popularity. (See: Adios, and Ain't It a Shame, below, for two variations of this type. As indicated, Adios was repopularized while Ain't It a Shame was not, but is listed as one of many older songs which were heard from time to time.)

3. Titles of "Collector's Item" songs, which may either have been pre-Big Band Era songs which were given swing arrangements or newly-written songs. These are followed by the year they were written and/or introduced and the artist's name. An asterisk further identifies them as "Collector's Items." All available information about such songs is contained in the index listing. For example, the listing for After You've Gone (below) shows that it was written in 1918, was given a swing treatment on three different occasions by Benny Goodman and once each by Tommy Dorsey and Gene Krupa.

229

About a Quarter to Nine April-June, 1935
Absent-Minded Moon 1942 (Artie Shaw)*
Accent On Youth July-Sept., 1935
Ac-cent-tchuate the Positive Jan.-Mar., 1945
Address Unknown Oct.-Dec., 1939
Adios 1931; July-Sept., 1941
Admiration 1935 (Duke Ellington)*
Afraid to Dream July-Sept., 1937
After All Oct.-Dec., 1939; 1941 (Duke Ellington)*
After Hours 1940 (Erskine Hawkins)*
After You've Gone 1918,
    1935 (Benny Goodman Trio)*;
    1936 (Tommy Dorsey)*
    1941 (Gene Krupa)*
    1942 (Benny Goodman Full Band)*;
    1945 (Benny Goodman Sextet)*
Ain't It a Shame 1922
Ain't Misbehavin' 1929,
    1945 (Benny Goodman, Harry James)*
Ain't She Sweet? 1927
Ain't We Got Fun? 1921
Air Mail Special 1941 (Benny Goodman)*;
    1946 (Lionel Hampton)*
Air Mail Stomp 1939 (Bob Crosby)*
Alabamy Bound 1925
Alexander's Ragtime Band 1911,
    1936 (Benny Goodman)*
    July-Sept., 1938
Alice Blue Gown 1920
All Alone 1924
All Alone and Lonely July-Sept., 1941
All Ashore Oct.-Dec., 1938
All By Myself 1921, July-Sept., 1946
All God's Chillun Got Rhythm 1937 (Duke Ellington)*
All I Do Is Dream of You 1934

All I Need Is You April-June, 1942
All I Remember Is You April-June, 1939
All My Life April-June, 1936
All of Me 1931, April-June, 1939
All of My Life April-June, 1945
All Or Nothing At All (Recorded 1939) July-Sept., 1943
All the Things You Are Oct.-Dec., 1939
All This and Heaven Too July-Sept., 1940
All Through the Day April-June, 1946
All You Want To Do Is Dance July-Sept., 1937
Alone 1935 (Jimmie Lunceford)*; Jan.-Mar., 1936
Along the Navajo Trail July-Sept., 1945
Along the Santa Fe Trail Oct.-Dec., 1940
Always 1926, Oct.,-Dec., 1944
Always In My Heart April-June, 1942
Amapola 1924, Jan.-Mar., 1941
Amen April-June, 1942
American Patrol 1924, April-June, 1942
Am I Blue? 1929
Among My Souvenirs 1927
Amor April-June, 1944
An Apple For the Teacher July-Sept., 1939
And Her Tears Flowed Like Wine July-Sept., 1944
And So Do I Oct.-Dec., 1940
And the Angels Sing April-June, 1939
And Then Some July-Sept., 1935
Angels Came Thru, The July-Sept., 1941
Angels With Dirty Faces Oct.-Dec., 1938
Anniversary Waltz Jan.-Mar., 1942
Answer Man 1941 (Harry James)*

Basie Boogie 1941 (Count Basie)*
Basin Street Blues 1929
    (A later Jack Teagarden theme
    song) Hit revival: Oct.-Dec., 1937
Battle Axe 1941 (Jimmie Lunceford)*
Battle of Swing 1939 (Duke Ellington)*
Beale Street Blues 1916, 1937 (Tommy
    Dorsey)*
Bean At the Met 1944 (Coleman
    Hawkins)*
Bear Mash Blues 1942 (Erskine
    Hawkins)*
Beat Me Daddy, Eight to the Bar July-
    Sept., 1940
Beau Brummel 1941 (Count Basie)*
Beautiful Lady In Blue, A Jan.-Mar.,
    1936
Be Careful, It's My Heart July-Sept.,
    1942
Beer Barrel Polka April-June, 1939
Begin the Beguine Oct.-Dec., 1935;
    Oct.-Dec., 1938; April-June, 1945
Bei Mir Bist Du Schoen Jan.-Mar.,
    1938
Bell Bottom Trousers April-June, 1945
Bells of St. Mary's, The 1917, Jan.-
    Mar., 1946
Bells of San Raquel, The Oct.-Dec.,
    1941
Benny Rides Again 1940 (Benny
    Goodman)*
Besame Mucho Jan.-Mar., 1944
Best Man, The Oct.-Dec., 1946
Best Things in Life Are Free, The 1927
Betty Co-ed 1930
Between a Kiss and a Sigh Jan.-Mar.,
    1939
Between 18th and 19th On Chestnut
    Street Jan.-Mar., 1940
Between the Devil and the Deep Blue
    Sea 1931, Oct.-Dec., 1939

Beware, Brother, Beware April-June,
    1946
Bewitched (Bothered and Bewildered)
    Jan.-Mar., 1941
Beyond the Blue Horizon 1930, 1941
    (Artie Shaw)*
Bidin' My Time 1930
Big Apple, The July-Sept., 1937
Big Chief DeSoto 1936 (Bob Crosby)*
Big Dipper, The 1937 (Larry Clinton,
    Artie Shaw)*
Big John's Special 1936 (Erskine
    Hawkins)*; 1938 (Benny
    Goodman)*
Big Noise From Winnetka Oct.-Dec.,
    1940
Bigwig in the Wigwam 1939 (Woody
    Herman)*
Bijou 1945 (Woody Herman)*
Bill Bailey, Won't You Please Come
    Home? 1902
Birmingham Breakdown 1941 (Charlie
    Barnet)*
Birth of the Blues 1926, April-June,
    1941
Bishop's Blues 1941 (Woody Herman)*
Bizet Has His Day 1941, 1944 (Les
    Brown)*
Black and Blue 1929
Black and Tan Fantasy 1935 (Jimmie
    Lunceford)*
Black Butterfly 1937 (Duke Ellington)*
Black Zephyr 1942 (Bob Crosby)*
Blame It On My Last Affair Jan.-Mar.,
    1939
Bless 'Em All April-June, 1941
Blossoms On Broadway Oct.-Dec.,
    1937
Blowin' Up a Storm 1946 (Woody
    Herman)*
Blow Top 1940 (Count Basie)*

Boy Meets Girl (a.k.a. Grand Slam) 1940 (Benny Goodman)*
Boy Meets Horn 1939 (Duke Ellington)*; (Benny Goodman)*
Boy Next Door, The Oct.-Dec., 1944
Braggin' in Brass 1938 (Duke Ellington)*
Brass Boogie (1& 2) 1942 (Bob Crosby)*
Brazil Jan.-Mar., 1943
Breeze and I, The April-June, 1940
Breezin' Along With the Breeze 1926
Broadway Rhythm Oct.-Dec., 1935
Broken Record, The Jan.-Mar., 1936
Brown Skin Gal, The 1941 (Duke Ellington)*
Buckle Down Winsocki July-Sept., 1941
Buffet Flat 1938 (Duke Ellington)*
Bugle Blues 1942 (Count Basie)*
Bugle Call Rag 1923, 1935 (Ray Noble)*;
   1936 (Benny Goodman)*;
   1940 (Glenn Miller)*
Bumble Bee Stomp 1938 (Benny Goodman)*
Bumble Boogie April-June, 1946
Busy as a Bee 1940 (Benny Goodman)*
But Not For Me 1930, July-Sept., 1942
Button Up Your Overcoat 1928
Buzz, Buzz, Buzz 1940 (Bob Chester)*
Bye-Bye, Baby July-Sept., 1936
Bye-Bye, Blackbird 1926
Bye-Bye Blues 1930, 1938 (Gene Krupa)*
By the Beautiful Sea 1914
By the Light of the Silv'ry Moon 1909, Jan.-Mar., 1942
By the River Sainte Marie 1931, 1939 (Tommy Dorsey)*
By the Waters of Minnetonka 1915, 1938 (Glenn Miller)*

Cabin in the Sky Oct.-Dec., 1940; April-June, 1943
Cafe Society Blues 1942 (Count Basie)*
Caldonia April-June, 1945
California, Here I Come 1921
Calliope Blues 1938 (Woody Herman)*
Call of the Canyon Oct.-Dec., 1940
Call of the Freaks, The 1938 (Artie Shaw)*
Canadian Capers 1922, 1937 (Tommy Dorsey)*
Candy Jan.-Mar., 1945
Can I Forget You? Oct.-Dec., 1937
Can I Help It? Oct.-Dec., 1939
Can't Get Out of This Mood Jan.-Mar., 1943
Can't Help Lovin' Dat Man 1927
Can't We Be Friends? 1938 (Bob Crosby)*
Can't You Read Between the Lines? July-Sept., 1945
Caravan July-Sept., 1937
Careless Oct.-Dec., 1939 (Eddy Howard Theme Song)
Careless Love 1921
Carelessly April-June, 1937
Caribbean Clipper 1942 (Glenn Miller)*
Carioca, The 1933, 1939 (Artie Shaw)*
Carnival 1942 (Artie Shaw)*
Carnival of Venice 1940 (Larry Clinton)*;
   1941 (Harry James)*
Carolina in the Morning 1922
Carolina Moon 1928
Casa Loma Stomp 1937 (Glen Gray)*
Casbah Blues 1939 (Woody Herman)*
Cathedral in the Pines April-June, 1938
Cecelia 1925, April-June, 1940
Celery Stalks at Midnight Oct.-Dec., 1940
Cement Mixer (Put-ti, Put-ti) April-June, 1946

Concerto For Trumpet 1939 (Harry James)*
Concerto to End All Concertos 1946 (Stan Kenton)*
Confessin' (That I Love You) 1930, 1941 (Artie Shaw)*; Oct.-Dec., 1944
Conga Brava 1940 (Duke Ellington)*
Constantinople 1928
Continental, The 1934
Contrasts 1940 (Jimmy Dorsey Signature Tune)*
Copenhagen 1925, 1937 (Artie Shaw)*
Coquette 1928 (Guy Lombardo Signature Tune)*; July-Sept., 1939
Cottage For Sale 1930, Oct.-Dec., 1945
Cotton Club Stomp 1939 (Duke Ellington)*
Cotton Tail 1940 (Duke Ellington)*
Could Be Jan.-Mar., 1939
Count, The 1941 (Benny Goodman)*
Count's Idea, The 1939 (Charlie Barnet)*
Cow Cow Boogie July-Sept., 1942
Crazy Rhythm 1928, 1940 Benny Goodman)*; 1942 (Harry James)*
Cream Puff 1937 (Artie Shaw)*
Crescendo in Blue 1937 (Duke Ellington)*
Cross-Country Jump 1939 (Harry James)*
Cross Patch July-Sept., 1936
Cross Your Heart 1940 & 1943 (Artie Shaw Gramercy Five)*
Cry, Baby, Cry April-June, 1938
Cryin' For the Carolines 1930
Cuban Sugar Mill 1944 (Freddy Slack)*
Cucaracha, La 1916
Cuckoo in the Clock Jan.-Mar., 1939

Cuddle Up a Little Closer 1908, Oct.-Dec., 1943
Cup of Coffee, a Sandwich and You, A 1925

Daddy April-June, 1941
Dance of the Blue Devils 1937 (Les Brown's original Signature Tune)*
Dance With a Dolly Oct.-Dec., 1944
Dancing in the Dark 1931, Jan.-Mar., 1941; 1944 (Artie Shaw reissue)*
Dancing With Tears in My Eyes 1930
Danny Boy (See: Londonderry Air)
Danza Lucumi 1940 (Artie Shaw)*
Dardanella 1919
Dark Eyes 1926, 1945 (Gene Krupa Trio)*
(When it's) Darkness on the Delta 1932
Darktown Poker Club, The Jan.-Mar., 1946
Darktown Strutters' Ball, The 1917; 1938 (Jimmy Dorsey)*
Darling Je Vous Aime Beaucoup Oct.-Dec., 1943
Darn That Dream Oct.-Dec., 1939
Davenport Blues 1925, 1938 (Tommy Dorsey)*
Day After Day 1932, Oct.-Dec., 1938
Day After Forever, The July-Sept., 1944
Daybreak Oct.-Dec., 1942
Daybreak Serenade 1945 (Les Brown)*
Day By Day Jan.-Mar., 1946
Day Dreaming Jan.-Mar., 1942
Day Dreams Come True at Night Oct.-Dec., 1939 (Dick Jurgens Theme Song)
Day In, Day Out July-Sept. 1939
Dearly Beloved July-Sept., 1942
Dear Mom Jan.-Mar., 1942
Dear Old Donegal Jan.-Mar., 1946

Dear Old Southland 1921,
    1935 & 1942 (Benny Goodman)*
Dedicated to You Jan.-Mar., 1937
'Deed I Do 1926
Deep in a Dream Oct.-Dec., 1938
Deep in the Blues 1941 (Count Basie)*
Deep in the Heart of Texas Jan.-Mar.,
    1942
Deep Night 1929, Oct.-Dec., 1939;
    1940 (Woody Herman)*
Deep Purple Jan.-Mar., 1939
Deep River 1917, 1941 (Tommy
    Dorsey)*
Delilah July-Sept., 1941
Der Fuehrer's Face July-Sept., 1942
Devil May Care April-June, 1940
Devil Sat Down and Cried, The Jan.-
    Mar., 1942
Diane 1927
Did I Remember? July-Sept., 1936
Did You Ever See a Dream Walking?
    1934
Did You Mean It? Oct.-Dec., 1936
Diga Diga Doo 1928, 1938 (Bob
    Crosby)*
Dig You Later (A-Hubba-Hubba-
    Hubba) Jan.-Mar., 1946
Diminuendo in Blue 1937 (Duke
    Ellington)*
Dinah 1925, 1935 (Ray Noble)*;
    1936 (Benny Goodman Quartet)*
Dinah's in a Jam 1938 (Duke
    Ellington)*
Ding-Dong, the Witch is Dead! July-
    Sept., 1939
Dinner For One, Please James Jan.-
    Mar., 1936
Dinner Music For a Pack of Hungry
    Cannibals 1937 (Raymond Scott
    Quintet)*

Dipper Mouth Blues 1924, 1936
    (Jimmy Dorsey)*; 1938 (Glenn
    Miller)*
Dipsy Doodle, The Jan.-Mar., 1938
    (Larry Clinton wrote it, used it as
    his signature tune, but was legally
    prevented from recording it.)
Dirty Dozens, The 1938 (Count Basie)*
Dixieland Shuffle 1936 (Bob Crosby)*
Doctor Jazz 1937 (Woody Herman)*
Doctor, Lawyer, Indian Chief Jan.-
    Mar., 1946
Doctor Livingstone, I Presume 1940
    (Artie Shaw Gramercy Five)*
Dodgers' Fan Dance 1941 (Harry
    James)*
Do-Do-Do 1926
Does Your Heart Beat For Me? Jan.-
    Mar., 1939 (Russ Morgan Theme
    Song)
Doggin' Around 1938 (Count Basie)*
Dogtown Blues 1938 (Bob Crosby)*
Do I Love You? Jan.-Mar., 1940
Doin' the Jive 1937 (Glenn Miller)*
Doin' What Comes Natur'lly July-
    Sept., 1946
(Please) Do it Again 1922
Do I Worry? April-June, 1941
Dolores April-June, 1941
Donkey Serenade, The April-June, 1937
Do Nothin' Till You Hear From Me
    Jan.-Mar., 1944 (Originally
    Concerto For Cootie 1940)
Don't Be a Baby, Baby April-June,
    1946
Don't Be That Way April-June, 1938
Don't Blame Me 1933
Don't Fence Me In Oct.-Dec., 1944
Don't Get Around Much Any More
    Jan.-Mar., 1943 (Originally Never
    No Lament 1940)

Don't Give Up the Ship Oct.-Dec., 1935

Don't Sit Under the Apple Tree April-June, 1942

Don't Take Your Love From Me 1940, Oct.-Dec., 1941; Oct.-Dec., 1944

Don't Worry 'Bout Me April-June, 1939

Doodle Doo Doo 1924 (Art Kassel Signature Tune)

Doo Wacka Doo 1924

Double or Nothing 1937 (Woody Herman)*

Double Trouble July-Sept., 1935

Down Among the Sheltering Palms 1914

Down Argentina Way Oct.-Dec., 1940

Down By the O-Hi-O 1920

Down By the Old Ox Road 1933

Down By the River Jan.-Mar., 1935

Down For Double 1941(Count Basie)*

Down Home Rag 1938 (Tommy Dorsey)*

Down the Road A Piece Oct.-Dec., 1940

Down Under 1942 (Woody Herman)*

Do You Care? July-Sept., 1941

Do You Ever Think of Me? 1920, July-Sept., 1940

Do You Know Why? Oct.-Dec., 1940

Do You Wanna Jump, Chillun? 1939 (Erskine Hawkins)*

Do You Want to Jump, Children? 1938 (Charlie Barnet)*

Dracula 1939 (Gene Krupa)*

Dream April-June, 1945

Dream a Little Dream of Me 1931

Dreamer, The Oct.-Dec., 1943

Dreamsville, Ohio Oct.-Dec., 1941

Drifting and Dreaming 1925 (Orrin Tucker Signature Tune)

Drum Boogie April-June, 1941

Duke's Idea, The 1939 (Charlie Barnet)*

Duke's Mixture 1941 (Harry James)*

Dupree Blues 1937 (Woody Herman)*

Dusk 1940 (Duke Ellington)*; 1942 (Artie Shaw)*

Dusk in the Desert 1937 (Duke Ellington)*

Dusk in Upper Sandusky 1935 (Jimmy Dorsey)*

Eager Beaver 1944 (Stan Kenton)*

Earl, The 1941 (Benny Goodman, Earl Hines)*

Easter Parade 1933, April-June, 1942

East of the Sun (and West of the Moon) July-Sept., 1935; April-June, 1940)

East Side Kick 1939 (Woody Herman)*

East Side of Heaven April-June, 1939

Easy Does It 1939 (Tommy Dorsey*; 1940 (Count Basie)*

Easy to Love Oct.-Dec., 1936

Ebb Tide Oct.-Dec., 1937

Eccentric 1942 (Bob Crosby)*

Echoes of Harlem 1936 (Duke Ellington)*

Ec-Stacy 1942 (Bob Crosby)*

Eenie, Meenie, Miney, Mo Oct.-Dec., 1935

11:60 P. M. July-Sept., 1945

Eli-Eli 1941 (Harry James)*

Elks' Parade 1942 (Bobby Sherwood Signature Tune)*

Elmer's Tune Oct.-Dec., 1941

(Alla En) El Rancho Grande 1934, April-June, 1939

Embraceable You 1930, July-Sept., 1941

Empty Saddles July-Sept., 1936

Especially For You July-Sept., 1939

Estrellita 1914, 1942 (Harry James)*; July-Sept., 1944

For the First Time Oct.-Dec., 1943
Forty Second Street 1932
For You 1930, Jan.-Mar., 1941
For You, For Me, Forevermore Oct.-
Dec., 1946
Four or Five Times 1927
Frenesi Oct.-Dec., 1940
Friendship April-June, 1940
Frim Fram Sauce, The Jan.-Mar., 1946
Froggy Bottom 1936 (Andy Kirk)*
From Now On July-Sept., 1938
From the Top of Your Head to the Tip
of your Toes July-Sept., 1935
Full Dress Hop 1940 (Gene Krupa)*
Full Moon and Empty Arms April-June,
1946
Funny Old Hills, The Oct.-Dec., 1938
Furlough Fling 1943 (Freddy Slack)*
Fur Trappers' Ball 1941 (Woody
Herman)*
Futuristic Shuffle 1938 (Jan Savitt)*

Gal in Calico, A Oct.-Dec., 1946
Gang That Sang Heart of My Heart,
The 1926
Garden in the Rain, A 1929
Garden of the Moon July-Sept., 1938
Gaucho Serenade Jan.-Mar., 1940
G'Bye Now April-June, 1941
Gentleman Obviously Doesn't Believe
(in Love), The Oct.-Dec., 1935
Georgia on My Mind 1930, April-June,
1941; 1941Artie Shaw*
Get Happy 1930, 1936 (Benny
Goodman)*; 1939 (Jan Savitt)
Get Out and Get Under the Moon 1928
Get Out of Town Oct.-Dec., 1938
Get Your Boots Laced, Papa
1940 (Woody Herman)*
Ghost of a Chance, A 1933
Giddybug Gallop, The 1941 (Duke
Ellington)*

G. I. Jive, The April-June, 1944
Gimme a Little Kiss, Will Ya, Huh?
1926, April-June, 1940
Gin Mill Blues 1937 (Bob Crosby)*
Girl Friend of the Whirling Dervish
Oct.-Dec., 1938
Girl of My Dreams 1928, July-Sept.,
1939
Girl That I Marry, The April-June,
1946
Give a Little Whistle Jan.-Mar., 1940
Give Me the Simple Life Jan.-Mar.,
1946
Give My Regards to Broadway 1904
Glen Island Special 1939 (Glenn
Miller)*
Glory of Love, The April-June, 1936
Glow Worm 1907
Gobs of Love April-June, 1943
God Bless America, 1918, April-June,
1939
Going My Way July-Sept., 1944
Goin' to Chicago Blues 1941 (Count
Basie)*
Golden Bantam 1939 (Larry Clinton)*
Golden Wedding, The 1941 (Woody
Herman)*
Golondrina, La 1883
Gone 1941 (Jimmie Lunceford)*
Gone With the Wind July-Sept., 1937
Gone With What Wind? 1940 (Benny
Goodman)*
Goodbye, Little Darlin', Goodbye-July
Sept., 1940
Goodnight Angel Jan.-Mar., 1938
Goodnight, My Love Jan.-Mar., 1937
Goodnight, Sweetheart 1931
Goodnight, Wherever You Are April-
June, 1944
Goody Goody Jan.-Mar., 1936
Goose Hangs High, The 1936 (Woody
Herman)*

Hold Tight, Hold Tight April-June, 1939

Holiday For Strings April-June, 1943

Holy Smoke! (Can't Ya Take a Joke?) Oct.-Dec., 1939

Homesick, That's All Oct.-Dec., 1945

Honeysuckle Rose 1929, 1937 (Count Basie)*; 1939 (Benny Goodman Sextet)*

Honky Tonk Train Blues 1938 (Bob Crosby)*

Hooray For Hollywood Oct.-Dec., 1938

Hot Chestnuts 1941 (Woody Herman)*

Hot Lips 1922 (Henry Busse Signature Tune)*

Hot Time in the Town of Berlin July-Sept., 1944

House of Blue Lights, The Jan.-Mar., 1946

How About You? Jan.-Mar., 1942

How Blue the Night April-June, 1944

How Deep is The Ocean? 1932

How'dja Like to Love Me? Jan.-Mar., 1938

How High the Moon? April-June, 1940

How Long Blues 1938, 1942 (Count Basie)*

How Long Has This Been Going On? Oct.-Dec., 1939

How Many Hearts Have You Broken? July-Sept., 1944

Huggin' and Chalkin' Oct.-Dec., 1946

Humoresque 1894, 1944 (Guy Lombardo)*

Humpty Dumpty Heart Jan.-Mar., 1942

Hurry Home Jan.-Mar., 1939

Hut Sut Song, The April-June, 1941

I Came Here to Talk For Joe Oct.-Dec., 1942

I Can Dream, Can't I? Jan.-Mar., 1938

I Can't Begin to Tell You Oct.-Dec., 1945

I Can't Believe That You're in Love With Me 1927; 1938 (Artie Shaw)*; July-Sept., 1945

I Can't Escape From You July-Sept., 1936

I Can't Get Started (With You) Jan.-Feb., 1938 (Bunny Berigan Theme Song)

I Can't Give You Anything But Love 1928, 1941 (Benny Goodman Sextet)*; April-June, 1942

I Can't Love You Any More April-June, 1940

I Concentrate On You April-June, 1940

I Could Make You Care Oct.-Dec., 1940

I Couldn't Believe My Eyes July-Sept., 1935

I Couldn't Sleep a Wink Last Night Jan.-Mar., 1944

I Could Write a Book April-June, 1941

I Cover the Waterfront 1933, 1941 (Artie Shaw)*

I Cried For You 1923, Jan.-Mar., 1939; July-Sept., 1942

Idaho April-June, 1942

Ida, Sweet as Apple Cider 1903, 1937 (Benny Goodman Quartet)*; April-June, 1941

I Didn't Know About You 1942 (Duke Ellington)*; Jan.-Mar., 1945

I Didn't Know What Time it Was Oct.-Dec., 1939

I'd Know You Anywhere Oct.-Dec., 1940

I Don't Care Who Knows It July-Sept., 1945

I Don't Know Enough About You April-June, 1946

I Don't Know Why 1931

I Know Now July-Sept., 1937

I Know That You Know 1926, 1936 (Benny Goodman)*

I Know Why Oct.-Dec., 1941

I Left My Heart at the Stage Door Canteen July-Sept., 1942

I Let a Song Go Out of My Heart April-June, 1938

(I, Yi, Yi, Yi, Yi,) I Like You Very Much April-June, 1941

I'll Always Be in Love With You 1929, 1938 (Benny Goodman)*

I'll Be Around Oct.-Dec., 1943

I'll Be Home For Christmas Oct.-Dec., 1943

I'll Be Seeing You 1938, April-June, 1944

I'll Be With You in Apple Blossom Time 1920, April-June, 1941

I'll Buy That Dream July-Sept., 1945

I'll Get By 1928, April-June, 1944

I'll Never Be the Same 1932, 1945 (Artie Shaw)*

I'll Never Say "Never Again" Again April-June, 1935

I'll Never Smile Again July-Sept., 1940

I'll Remember April Jan.-Mar., 1942

I'll See You in My Dreams 1924, July-Sept., 1938

I'll Sing You a Thousand Love Songs Oct.-Dec., 1936

I'll String Along With You 1934

I'll Walk Alone July-Sept., 1944

I Lost My Sugar in Salt Lake City Jan.-Mar., 1943

I Love You (Oh! How I Love You) 1935 (Tommy Tucker Theme Song)

I Love You (..."hums the April breeze") Jan.-Mar., 1944

I'm a Big Girl Now Jan.-Mar., 1946

I'm a Ding-Dong Daddy From Dumas 1930, 1937 (Benny Goodman Quartet)*

I'm a Dreamer (Aren't We All?) 1929

Imagination April-June, 1940

I'm Always Chasing Rainbows 1918, Jan.-Mar., 1946

I'm an Old Cowhand July-Sept., 1936

I Married an Angel July-Sept., 1938

I May Be Wrong, But I Think You're Wonderful 1929

I'm Beginning to See the Light Jan.-Mar., 1945

I'm Building Up to an Awful Letdown Jan.-Mar., 1936

I'm Coming Virginia 1926, 1939 (Artie Shaw)*

I'm Confessin' That I Love You (See: Confessin')

I'm Dancing With Tears in My Eyes 1930

I'm Forever Blowing Bubbles 1919

I'm Getting Sentimental Over You 1932 (Tommy Dorsey Theme Song)

I'm Glad I Waited For You Jan.-Mar., 1946

I'm Glad There is You Jan.-Mar., 1942

I'm Gonna Lock My Heart July-Sept., 1938

I'm Gonna Love That Guy (Like He's Never Been Loved Before) July-Sept., 1945

I'm Gonna Sit Right Down and Write Myself a Letter July-Sept., 1935; Jan.-Mar., 1936

I'm in Love With the Honorable Mr. So and So Jan.-Mar., 1939

I'm in the Market For You 1939 (Harry James)*

I'm in the Mood For Love July-Sept., 1935; 1944 (Coleman Hawkins)*

I Still Love to Kiss You Goodnight
Oct.-Dec., 1937

I Surrender Dear 1930, 1937 (Artie
Shaw)*; April-June, 1939; 1940
(Benny Goodman)*

Is You Is, Or Is You Ain't My Baby?
July-Sept., 1944

It Ain't Necessarily So April-June,
1936

It All Comes Back to Me Now Jan.-
Mar., 1941

It All Depends on You 1927

It Can't Be Wrong Jan.-Mar., 1943

It Could Happen to You July-Sept.,
1944

It Don't Mean a Thing (If it Ain't Got
That Swing) 1932

It Had to Be You 1924, 1938 (Benny
Goodman)*; 1939 & 1941 (Artie
Shaw)*; July-Sept., 1944

It Happened Down in Dixieland
1937 (Woody Herman)*

It Happened in Monterrey 1930

It Happened in Sun Valley Oct.-Dec.,
1941

I Thought About You Oct.-Dec., 1939

It Isn't Fair 1933 (Richard Himber
Theme Song)

It Looks Like Rain in Cherry Blossom
Lane April-June, 1937

It Might as Well Be Spring Oct.-Dec.,
1945

It Must Be Jelly, 'Cause Jam Don't
Shake Like That July-Sept., 1942

It's a Blue World Jan.-Mar., 1940

It's a Grand Night For Singing Jan.-
Mar., 1946

It's a Lonesome Old Town 1930 (Ben
Bernie Theme Song)

It's Always You April-June, 1941;
April-June, 1943

It's a Pity to Say Goodnight Jan.-Mar.,
1946

It's a Sin to Tell a Lie April-June, 1936

It's a Wonderful World 1931, April-
June, 1940 (Jan Savitt Theme Song)

It's Been a Long, Long Time July-
Sept., 1945

It's Been So Long Jan.-Mar., 1936

It's De-Lovely Oct.-Dec., 1936

It's Easy to Remember (and So Hard to
Forget) Jan.-Mar., 1935

It's Funny to Everyone But Me July-
Sept., 1939; Oct.-Dec., 1944

It's Love, Love, Love Jan.-Mar., 1944

It's Only a Paper Moon 1933, Oct.-
Dec., 1945

It's So Peaceful in the Country July-
Sept., 1941

It's Square, But it Rocks 1941 (Count
Basie)*

It Started All Over Again Jan.-Mar.,
1943

It's the Dreamer in Me April-June,
1938

It's the Natural Thing to Do July-Sept.,
1937

It's the Talk of the Town 1933,
1945 (Coleman Hawkins)*

It's Time to Jump and Shout 1940 (Jan
Savitt)*

I Understand April-June, 1941

I Used to Be Color Blind Oct.-Dec.,
1938

I've Got a Crush on You 1930

I've Got a Date With a Dream July-
Sept., 1938

I've Got a Feeling I'm Falling 1929

I've Got a Feelin' You're Foolin' Oct.-
Dec., 1935

I've Got a Gal in Kalamazoo
(See: (I've Got a Gal in)
Kalamazoo)

Jump-Jump's Here 1938 (Charlie
Barnet)*
Jump Session 1939 (Charlie Barnet)*
Jump the Blues Away 1941 (Count
Basie)*
Jump Town 1942 & 1943 (Harry
James)*
June in January Jan.-Mar., 1935
June is Bustin' Out All Over July-Sept.,
1945
Jungle Drums 1939 (Artie Shaw)*
Jungle Madness 1939 (Gene Krupa)*
Just a Gigolo 1930
Just a Kid Named Joe Oct.-Dec., 1938
Just a Little Bit South of North Carolina
April-June, 1941
Just a Little Fond Affection Oct.-Dec.,
1945
Just a Prayer Away April-June, 1945
Just A-Sittin' and A-Rockin' Jan.-Mar.,
1946
Just as Though You Were Here July-
Sept., 1942
Just For a Thrill July-Sept., 1939
Just One More Chance 1931, July-
Sept., 1939
Just One of Those Things Oct.-Dec.,
1935; 1945 (Benny Goodman
Sextet)*
Just Plain Lonesome April-June, 1942
Just You, Just Me 1945 (Benny
Goodman)*

(I've Got a Gal in) Kalamazoo July-
Sept., 1942
Kansas City Moods 1940 (Jan Savitt)*
Keepin' Myself For You 1940
(Artie Shaw Gramercy Five)*
Keep Your Sunny Side Up (See: Sunny
Side Up)
Kick It 1941 (Gene Krupa)*
King, The 1946 (Count Basie)*

King Porter Stomp 1924, 1935 (Benny
Goodman)*; 1938 (Glenn Miller)*;
1939 (Harry James)*
Kiss Goodnight, A July-Sept., 1945
Kiss the Boys Goodbye July-Sept., 1941
Knockin' at the Famous Door 1939
(Charlie Barnet)*
Knock, Knock, Who's There? July-
Sept., 1936
Ko-Ko 1940 (Duke Ellington)*

Lady in Blue 1939 (Duke Ellington)*
Lady in Red, The April-June, 1935
Lady is a Tramp, The Oct.-Dec., 1937
Lady's in Love With You, The April-
June, 1939
Lambeth Walk, The Oct.-Dec., 1938;
1938 (Duke Ellington)*
Lament For a Lost Love 1939 (Charlie
Barnet)*
Lament to Love 1941 (Harry James)*
Lamp is Low, The July-Sept., 1939
Lamplight Jan.-Mar., 1937
Lamplighter's Serenade, The April-
June, 1942
Last Call For Love, The April-June,
1942
Last Jump, The 1939 (Charlie Barnet)*
(Why Couldn't it Last) Last Night Oct.-
Dec., 1939
Last Roundup, The 1933
Last Time I Saw Paris, The Jan.-Mar.,
1941
Laughing Boy Blues 1938 (Woody
Herman)*
Laughing on the Outside (Crying on the
Inside) April-June, 1946
Laura April-June, 1945
Lazy Bones 1933, Jan.-Mar., 1939
Lazy Rhapsody 1941 (Woody Herman)*
Lazy River 1931

Long Ago and Far Away April-June, 1944
Long Tall Mama 1941 (Glenn Miller)*
Look For the Silver Lining 1921
Lookie, Lookie, Lookie, Here Comes Cookie Jan.-Mar., 1935
Loose Lid Special 1941 (Tommy Dorsey)*
Loose Wig 1944 (Lionel Hampton)*
Lost Jan.-Mar., 1936
Lost in Love 1941 (Harry James)*
Lost in Meditation 1938 (Duke Ellington)*
Lost in the Shuffle 1938 (Artie Shaw)*
Louise 1929
Louise, Louise 1938 (Bob Crosby)*
Louisiana 1940 (Count Basie)*
Louisiana Hayride 1932
Love and a Dime April-June, 1935
Love Bug Will Bite You, The April-June., 1937
Love For Sale 1920
Love in Bloom 1934
(Our) Love is Here to Stay Jan.-Mar., 1938
Love is Just Around the Corner Jan.-Mar., 1935
Love is Like a Cigarette April-June, 1936
Love is Sweeping the Country 1931
Love is Where You Find It July-Sept., 1938
Love Letters (Straight From My Heart) Oct.-Dec., 1945
Lovelight in the Starlight April-June, 1938
Loveliness of You, The July-Sept., 1937
Lovely to Look At Jan.-Mar., 1935
Lovely Way to Spend an Evening, A Jan.-Mar., 1944
Love Me Forever July-Sept., 1935

Love Me or Leave Me 1928, 1936 (Benny Goodman)*
Lover 1933
Lover Come Back to Me 1928, 1939 (Artie Shaw)*
Lover Man (Oh Where Can You Be?) April-June, 1945
Love Walked In April-June, 1938; 1945 (Benny Goodman)*
Lucky Day 1926
Lullaby in Rhythm 1938 (Benny Goodman, Woody Herman)*
Lullaby of Broadway Jan.-Mar., 1935
Lullaby of the Leaves 1932
Lulu's Back in Town July-Sept., 1935

Macumba 1941 (Charlie Barnet)*
Mad About Him, Sad Without Him, How Can I Be Glad Without Him Blues July-Sept., 1942
Madam Swings It, The 1939 (Gene Krupa)*
Mad Boogie 1946 (Count Basie)*
Magic is the Moonlight 1930
Ma! He's Makin' Eyes at Me 1921, Jan.-Mar., 1940
Main Stem 1942 (Duke Ellington)*
Mairzy Doats Jan.-Mar., 1944
Major and Minor Stomp 1939 (Jimmy Dorsey)*
Make Believe 1928, 1938 (Benny Goodman)*
Make Believe Island April-June, 1940
Makin' Whoopee 1928
Mama Yo Quiero (See: I Want My Mama)
Man and His Dream, A July-Sept., 1939
Man and His Drum, A 1939 (Jimmy Dorsey)*
Mandy 1918

Mister Meadowlark July-Sept., 1940
Mole, The 1942 (Harry James)*
Mood Indigo 1931
Moon Glow 1934,
    1936 (Benny Goodman Quartet)*;
    1941 (Artie Shaw)*
Moon Got in My Eyes, The July-Sept.,
    1937
Moonlight and Roses 1925
Moonlight and Shadows Jan.-Mar.,
    1937
(On) Moonlight Bay 1912
Moonlight Becomes You Oct.-Dec.,
    1942
Moonlight Cocktail Jan.-Mar., 1942
Moonlight Fiesta 1935 (Duke
    Ellington)*
Moonlight in Vermont Jan.-Mar., 1945
Moonlight Mood Jan.-Mar., 1943
Moonlight on the Ganges 1926,
    1941 (Benny Goodman)*;
    1942 (Tommy Dorsey)*
Moonlight Serenade July-Sept., 1939
    (Glenn Miller Theme Song)
Moon Love July-Sept., 1939
Moon Mist 1942 (Duke Ellington)*
Moon of Manakoora Jan.-Mar., 1938
Moon Over Cuba 1941 (Duke
    Ellington)*
Moon Over Miami Jan.-Mar., 1936
Moon Song (That Wasn't Meant For
    Me) 1933
Moon Was Yellow, The 1934
More and More Jan.-Mar., 1945
More I See You, The April-June, 1945
More Than You Know 1929,
    1936 (Benny Goodman Trio)*
Most Beautiful Girl in the World, The
    Jan.-Mar., 1936
Moten Swing 1940 (Count Basie)*
Murder at Peyton Hall 1941 (Charlie
    Barnet)*

"Murder" He Says July-Sept., 1942
Music Goes 'Round and Around, The
    Oct.-Dec., 1935
Music, Maestro, Please April-June,
    1938
Music Makers April-June, 1941
Music Stopped, The Jan.-Mar., 1944
Muskrat Ramble 1926, 1936 (Bob
    Crosby)*
Mutiny in the Brass Section 1936
    (Jimmy Dorsey)*
My Baby Just Cares For Me 1930
My Blue Heaven 1927, 1936 (Jimmie
    Lunceford)*; 1937 (Artie Shaw)*;
    1940 (Glenn Miller)*; Jan.-Mar.,
    1941
My Buddy 1922
My Cabin of Dreams July-Sept., 1937
My Devotion July-Sept., 1942
My Dreams Are Getting Better All the
    Time Jan.-Mar., 1945
My Funny Valentine Jan.-Mar., 1945
My Greatest Mistake Oct.-Dec., 1940
My Guy's Come Back Oct.-Dec., 1945
My Heart Belongs to Daddy Oct.-Dec.,
    1938
My Heart is Taking Lessons April-June,
    1938
My Heart Stood Still 1927, 1939 (Artie
    Shaw)*
My Heart Tells Me Oct.-Dec., 1943
My Honey's Lovin' Arms 1922,
    1938 (Benny Goodman)*
My Ideal 1930, Oct.-Dec., 1943
My Isle of Golden Dreams 1919, July-
    Sept., 1939
My Last Goodbye July-Sept., 1939
My Little Brown Book 1942 (Duke
    Ellington)*
My Little Grass Shack in Kealakekua,
    Hawaii 1934
My Man 1921

Oh, Baby! (1 & 2) 1946 (Benny
   Goodman)*
Oh, But I Do April-June, 1946
Oh! Johnny, Oh! Johnny, Oh! 1917,
   Oct.-Dec., 1939
Oh! Lady Be Good 1924,
   1936 (Benny Goodman Trio)*;
   1936 & 1939 (Red Norvo)*;
   1939 (Artie Shaw)*
Oh! Look at Me Now Jan.-Mar., 1941
Oh, Ma-Ma! (The Butcher Boy) April-
   June, 1938
Oh! What a Beautiful Mornin' Oct.-
   Dec., 1943
Oh! What it Seemed to Be Jan.-Mar.,
   1946
Oh! You Beautiful Doll 1911
Oh! You Crazy Moon July-Sept., 1939
Old Fashioned Swing 1936 (Woody
   Herman)*
Old Folks Oct.-Dec., 1938
Old Lamplighter, The Oct.-Dec., 1946
Ole Buttermilk Sky Oct.-Dec., 1946
Ol' Man River 1927
On a Cocoanut Island Oct.-Dec., 1936
On a Little Street in Singapore Jan.-
   Mar., 1940
Once in Awhile Oct.-Dec., 1937
One Dozen Roses April-June, 1942
One Foot in the Groove 1939 (Artie
   Shaw)*
One For My Baby Jan.-Mar., 1945
One Hour With You 1932
One I Love Belongs to Somebody Else,
   The 1924, July-Sept., 1940
One Meat Ball Jan.-Mar., 1945
One Night Stand 1939 (Artie Shaw)*
One O'Clock Jump
   1937 (Count Basie Signature Tune)*
   1938 (Benny Goodman; Harry
   James All-Stars)*

One Rose, The (That's Left in My
   Heart) 1929, Oct.-Dec., 1937
One, Two, Button Your Shoe Oct.-
   Dec., 1936
One-zy, Two-zy April-June, 1946
Only a Rose 1926, April-June, 1940
Only Forever Oct.-Dec., 1940
On the Alamo 1922, 1941 (Tommy
   Dorsey, Benny Goodman)*; July-
   Sept., 1946
On the Atchison, Topeka and the Santa
   Fe July-Sept., 1945
On the Beach at Bali-Bali April-June,
   1936
On the Beam 1939 (Gene Krupa)*
On the Bumpy Road to Love July-Sept.,
   1938
On the Good Ship Lollipop Jan.-Mar.,
   1935
On the Isle of May Jan.-Mar., 1940
On the Sentimental Side April-June,
   1938
On the Sunny Side of the Street April-
   June, 1945
On Treasure Island Oct.-Dec., 1935
Oomph Fah Fah 1945 (Benny
   Goodman)*
Opus Local 802 1940 (Benny
   Goodman)*
Opus No. 1 Jan.-Mar., 1945
Orange Blossom Lane Oct.-Dec., 1941
Orchids For Remembrance July-Sept.,
   1940
Orchids in the Moonlight 1933
Organ Grinder's Swing Oct.-Dec., 1936
Original Dixieland One-Step 1942 (Bob
   Crosby)*
Our Love April-June, 1939
Our Love Affair July-Sept., 1940
Our Love is Here to Stay (See: (Our)
   Love is Here to Stay)

Prelude in C-Major 1941 (Artie Shaw)*
Prelude to a Kiss 1938 (Duke
    Ellington)*
Prelude to a Stomp 1938 (Gene Krupa)*
Pretty Baby 1916
Pretty Girl is Like a Melody, A 1919
Prince Charming 1942 & 1943 (Harry
    James)*
Prisoner of Love 1931, April-June,
    1946
P. S., I Love You 1934, Jan.-Mar.,
    1935
Pushin' Sand 1942 (Kay Kyser)*
Puttin' on the Ritz 1929
Put Your Arms Around Me, Honey
    July-Sept., 1943
Put Your Dreams Away July-Sept.,
    1946
Pyramid 1938 (Duke Ellington)*;
    1941 (Artie Shaw)*

Quaker City Jazz 1938
    (Early Jan Savitt Signature Tune)
Quiet and Roll 'em 1939 (Gene Krupa)*
Quiet, Please! 1940, 1942 (Tommy
    Dorsey)*

Rachel's Dream 1945 (Benny
    Goodman)*
Racing With the Moon April-June,
    1941 (Vaughn Monroe Theme Song)
Ragtime Cowboy Joe 1912, April-June,
    1939
Rain 1934
Rainbow Rhapsody 1942 (Glenn
    Miller)*
Raincheck 1941 (Duke Ellington)*
Ramona 1927, 1942 (Benny Goodman)*
Ration Blues Jan.-Mar., 1944
Record Session 1941 (Harry James)*
Red Sails in the Sunset Oct.-Dec., 1935

Redskin Rhumba Oct.-Dec., 1940
    (Adopted as his signature tune by
    Charlie Barnet)
Remember 1925, 1945 (Erskine
    Hawkins)*
Remember Me? July-Sept., 1937
Remember Pearl Harbor Jan.-Mar.,
    1942
Reminiscing in Tempo 1935 (Duke
    Ellington)*
Rendezvous With a Dream July-Sept.,
    1936
Rhapsody in Blue 1924, 1942 (Glenn
    Miller)*
Rhumboogie April-June, 1940
Rhythm and Romance July-Sept., 1935
Rhythm is Our Business 1935
    (Jimmie Lunceford Signature
    Tune)*
Rhythm Jam 1938 (Gene Krupa)*
Rhythm of the Rain April-June, 1935
Riding on a Blue Note 1938 (Duke
    Ellington)*
Riffette 1943 (Freddy Slack)*
Riff Interlude 1939 (Count Basie)*
Rigamarole/Rigmarole 1937 (Les
    Brown)*; 1939 (Jimmy Dorsey)*
Ring Dem Bells 1940 (Charlie Barnet)*
Rio Rita 1927 (Ted Fio Rito Theme
    Song)
Riverboat Shuffle 1939 (Glen Gray)*
River, Stay Away From My Door 1931
Robin Hood Jan.-Mar., 1945
Robins and Roses April-June, 1936
Rock-a-Bye Basie 1939 (Count Basie)*
Rock-a-Bye Your Baby With a Dixie
    Melody 1918
Rockin' Chair 1930; April-June, 1937;
    1941 (Artie Shaw)*
Rockin' in Rhythm 1937 (Duke
    Ellington)*; 1940 (Charlie Barnet)*
Rockin' the Blues 1940 (Count Basie)*

Sentimental Lady 1942 & 1943 (Duke
    Ellington)*
Sepia Panorama 1940 (Duke Ellington)*
September in the Rain April-June, 1937
September Song Oct.-Dec., 1938;
    1945 (Artie Shaw)*
Serenade in Blue July-Sept., 1942
Serenade in the Night Jan.-Mar., 1937
Serenade to a Savage 1939 (Artie
    Shaw)*
Serenade to the Spot 1941 (Tommy
    Dorsey)*
Seven Come Eleven 1939 (Benny
    Goodman)*; 1944 (Red Norvo)*
720 in the Books Oct.-Dec., 1939
Shadrach 1931, Oct.-Dec., 1938
Shady Lady 1942 (Charlie Barnet)*
Shake Down the Stars April-June, 1940
Shall We Dance? April-June, 1937
Sharp as a Tack 1941 (Harry James)*
Sheik, The 1940 (Benny Goodman)*
Sheik of Araby, The 1921, 1938
    (Tommy Dorsey)*; 1939 (Woody
    Herman)*; 1940 (Harry James)*
She'll Always Remember April-June,
    1942
Shepherd Serenade Oct.-Dec., 1941
Sherman Shuffle 1942 (Duke Ellington)*
Sherwood's Forest 1946 (Bobby
    Sherwood)*
She's a Latin From Manhattan April-
    June, 1935
She's Funny That Way 1928
She Shall Have Music April-June, 1936
Shindig 1937 (Artie Shaw)*
Shine 1924, 1945 (Benny Goodman
    Sextet)*
Shine on, Harvest Moon 1908
Shoe Shine Boy July-Sept., 1936
Shoo Fly Pie and Apple Pan Dowdy
    April-June, 1946
Shoo, Shoo, Baby Oct.-Dec., 1943

Shorty George 1938 (Count Basie)*
Showboat Shuffle 1935 (Duke
    Ellington)*
Show Me the Way to Go Home 1925
Shrine of St. Cecilia Jan-Mar., 1942
Siboney 1929
Side By Side 1927
Sidewalks of New York, The 1894,
    1941 (Duke Ellington)*
Sidewalks of Cuba 1946 (Woody
    Herman)*
Sierra Sue April-June, 1940
Silver on the Sage Oct.-Dec., 1938
Sing, Baby, Sing July-Sept., 1936
Sing For Your Supper Oct.-Dec., 1938
Singing Hills, The April-June, 1940
Singing Sands of Alamosa, The 1942
    (Woody Herman)*
Singin' in the Rain 1929
Sing, Sing, Sing 1937 (Benny
    Goodman)*
Sing You Sinners 1930
Sinner Kissed an Angel, A Oct.-Dec.,
    1941
Sioux City Sue April-June, 1946
Siren Serenade 1941 (Gene Krupa)*
Siren's Song, The 1939 (Benny
    Goodman)*
Six Appeal 1940 (Benny Goodman)*
Six Flats Unfurnished 1942 (Benny
    Goodman)*
Six Lessons From Madame La Zonga
    July-Sept., 1940
Sixty Seconds Got Together Oct.-Dec.,
    1938
Skeleton in the Closet 1936 (Jimmy
    Dorsey)*; 1937 (Artie Shaw)*
Sky Fell Down, The April-June, 1940
Skylark April-June, 1942
Skyliner 1945 (Charlie Barnet)*
Sleep 1924 (Fred Waring Theme Song)

(By the) Sleepy Lagoon April-June, 1942

Sleepy Time Gal 1925, July-Sept., 1944

Sleepy Town Train 1942 (Glenn Miller)*

Sleigh Ride in July Jan.-Mar., 1945

Slip Horn Jive 1939 (lenn Miller)*

Slip Horn Sam 1935 (Russ Morgan)*

Slipped Disc 1945 (Benny Goodman)*

Slow Freight 1940 (Glenn Miller)*

Slumber Song 1940
(A temporary Glenn Miller signature tune, then used only to close.)*

Slumming on Park Avenue Jan.-Mar., 1937

Small Fry Oct.-Dec., 1938

Smarty July-Sept., 1937

Smile, Darn Ya, Smile 1931

Smiles 1918, 1937 (Benny Goodman Quartet)*

Smoke Gets in Your Eyes 1933, 1940 (Artie Shaw Gramercy Five)*

Smoke House 1938 (benny Goodman)*

Smoke Rings 1930
(Glen Gray Casa Loma Signature Tune)*

Smo-o-o-oth One, A 1941 (Benny Goodman Sextet)*

Smorgasbord and Schnapps 1939 (Duke Ellington)*

Snake Charmer 1938 (Jerry Blaine)*

Snootie Little Cutie Jan.-Mar., 1942

Snowfall 1941 (Claude Thornhill Signature Tune)*

Sobbin' Blues 1937 (Artie Shaw)*; 1938 (Les Brown)*

So Do I Oct.-Dec., 1936

Softly, As in a Morning Sunrise 1928, 1938 (Artie Shaw)*

So Help Me July-Sept., 1938

Solid Old Man 1939 (Duke Ellington)*

Solitude 1934, Jan.-Mar., 1935
(Once the theme song of Duke Ellington)

Solo Flight 1941, 1944 (Benny Goodman)*

So Long Jan.-Mar., 1940

Somebody Else is Taking My Place Jan.-Mar., 1942

Somebody Loves Me 1924, 1936 (Benny Goodman)*

Somebody Stole My Gal 1918

Some Day, Sweetheart 1931, 1935 (Benny Goodman Trio)*; 1937 (Artie Shaw)*; 1946 (Woody Herman Woodchoppers)*

Some Like it Hot 1939 (Gene Krupa)*

Some of These Days 1910

Someone 1942 (Duke Ellington)*

Someone's Rocking My Dreamboat Oct.-Dec., 1941

Someone to Watch Over Me 1926

Something to Remember You By 1931, April-June, 1943

Sometimes I'm Happy 1927
(Blue Barron Signature Tune); 1935 (Benny Goodman)*

Song is Ended, The (But the Melody Lingers On) 1927

Song is You, The 1932, Oct.-Dec., 1942

Song of India 1921, Jan.-Mar., 1937; 1943 (Tommy Dorsey reissue)*

Song of the Islands Oct.-Dec., 1936

Song of the Volga Boatmen Jan.-Mar., 1941

Sonny Boy 1928

Soon Jan.-Mar., 1935

Sophisticated Lady 1933, 1938 (Bunny Berigan)* 1940 (Duke Ellington)*

So Rare July-Sept., 1937

Sorghum Switch 1942 (Jimmy Dorsey)*

South 1941 (Woody Herman's Woodchoppers)*
South American Way July-Sept., 1939
South America, Take it Away July-Sept., 1946
Southern Fried 1940 (Charlie Barnet)*
Southern Scandal 1945 (Stan Kenton)*
Southland Shuffle 1940 (Charlie Barnet)*
South of the Border Oct.-Dec., 1939
South Rampart St. Parade 1937 (Bob Crosby)*
South Sea Island Magic Oct.-Dec., 1936
So What? 1940 (Tommy Dorsey)*
So You're the One Jan.-Mar., 1941
Spanish Kick 1941 (Charlie Barnet)*
Speaking of Heaven Oct.-Dec., 1939
Speak Low Oct.-Dec., 1943
Special Delivery Stomp 1940 (Artie Shaw)*
Spirit is Willing, The 1941 (Glenn Miller)*
S'Posin' 1929, April-June, 1939
Spring is Here July-Sept., 1938
Spring Will Be a Little Late This Year Oct.-Dec., 1944
Squeeze Me 1925, 1938 (Bob Crosby)*
Stairway to the Stars April-June, 1939
Stampede in G Minor 1940 (Count Basie)*
Star Dust 1929, Jan.-Mar., 1939; Jan.-Mar., 1941
Stardust on the Moon July-Sept., 1937
Star Eyes Jan.-Mar., 1944
Star Fell Out of Heaven, A July-Sept., 1936
Starlit Hour, The Jan.-Mar., 1940
Stars Fell on Alabama 1934
Stay as Sweet as You Are 1934, Jan.-Mar., 1935

Stealin' Apples 1939 (Benny Goodman)*
Stein Song, The 1930
Steppin' into Swing Society 1938 (Duke Ellington)*
Stompin' at the Savoy July-Sept., 1936
Stomp it Off 1939 (Tommy Dorsey)*
Stone Cold Dead in the Market July-Sept., 1946
Stone's Throw From Heaven, A Oct.-Dec., 1940
Stop Beatin' 'Round the Mulberry Bush July-Sept., 1938
Stop! It's Wonderful! Jan.-Mar., 1940
Stop, Look and Listen 1935 (Jimmy Dorsey)*; 1937 (Tommy Dorsey)*; 1938 (Charlie Barnet)*
Stormy Weather 1933; July-Sept., 1943
Story of a Starry Night, The April-June, 1942
Straighten Up and Fly Right April-June, 1944
Strange Enchantment April-June, 1939
Strange Music Oct.-Dec., 1944
Stranger in Town, A July-Sept., 1945
Street of Dreams 1933, July-Sept., 1942
Strictly Instrumental July-Sept., 1942
Strike Up the Band 1930
String of Pearls, A Jan.-Mar., 1942; 1942 (Benny Goodman, Woody Herman)*
Strip Polka Oct.-Dec., 1942
Struttin' With Some Barbecue 1938 (Louis Armstrong)*
Study in Blue, A 1938 (Larry Clinton)*
Study in Brown, A 1937 (Early Larry Clinton Signature Tune)*
Study in Green, A 1939 (Larry Clinton)*

Swing Low, Sweet Chariot 1872, 1939
& 1941 (Tommy Dorsey)*
Swing Street Strut 1939 (Charlie
Barnet)*
Swingtime in Honolulu 1938 (Duke
Ellington)*
Swingtime in the Rockies 1936 (Benny
Goodman)*
Swing Tonic 1941 (Glen Gray)*
'S Wonderful 1927, 1938 (Benny
Goodman)*;
1944 (Coleman Hawkins)*; 1945
(Artie Shaw)*
Symphony Jan.-Mar., 1946
Symphony in Riffs 1937 (Artie Shaw)*;
1938 (Tommy Dorsey)*; 1939
(Gene Krupa)*

'Tain't What You Do (It's the Way
That You Do It) Jan.-Mar., 1939
Take Me July-Sept., 1942
Take Me Back to My Boots and Saddle
Oct.-Dec., 1935
Take Me in Your Arms 1932
Take My Heart April-June, 1936
Take the "A" Train July-Sept., 1941
(Subsequently Duke Ellington's
Signature Tune)
Taking a Chance on Love Jan.-Mar.,
1943 (Recorded 1940, far more
popular 1943)
Tampico July-Sept., 1945
Tangerine Jan.-Mar., 1942
Tappin' at the Tappa 1940 (Charlie
Barnet)*
Taxi War Dance 1939 (Count Basie)*
Tea For Two 1924, 1937 (Benny
Goodman)*
Tears From My Inkwell April-June,
1939
Tell Me That You Love Me April-
June, 1935

Tempo De Luxe 1940 (Harry James)*
Temptation 1933, Oct.-Dec., 1940;
1944 (Artie Shaw reissue)*; April-
June, 1945
Ten-Day Furlough 1941 (Woody
Herman)*
Ten Mile Hop 1940 (Larry Clinton)*
Texas Shufle 1938 (Count Basie)*
Thanks a Million Oct.-Dec., 1935
Thanks For Everything Jan.-Mar., 1939
Thanks For the Memory Jan.-Mar.,
1938
That Drummer's Band 1942
(Gene Krupa's signature tune,
following "Apurksody" and
"Starburst.")
(Did You Ever Get) That Feeling in the
Moonlight? Oct.-Dec., 1945
That Old Black Magic Jan.-Mar., 1943
That Old Feeling July-Sept., 1937
That's A-Plenty 1936 (Tommy
Dorsey)*; 1939 (Jan Savitt)*
That's For Me 1940, July-Sept., 1945
That Sly Old Gentleman April-June,
1939
That's My Desire 1931
That Soldier of Mine July-Sept., 1942
Them There Eyes 1930
Then I'll Be Happy 1925, 1946
(Tommy Dorsey)*
There Are Such Things Oct.-Dec., 1942
There Goes My Heart 1934
There Goes That Song Again Oct.-
Dec., 1944
There I Go Oct.-Dec., 1940
There is a Tavern in the Town 1883
There is No Greater Love
(See: (There is) No Greater Love)
There, I've Said it Again April-June,
1945
There'll Be Some Changes Made 1921,
Jan.-Mar., 1941

Too-Ra-Loo-Ra-Loo-Ral 1914, Oct.-Dec., 1944

Too Romantic April-June, 1940

Toot Toot Tootsie 1921

Top Hat, White Tie and Tails July-Sept., 1935

Topsy 1937 (Count Basie)*; 1938 (Benny Goodman)*

Tormented April-June, 1936

Touch of Your Hand, The 1933

Touch of Your Lips, The April-June, 1936

To You July-Sept., 1939

To You, Sweetheart, Aloha Oct.-Dec., 1936; Jan.-Mar., 1940

Toy Trumpet 1938 (Artie Shaw)*

Trade Winds July-Sept., 1940

Traffic Jam July-Sept., 1939

Trolley Song, The Oct.-Dec., 1944

Truckin' July-Sept., 1935

True Confession Oct.-Dec., 1937

Trumpet Blues April-June, 1942

Trumpet Rhapsody (1 & 2) Oct.-Dec., 1941

Trust in Me Jan.-Mar., 1937

Try a Little Tenderness 1932

Tumbling Tumbleweeds 1934

Tune Town Shuffle 1941 (Count Basie)*

Tunin' Up 1941 (Gene Krupa)*

Tuxedo Junction Jan.-Mar., 1940 (Became Erskine Hawkins' Signature Tune)

Twelfth Street Rag 1917, 1939 (Count Basie)*

Twenty Four Hours a Day Oct.-Dec., 1935

Twilight in Turkey April-June, 1937

Twilight on the Trail April-June, 1936

Twilight Time Oct.-Dec., 1944 (Signature Tune of The Three Suns)

Twin City Blues 1938 (Woody Herman)*

Two Cigarettes in the Dark 1934

Two in One Blues 1942 (Artie Shaw)*

Two O'Clock Jump Jan.-Mar., 1939; 1943 (Harry James reissue)*

Two Sleepy People Oct.-Dec., 1938

Two Tickets to Georgia 1933

Ubangi 1937 (Artie Shaw)*

Umbrella Man, The Jan.-Mar., 1939

Undecided 1938 (Benny Goodman)*; Jan.-Mar., 1939

Under a Blanket of Blue 1933, Oct.-Dec., 1939

Under Blue Canadian Skies July-Sept., 1941

Underneath the Arches 1932

Until the Real Thing Comes Along July-Sept., 1936 (Andy Kirk Theme Song)

Until Today July-Sept., 1936

Until Tomorrow April-June, 1941

Uptown Downbeat 1936 (Duke Ellington)*

Velvet Moon July-Sept., 1942

Very Thought of You, The 1934 (Ray Noble Theme Song); Oct.-Dec., 1944

Victory Polka, The Oct.-Dec., 1943

Vieni Vieni Oct.-Dec., 1937

Vilia 1939 (Artie Shaw)*

Violets For Your Furs Oct.-Dec., 1941

Volcano 1939 (Count Basie)*

Wabash Blues 1921

Wagon Whels 1934

Wah Hoo Jan.-Mar., 1936

Waitin' For the Train to Come In Oct.-Dec., 1945

Wait Till the Sun Shines Nellie 1905

When Mother Nature Sings Her Lullaby
July-Sept., 1938

When My Baby Smiles at Me 1920

When My Dream Boat Comes Home
Jan.-Mar., 1937

When My Sugar Walks Down the Street
1924

When the Lights Go on Again (All Over
the World) Oct.-Dec., 1942

When the Lilacs Bloom Again April-
June, 1941

When the Midnight Choo Choo
Leaves For Alabam' 1912

When the Moon Comes Over the
Mountain 1931 (Theme Song of
singer Kate Smith)

When the Quail Come Back to San
Quentin 1940 (Artie Shaw
Gramercy Five)*

When the Red Red Robin Comes
Bob-Bob-Bobbin' Along 1926

When the Roses Bloom Again April-
June, 1942

When the Swallows Come Back to
Capistrano July-Sept., 1940

When They Ask About You Jan.-Mar.,
1944

When We're Alone (See: Penthouse
Serenade)

When You're a Long, Long Way From
Home April-June, 1942

When You're Smiling 1928

When Your Lover Has Gone 1931

When You Wish Upon a Star Jan.-
Mar., 1940

When You Wore a Tulip
and I Wore a Big Red Rose 1914

Where Am I? Oct.-Dec., 1935

Where Are You? April-June, 1937

Where Do I Go From You? April-June,
1940

Where'd You Get Those Eyes? 1926

Where or When July-Sept., 1937

Where the Blue of the Night Meets the
Gold of the Day 1932 (Bing Crosby
radio Theme Song)

Where Was I? April-June, 1940

Whiffenpoof Song, The 1911

While a Cigarette Was Burning Oct.-
Dec., 1938

Whispering 1920, 1936 (Benny
Goodman Quartet)*

Whispering Grass July-Sept., 1940

Whispers in the Dark July-Sept., 1937

Whistle Stop 1940 (Woody Herman)*

Whistle While You Work Jan.-Mar.,
1938

White Christmas Oct.-Dec., 1942

White Cliffs of Dover, The Jan.-Mar.,
1942

White Sails (Beneath a Yellow Moon)
July-Sept., 1939

Without a Song 1929, April-June, 1941

Without a Word of Warning July-Sept.,
1935

With Plenty of Money and You Jan.-
Mar., 1937

Who? 1925, 1935 (Benny Goodman
Trio)*; Oct.-Dec., 1937; 1940
(Gene Krupa)*

Who Blew Out the Flame? Oct.-Dec.,
1938

Whole World is Singing My Song, The
Oct.-Dec., 1946

Wholly Cats 1940 (Benny Goodman)*

Who's Sorry Now? 1923, July-Sept.,
1939; 1946 (Harry James)*

Who's Your Little Who-Zis? 1931

Who Wouldn't Love You? April-June,
1942

Why Do I Love You? 1927

Why Don't We Do This More Often?
July-Sept., 1941

You Call it Madness (But I Call it Love) 1931, July-Sept., 1946

You Can Depend on Me 1932, July-Sept., 1939; Oct.-Dec., 1942

You Can't Have Everything July-Sept., 1937

You Can't Pull the Wool Over My Eyes April-June, 1936

You Can't Stop Me From Dreaming Oct.-Dec., 1937

You Couldn't Be Cuter April-June, 1938

You'd Be So Nice to Come Home To Jan.-Mar., 1943

You'd Be Surprised Jan.-Mar., 1940

You Don't Know What Love Is Oct.-Dec., 1941

You Do Something to Me 1929

You Forgot About Me Oct.-Dec., 1940

You Go to My Head July-Sept., 1938 (Mitchell Ayres' Theme Song)

You Gotta Be a Football Hero (To Get Along With the Beautiful Girls) 1933

You Hit the Spot Jan.-Mar., 1936

You Keep Coming Back Like a Song Oct.-Dec., 1946

You Leave Me Breathless April-June, 1938

You'll Have to Swing It Oct.-Dec., 1936

You'll Never Know April-June, 1943

You Made Me Love You 1913, Oct.-Dec., 1941

You Make Me Feel So Young Oct.-Dec., 1946

You Must Have Been a Beautiful Baby Oct.-Dec., 1938

You Oughta Be in Pictures 1934

You're a Heavenly Thing April-June, 1935

You're All I Need July-Sept., 1935

You're an Education Jan.-Mar., 1938

You're an Old Smoothie 1932

You're a Sweetheart Jan.-Mar., 1938

You're a Sweet Little Headache Jan.-Mar., 1939

You're Driving Me Crazy 1930, 1938 (Bob Crosby)*

You're Getting to Be a Habit With Me 1933

You're Laughing at Me Jan.-Mar., 1937

You're Lonely and I'm Lonely April-June, 1940

You're My Everything 1931

You're My Thrill 1933, Jan.-Mar., 1941

You're Nobody 'Til Somebody Loves You Jan.-Mar., 1946

You're Not the Kind July-Sept., 1936

You're the Cream in My Coffee 1928

You're the Top Jan.-Mar., 1935

Yours 1932, July-Sept., 1941

Yours is My Heart Alone 1929

You Started Me Dreaming April-June, 1936

You Stepped Out of a Dream Jan.-Mar., 1941

You Taught Me to Love Again July-Sept., 1939

You Took Advantage of Me 1927

You Turned the Tables on Me Oct.-Dec., 1936

You've Changed Oct.-Dec., 1941

You've Got Me This Way Jan.-Mar., 1941

You Walk By Jan.-Mar., 1941

You Were Meant For Me 1929

You Were Never Lovelier July-Sept., 1942

You Won't Be Satisfied (Until You Break My Heart) Jan.-Mar., 1946